Literature and Computation

Literature and Computation presents some of the most relevantly innovative recent approaches to literary practice, theory, and criticism as driven by computation and situated in digital environments. These approaches rely on automated analyses, but use them creatively, engage in text modeling but inform it with qualitative[-interpretive] critical possibilities, and contribute to present-day platform culture in revolutionizing intermedial ways. While such new directions involve more and more sophisticated machine learning and artificial intelligence, they also mark a spectacular return of the (trans) human(istic) and of traditional-modern literary or urgent political, gender, and minority-related concerns and modes now addressed in ever subtler and more nuanced ways within human-computer interaction frameworks. Expanding the boundaries of literary and data studies, digital humanities, and electronic literature, the featured contributions unveil an emerging landscape of trailblazing practice and theoretical crossovers ready and able to spawn and/or chart the witness literature of our age and cultures.

Chris Tanasescu is a poet and academic with backgrounds in English and computer science. The *Graph Poem* project he started 15 years ago has outputted natural language processing and network science-based poetry classifiers, intermedia performances, and computationally assembled poetry anthologies. His alias MARGENTO refers to a cyber cross-artform ensemble and international coalition of poets-translators, visual artists/ musicians, and coders throwing events and launching publications on and off-line in four continents. Chris is currently a research scientist on the *PIETRA* project at the University of Galway. Previous or ongoing positions and affiliations include Coordinator of Digital Humanities at the University of Ottawa, Altissia Chair in Digital Cultures and Ethics at Université Catholique de Louvain, Senior Researcher in Global Literary Studies and Complex Systems at Universitat Oberta de Catalunya, and Visiting Scholar at the Electronic Textual Cultures Lab, University of Victoria. He is an *Asymptote* Editor-at-Large.

Routledge New Textual Studies in Literature
Series Editors: Jane Potter, Bonnie Latimer and Kevin Killeen

The Collaborative Literary Relationship of Percy Bysshe Shelley and Mary Wollstonecraft Shelley
Anna Mercer

Richard Polwhele and Romantic Culture
The Politics of Reaction and the Poetics of Place
Dafydd Moore

The Mini-Cycle
Allan Weiss

Criticism After Theory from Shakespeare to Virginia Woolf
Perry Meisel

Historical Research, Creative Writing, and the Past
Methods of Knowing
Edited by Kevin A. Morrison and Pälvi Rantala

The British and Anglo-Irish Thing-Essay from 1701 to 2021
Of Broomsticks and Doughnuts
Daniel Schneider

Literature and Computation
Platform Intermediality, Hermeneutic Modeling, and Analytical-Creative Approaches
Edited by Chris Tanasescu

For more information about this series, please visit: https://www.routledge.com/Routledge-New-Textual-Studies-in-Literature/book-series/NTSL

Literature and Computation

Platform Intermediality, Hermeneutic Modeling, and Analytical-Creative Approaches

Edited by Chris Tanasescu

Routledge
Taylor & Francis Group
NEW YORK AND LONDON

First published 2024
by Routledge
605 Third Avenue, New York, NY 10158

and by Routledge
4 Park Square, Milton Park, Abingdon, Oxon, OX14 4RN

Routledge is an imprint of the Taylor & Francis Group,
an informa business

ISBN: 978-1-032-34166-8 (hbk)
ISBN: 978-1-032-34167-5 (pbk)
ISBN: 978-1-003-32083-8 (ebk)

DOI: 10.4324/9781003320838

The Open Access version of the Introduction and Chapter 3 are
funded by The University of Galway.

Contents

Figures

Tables

Notes on Contributors

Rosario Arias is Full Professor of English Literature at the University of Málaga. She has published on neo-Victorian fiction, and on the work of contemporary writers. She has co-edited (with Patricia Pulham) *Haunting and Spectrality in Neo-Victorian Fiction* (Palgrave 2010), and she has also published *Science, Spiritualism and Technology* (Routledge 2014). Among her most recent publications are two volumes, *Reading the Trace in Modern and Contemporary Fiction* (co-edited with Lin Pettersson, Gylphi 2022) and *Spanish Spiritualist Writing and Its Dissemination through Translations* (co-edited with Juan Jesús Zaro, Reichenberger 2023). She is an active member of the Centre for Feminist and Gender Studies at the University of Málaga, as well as a member of Academia Europaea. Rosario Arias has directed several funded projects, she leads the Literary Assemblage Project (RELY), the LITCAE research group, and she is currently the President of the Spanish Association of Anglo-American Studies (AEDEAN) and of the Victorian and Neo-Victorian Society in Spain (VINS).

Florentina Armaselu, PhD, is Research Scientist at the Luxembourg Centre for Contemporary and Digital History (C²DH) of the University of Luxembourg. Her educational background includes a PhD in comparative literature and an MSc in computer science, from the University of Montreal, Canada, and studies in computer science and philology at the University of Craiova, Romania. She was involved in teaching and research projects in computer-assisted language learning, natural language processing, digital editions, and interface design at the Faculty of Letters, University of Craiova, Romania, the Department of Computer Science and Operations Research of the University of Montreal, North Side Inc., R&D, Montreal, Canada, and the Centre Virtuel de la Connaissance sur l'Europe (CVCE), Luxembourg. Currently, her research and teaching involve areas such as computational text analysis and text interpretation, text encoding and human-computer interaction, and their applications in digital history and digital humanities.

Johanna Drucker is Distinguished Professor and Breslauer Professor Emerita, Department of Information Studies, UCLA. She is internationally known for her work in the history of graphic design, typography, experimental poetry, fine art, and digital humanities, as well as for her artist's books, which are featured in many special collections in museums and libraries in North America and elsewhere. Recent titles include *Visualization and Interpretation* (MIT Press 2020), and *Iliazd: Meta-Biography of a Modernist* (Johns Hopkins University Press 2020), *Digital Humanities 101: An Introduction to Digital Methods* (Routledge 2021), and *Inventing the Alphabet* (University of Chicago Press 2022).

Javier Fernández-Cruz is a Margarita Salas researcher in the Department of English Philology at the University of Málaga and a member of the Tecnolengua research group. For the last decade he has taught at the Pontificia Universidad Católica del Ecuador and has been a Visiting Professor at the University of Bergamo and the University of Burgundy. His studies focus on corpus linguistics, sentiment analysis, and digital humanities.

Ioana Galleron is Full Professor of French Literature and Digital Humanities at Sorbonne Nouvelle. She has published studies and books about the French comedy of the 17th and 18th centuries, which she approached by combining a close-reading perspective with digital tools and methods (*La Comédie de mœurs sous l'Ancien régime: poétique et histoire*, Oxford University 2017; *Dictionnaires et réseaux des lexicographes aux XVIIe et XVIIIe siècles*, Honoré Champion 2023). Ioana Galleron has consistently contributed to several scholarly editions (in both digital and print) and other digital resources: Louis de Boissy, *Théâtre complet*, Classiques Garnier 2020; Michel Baron, *Théâtre complet*, Classiques Garnier 2018; *HAIRO: corpus de romane haiduceşti (1850–1950)*, *https://www.nakala.fr/search/?q=HAIRO* 2020). Her next book, *Les Comptes de Thalie* (Presses Universitaires de Rennes), is due by the end of 2023.

Andrew Klobucar is Associate Professor at the New Jersey Institute of Technology and director of communication and media program. His research continues to advance along two distinct but strongly interrelated lines of study: the development and application of digital programming and multimedia technologies in the literary arts and the continued refinement of social media networking in university-level pedagogy through ongoing advancements in software development. His latest work is an anthology of essays entitled, *Narrative Play and Interactivity in the Art of Digital Storytelling* due to be published in 2024 by Intellect Press, distributed by the University of Chicago.

Frédérique Mélanie-Becquet is Research Engineer at Centre National de Recherche Scientifique (CNRS) and Laboratoire Langues, Textes, Traitements informatiques, Cognition (LATTICE), where she provides expertise in corpus linguistics and database management. She collaborated in the constitution of digitally enhanced resources and published extensively about *Données vérité de terrain HTR+ Annuaire des propriétaires et des propriétés de Paris et du département de la Seine 1898-1923; Parasol (A Parallel Corpus of Slavic and Other Languages); Oupoco; Democrat; BSP(Base de Syntagmes Prépositionnels); EIOM-SIT (Eléments Initiaux, Ordre des Mots, Structures Informationnelle et Textuelle); ETE (Espace Temps Existence); SCF (Structures comparatives en français).*

Servanne Monjour is Associate Professor of French Literature at the Sorbonne. Her research focuses on new forms of literary production and publishing in the 21st century as relevant, for instance, to digital literature and single-source publishing. She has recently also developed an interest in how literary writing is inspired or informed by platform-based computing protocols (e.g. Twitter-X, Instagram, and GitLab). Her conceptual thinking draws on her own personal practice and experimenting with digital writing tools and formats, while other chapters of her academic work focus on the preservation of online literary corpora, particularly those published on social media.

Roxana Patras is Senior Researcher (I) at the Institute of Interdisciplinary Research, "Alexandru Ioan Cuza" University of Iaşi, where she coordinates the Digital Humanities Laboratory. She has published books and studies on the 19th-century European and Romanian literature and co-authored several scholarly editions: *Spaţii eminesciene. Studii de poetică şi stilistică* (Timpul 2017), *The Remains of the Day: Literature and Political Eloquence in 19th-Century Romania* (Aracne 2018), *Oratorie politică românească* (Editura Universităţii din Iaşi 2016), C. D. Aricescu, *Misterele căsătoriei* (Timpul 2020). Roxana Patras is interested in the alchemy of mercurial computationality with modern literature's gold nuggets and has therefore focused on remixing the theories of the para-literary field (titling practices, illustrations, prefaces, popular novels/genre fiction) and on creating digital literary corpora with a view to a context-sensitive study of lesser-resourced languages (ELTEC-rom, HAIRO, Pop-Lite).

Nicolas Sauret is Associate Professor of Information and Communication Sciences at Université Paris 8 Vincennes—Saint-Denis, where he teaches in the Digital Humanities department. His research focuses on the digital materiality of writing and publishing. He is particularly interested in collective writing and its conversational dynamics in digital environments. By means of research-action, he explores the practices of various writing communities—digital-literature, online-commons, and academic ones—with and for whom he co-designs shared open-source writing and publishing spaces. This work is part of an epistemological reflection on knowledge production, dissemination, and legitimization in digital environments.

Olga Seminck is Research Engineer at Centre National de Recherche Scientifique (CNRS) and Laboratoire Langues, Textes, Traitements informatiques, Cognition (LATTICE), where she provides expertise in cognitive computational models, artificial intelligence, and statistics. She has been involved in various digital projects such as *Mind-it: Detection automatique de la maladie d'Alzheimer dans des messages electroniques* (2020), *DoRANum-Donnees de la recherche: Apprentissage Numerique* (2022), CIDRE: *The Corpus for Idiolectal Research* (2021), GIRLS: *The Gender Identification Resource for Literature and Style* (2022). Olga Seminck has published articles and participated in conferences with talks on topics such as gendered literary idiolects, pronoun anaphora, and coreference.

Jan-Erik Stange is a data visualization and user experience design researcher at the University and State Library of Münster. In his research he investigates the role of interactive visual representations as devices for modeling in the digital humanities. As a professional designer Jan-Erik draws from design practice and research in order to conceptualize modeling as a creative, iterative process of interpretation, in which visual representations are not end results showing "the" data but rather steps in the process of producing data in a performative way. He holds a Bachelor's in Industrial Design (Muthesius Kunsthochschule Kiel) and a Master's degree in Interface Design (Fachhochschule Potsdam), and he worked in design studios in Germany and the USA. He previously filled several Research Associate positions at FU Berlin (Excellence Cluster EXC2020 "Temporal Communities"), Universität Hamburg, and Fachhochschule Potsdam.

Raluca Tanasescu is Researcher in Translation and Global Media in the School of Languages, Literatures, and Cultures at the University of Galway, Ireland. After obtaining a doctoral degree in Translation Studies from the University of Ottawa in Canada, she worked as a Postdoctoral Researcher in digital methods applied in early modern science history at the University of Groningen. Her scholarly work is situated at the nexus of translation, complexity, and digital humanities. Raluca is mainly interested in the dynamics between translation and the digital as well as the essential role played by the two in creating more sustainable and just communities. She is currently working on the European Research Council-funded project *PIETRA: Translation and Communication* and serves as the Chair of the Multilingualism and Multiculturalism Committee for the Alliance of Digital Humanities Organizations.

Introduction

Chris Tanasescu

Platform Intermediality, Hermeneutic Modeling, and Analytical-Creative Approaches

Where is literature nowadays? Even those who only believe in 'serious' literature that always comes in traditional/print form from mainstream publishers are aware that every now and then they do need to check out 'untraditional' literary venues such as social media (SM), blogs, and various other kinds of websites for potentially relevant news about, insight into, or even pieces of, such literature. On the other hand, boundaries or gaps that seemed to be here to stay are now crossed in all, and at times, the most unexpected directions. Literature initially published, for instance, on SM as such, as belonging there, e.g., Instapoetry, was once in a while reissued in print book form, in certain cases, to huge market success. Poetry "of the Web, by the Web, for the Web" (Funkhouser "Digital Poetry") is itself featured in anthologies and handbooks to much critical acclaim and/or academic/educational popularity, while classics make popular YouTube videos, new-media artworks (Schaefer), and viral memes. Given such perhaps unprecedented versatility, one could very well reframe the question above as, rather, where isn't literature nowadays....

And yet, it may turn out neither the question nor the answer is that simple. If literature is everywhere (and everything?),[1] then it may be nowhere (to find). In speaking of space and place more specifically, if literature is the space of our culture, if it is digital space (Kennedy; Monjour and Vitali-Rosati "Pour une redéfinition"), does it also have a place, a realm of its own? Where and how is it, if it is, collected, stored, saved, archived, maintained (Vauthier and Kirschenbaum's textual condition)? If it is (about) the space of its culture and age, then contemporary literature is surely also about that, about the huge and largely unaddressed challenge of saving, archiving, making accessible. Literature and, thus, the Web, the locus and life of our cultures. And as *the* locus is the digital platform, the life is one of resistance to (and/or compliance with) hegemony,

DOI: 10.4324/9781003320838-1

resource extraction (Sadowski), algorithmic oppression (Noble), and control (Franklin). Agent, testimony, and witness at the same time of such resistance, literature needs to endure in such environments beyond the rare oases of the Internet Archive and its Wayback Machine and other Web (or) heritage preservation havens.

A salient feature of literature in digital space (and not only) is its double capacity as record and event. Literature is remembering and recording, and as such it exercises the paradox of preservation and loss, of memory and its decay and disappearance; once written down, history and 'reality' do not have to be remembered anymore (Plato, Derrida). As digital record or inscription therefore, it speaks to the timely issues of digital memory and existence as technological embodiment and process (Lagerkvist), the performed history of communities as networks (Lievrouw and Loader), and of networks as emerging techno-human or, more precisely, data-AI-human communities (Tanasescu *et al.* "A-poetic Technology"). By mediating the digital medium—medium as both flux (Andersen) and environment or milieu—by writing the social dimension of media and the mediation in the societal, literature is a metarecord, the documenting of its own documentation. Literary datasets, collections, archives, and anthologies are ways of communal and computational association: the record equals ways of connecting with the other in collecting and algorithmically analyzing and classifying literature (e.g., *chinese-poetry*). And, at the same time, computationally analyzing literature is the way to collect and record it, and establish and expand social networks in the process. The platform thus becomes an anthology and the anthology emerges as a platform (see [R.] Tanasescu's chapter in this collection).

From the poem as fundamentally, radically, and technologically evental (Stefans *Word Toys*) to ephemerality as defining feature of electronic literature (e-lit) (Funkhouser) to events involving collectively and algorithmically (re)writing poems (Monjour and Sauret in this book) to data-commoning performances (Tanasescu "#GraphPoem @ DHSI" and the chapter in this collection), literature is pervasively performative and subversively mediatic (Monjour and Vitali-Rosati "Pour une redéfinition"). As all digital writing is a form of reading and vice versa ("readingwriting" in Emerson's terms, see also Jaramillo et al.), engaging with a piece of literature in digital environments, even by simply viewing it and/or clicking on its embedding link, is an event in and of itself that (re)shapes that piece and its place and role in the community-network. In SM in general, time and timing are of the essence in the economy of user content and the attention it does (or does not) draw to itself—e.g., the link to a Facebook post is a function of its date and time feature—and online literary communities and projects are critically aware of and informed by that. Both the way in which literary pieces are contributed or presented and the way in which the 'audience' reacts and interacts are typically staged and paced as evental and performative. The reading-writing dialectics and the networked complexity of digital writing per se (Tanasescu and Tanasescu "Complexity," see also below) play, in fact, a major role in the continued performativity definitory of literature in digital space and computing environments. A poem for instance in such environments is permanently performed and (re)written by the complex writing processes and networked textualities it is embedded in and accessed or updated by, and which, in its turn, the poem itself continuously reshapes.

Moreover, the above-mentioned record and event facets of literature actually work as a feedback loop: the Muse is urged to sing—here and now—as safest and most effective way to recount, and, indeed, record, past events (Homer); inscribing (making) history, on the other hand, is what occasions, fuels, and keeps the song going. While living archives are of significance in digital memory and culture studies (Hoskins), literature is also instrumental in, and as, *live* archive(ing), heritage, or, 'simply,' data (Tanasescu "Collection Computing"). The archives and repos of literature as record and memory are complemented by the very performativity and liveness of the literature involved per se, by its propulsiveness (Funkhouser), "intra-action" (Tanasescu "#GraphPoem"), and inherent determination to create something out of itself (Funkhouser "'US' Poets"). In such contexts, the two facets of literature, record and event, have been refined by drawing on performance studies concepts and thus developed into "performative relays" and "performances" (Tanasescu and Tanasescu "Complexity," and also, [C.] Tanasescu's chapter in this collection). The former are the live documents, the "text(s)" of a work that both record its ongoing performance and fuel its further iterative development. They are themselves iteratively reinscribed in the process as interrelated and networked pieces of digital writing. And the latter refer to the work's continuous performance as reperformance, its centripetal gravitation to the evolving "script(s)" or "text(s)" and its centrifugal computational expansion and intermedial alteration (their progress with, by means of, and into alterity).

Intermediality is, therefore, as this collection argues on a number of levels, a fundamental feature of contemporary literature, particularly on or combining multiple platforms. Tangibly speaking, in our cultures, text is published as or alongside visuals and/or audio, and literary works are usually presented as (collective) performances targeting, assembling, and/or developing/expanding certain multilayer data-community-networks. Literature is thus at times seen as being absorbed into the visual or video arts (Cytter *et al.*), or undistinguishable from digital art in general (Simanowski), so much the more so as established e-lit once in a while did away with (natural) language altogether (Hayles 4). On the other hand, to continue pursuing for now this sensorium-based acceptance of media and mediation, intermedia has also been seen as an integral and inherent part of literature. Sound has of course naturally been studied as such, as a standalone characteristic in poetics (e.g., Perloff and Dworkin, Leithauser). Visuality, on the other hand, has been described as an intrinsic, a-priori kind of feature of literature to the extent to which the latter culturally and aesthetically conditions the way we see and our relationship to images in general (Bodola and Isekenmeier). In more technology-informed if still, at times essentialist manners, intermedia has also been seen as a constitutive feature of global literature or literature in a global comparative perspective (see, for instance, Habjan and Imlinger, also Roig-Sanz and Rotger). And, most recently and closest to the vision informing the contributions to this collection, transmediality has been argued to be characteristic of literature not as a combination of, and thus demarcation between essentialized media and/as art forms or genres (see the criticism in [C.] Tanasescu's chapter in this book), but as a dynamic and adaptable heterogeneity of literature as "transmedial configuration and *network*" (Schaefer 169, my emphasis). In that perspective, intermediality is seen as a "constitutive element within the literary field itself," while the concept advanced for the literature accommodating such an updated "configuration" is the "network *model*."[2] (Schaefer 170, my emphasis; see also the "Hermeneutic Modeling" section of this collection as well as the above-cited chapter in relation to literary modeling).

Intermediality nevertheless means, from a philosophical and philosophy of media point of view, performativity in the uttermost sense of the word (Larrue and Vitali-Rosati). It comports a kind of dynamics that is not pre-established or in any way formulated beforehand but belongs completely in the moment, in the freedom of improvisation and unpredictability, in the Heraclitan flow of indetermination. It does away with any kind of essentialism related to either media ("media do not exist," says Larrue and Vitali-Rosati's title) or art forms and genres to the extent to which it is not even concerned whether intermediality is, for instance, as in Schaefer's contribution cited above, even "constitutive" of literature or not. Instead, it informs a poetics of performance involving "network walks," "stigmergy,"[3] accident, (Tanasescu "#GraphPoem") and complex-system-writing (Tanasescu and Tanasescu "Complexity").[4] Intermediality thus not only crosses the borders or gaps between various modes of mediation and/or digital apps (e.g., PowerPoint presentation, music videos livestreaming, and live interactive coding) but also correlates multiple platforms while subverting the control that informs them.

Computational analysis, more often than not in its computational literary studies (CLS) capacity, plays a major role in such performances and is, at times, the driving, creative force behind the above-described acceptance of intermediality (see the "Analytical-creative Approaches" section in this collection; also see below). As academic pursuit, computational analysis provides the methods, algorithms, and classifiers for reading, collecting, modeling, assembling, and expanding datasets, processes that can all involve or result in creative developments (see [R.] Tanasescu's chapter in this book). The links between CLS—or, in a more inclusive framework, digital humanities (DH)—and creative work, particularly literary creative work, have been explored before from two main angles. The first one was adopted by e-lit academics and practitioners that sought to find a spot for the subject under the more comprehensive—and chic, which often equates with better funded—umbrella of DH (Rettberg "Electronic Literature as Digital Humanities," Grigar and O'Sullivan). This is part of a more general inter- or post-disciplinary trend, e.g., remix studies as DH (Navas, Gallagher, and burrough). Pervasive and/or specific features of e-lit have been analyzed in the context as relevant from and consistent with the point(s) of view of DH, even as the lattter continues itself to be (re)defined and (re)shaped as a subject. Conversely, algorithms and tools developed in e-lit were appropriated and repurposed by scholars in CLS for their own analytical purposes related to, for instance, meter and rhyme detection and classification (e.g., Padget *et al.*'s repurposing Charles O. Hartman's *Scandroid*). The second angle made conspicuous certain instances of shared filiation between e-lit and (C)LS in either foregrounding the ways in which the former is historically and methodologically related to traditional avant-garde and experimental, procedural, or conceptual poetry (Funkhouser *Prehistoric Digital Poetry*, Rettberg *Electronic Literature)* or in arguing that a narrow understanding of the digital obscures its presence throughout the history of literature. Ignoring the foundationally geminate advents of structuralism—in both linguistics and poetics—and computational analysis for instance has been advanced as illustrative of the related shortsightedness in the field (Cramer). Cramer's once in a while tongue-in-cheek when not openly sarcastic argument is that, for instance, simply using the alphabet represents a digital approach to writing (12)... On a more sophisticated level, DH alongside CLS and e-lit is threatened by precariousness exactly because structuralism (and the computational implementations that followed) betrayed the initial non-semantic non-hermeneutic program; ironically, it is exactly that inconsistency that prevents computational analysis from handling subtle issues such as metaphors (14–16; Cramer is in fact quite wrong at least in this respect, see Shutova *et al.* or, more recently, Tanasescu *et al.* "Metaphor Detection" and Li *et al.*).

Yet as a recent contribution concluded after close scrutiny, CLS, while in certain respects obviously related, is actually in essential aspects paradigmatically and methodologically strange to structuralism (Gius and Jacke). While, in spite of the above-mentioned interdisciplinary advocacy and sparse cross-pollinations, the CLS-e-lit connection still remains to be reinforced, in its textual analysis, authorship attribution, and natural language processing or NLP-based focus, CLS is thriving across journals and, at times, languages and literatures (e.g., Patras *et al.*) as major milestones are passed (Primorac *et al.*). It perhaps falls short there where Cramer's above-referenced critique does as well: in addressing the relevant media(tion) issues (see Tanasescu "Literature and/as..." also for the difference in that respect between CLS and DLS, digital literary analysis). What indeed differentiates the digitality of... digital writing, for instance, from that of the alphabet used in print or, say, runic inscriptions, is the very kind of mediation involved, the intermediality along its spectrum of acceptances mentioned above, and, as also already hinted, its complexity.

Although traditionally mediation, mediality, and/or multimedia have been highlighted as distinctive features of e-lit from its earliest stages (see Funkhouser *Prehistoric...*), in these more recent DH tie-ins, it is precisely the approach to intermediality and particularly platform intermediality that seems to be lagging behind. Flores' widely cited article reissued as a book chapter as well (Flores "Third-Generation" 2019, "Third-Generation" 2020) advancing the idea of a third e-lit generation or wave that embraces platforms, understands intermedia as multimedia and the latter basically as "image macro memes" or as "upload[ing] a picture, put[ting] language in it, create[ing] an animation, and share[ing] it" (30). Working on platforms, on the other hand, involves "exploring existing forms, established platforms, and interfaces" (38). The issue with such statements and descriptions—besides representing another way of saying that (e-)literature is everywhere or everything is literature—is not their simplicity, but their incompleteness: intermediality, as stated above, can involve a good deal of other approaches. The platforms involved, for example, can (also) be coding platforms besides the more frequently researched SM (see Monjour and Sauret in this collection), (pre)established modes and roles can be (analytically-)creatively deformed or repurposed, and intermediality can span and interconnect multiple platforms ("interplatform intermediality," see the chapter "Dynamical Systems and Interplatform Intermediality") particularly in community-involving, culturally and politically subversive ways (Monjour and Sauret in this book).

A richer and, at the same time, more refined concept of intermediality could help to build stronger bridges between the various genres of digital-space-based literature and CLS/ digital literary studies (DLS)/ DH. While in these contemporary cultural/computational environments, literature can evolve and expand within, or alongside, communities without worrying about its own essential character—about whether, for instance, intermediality is an intrinsic literary feature or a rather more recent paradigm that expands literature's established boundaries—it can and it does nevertheless draw in the process on data and outputs coming from less dynamic approaches. (C)LS, text analysis (TA), NLP, network analysis, and, generally, computational-analysis-based approaches, for instance, have been used in literary projects/performances to build and run intermedia developments on (Tanasescu and Tanasescu "Complexity" Tanasescu and Tanasescu, "#GraphPoem: Holisme analytique-créatif," [R. and C.] Tanasescu's chapters) or for performative and reflective modeling (Stange's chapter in this collection).[5] Similarly, traditional hermeneutics has been revisited and reformulated for dynamic, adaptive, interactive, and/or multilayered modeling (Kleymann and Stange; see also Armaselu as well as Galleron *et al.*'s chapters in this collection). It is the intermediality and the relevant analytical-creativity of such approaches that turned visualization, in spite of the typical multiple pitfalls it can present when uncritically practiced (Drucker "Writing like a Machine"), into an adaptive and hermeneutically nuanced method (Kleymann and Stange). They also helped to develop types of hermeneutic modeling whereby visual metaphors such as zooming and (charting) scale acquired significant theoretical and practical meaning and utility (Armaselu in this collection).

These recent contributions strive to internalize sophisticated and subtle literary theory and specific hermeneutic concepts that generally have not been previously in the focus of the operational literary computational research. While theorists and practitioners have stated the necessity of including such issues in CLS/DLS for over a decade now (cf. for instance Ramsay), it is only relatively recently that actual significant steps have been taken down that path. Aspects of specialized scholarly literary criticism, qualitative, critically creative, and complex comparative interpretive assessment are now more and more being built into the overall computational approach. As a consequence, these new directions incorporate user's content, critical input, and creativity as an essential part of the modeling per se. This allows a kind of interactivity that accommodates users individually or collectively with their own reading of, or research into, the literary work(s) and with the secondary or comparative sources they want to include in that reading, a dimension that has been termed "digital hermeneutics" (see Armaselu; also van den Heuvel and Armaselu "Genetic Criticism"). Such projects alongside the attendant theory are much more than annotatable digital editions though as they involve specific a-priori modeling allowing text mining and "zoomability" (ibid.) and the implementation of sophisticated hermeneutic concepts such as multiperspectivity, ambiguity, and contradiction (Kleymann and Stange) as well as adaptive and interactive data development, processing, and analysis. In the case of authors like Armaselu, developing in-depth analysis tools for hermeneutic modeling purposes also has a pertinent creative dimension.

In fact, Armaselu's hermeneutic modeling is analytical-creative in quite a number of ways. As she delves, for instance, into what she calls the "conceptual" or "informational granularity" of the text, she discovers ways to (re)generate the latter as a "stratified *assemblage*" (Armaselu in this collection, my emphasis, also a term foregrounded as analytical-creativity-relevant by [R.] Tanasescu in her contribution). Armaselu thus computationally (re)reads/(re)writes/(re)assembles a literary text as a performative way to chart its semantic layers and the specific role played by details in them (while describing code itself as performance too). She also combines literary works with established critical readings of them (e.g., Balzac's *Sarrasine* and Barthes' analysis of it) as part of a "deformative-interpretive" process, and, last but not least, she writes her own (confessional) fiction as part of developing and testing the hermeneutic model. The latter, described as "model of textual zoom or z-text," is thus developed within, and by means of, a "*self-expanding* story" "answering readers' questions" (Armaselu in this collection, my emphasis). Both Armaselu and Stange (see his chapter in this collection) develop an implicit dialogue with Krämer's views on the often obscured relation between DH and the humanities as based on a "flattening technique." The diagrammatic informing both fields in Krämer's theory as a cultural and epistemic technique critically mirrors Armaselu's "zoomland" and Stange's "reflective [modeling] sketches" in ways that revisit and reform traditional hermeneutics from "deep" interpretation to "surface orientation" (Krämer; see also the concept of "orientation" of prefatory/liminal texts in the chapter by Galleron *et al.* in this book).

While, as in the case above, it can be present as a surprising enriching development in hermeneutic modeling, the automated (or self-)expansion of data is a most salient feature of analytical-creative approaches to contemporary literature more widely. Analysis in general and computational analysis in particular inevitably involve creativity, but especially given the prominence (if not primacy) of NLP and text analysis in DH, this has a particular relevance to literary practice. Creativity actually acquires new meanings and manifestations in the context as artificial intelligence (AI) can "learn" and quantify literary features from text corpora only, and by means of literary text datafication (Pold & Erslev). Creativity therefore involves in our current literary culture, on the one hand, data-analysis-driven computer and human-computer interaction or HCI-based writing mainly as sampling (Johnston) or translation ([R.] Tanasescu in this collection). Such approaches provide an algorithmic consistency and specific scalable methodology to the previously advanced but less articulate "uncreative" poetics (Perloff, Goldsmith, see also Monjour and Sauret in this collection). On the other hand, then, and arguably even more relevantly, creativity in literature gained new meanings and approaches, specifically related to generating or creating new literary or literature-relevant data. Significant contributions in this respect range from literary text maps (Eide) to computationally assembled literary anthologies (Sondheim *et al.*) to interactive and comparative web-based "editions of editions" of specific literary works (Raposo *et al.*).

Quite a number of relevant examples are analyzed in this collection as well. Literary corpora expand by algorithmically searching and including works that have certain features and/or contribute to a certain trend in the corpus ([R.] Tanasescu in this collection); in data-commoning projects or events, computational analysis is the driving force behind the interplatform intermediality and the dynamics informing both the accumulation of data and the related evolution of the network-community (chapter "Dynamical Systems and Interplatform Intermediality" in this volume); deep-learning algorithms "learn" poetry big data before collaboratively (re)writing them (as "re… rites") into new poems together with the programmer-performer and his audiences (Jhave *Big Data Poetry* and *ReRites*); a poet writes not like, but as a NLP compression algorithm (Drucker in this collection, also Drucker "Writing Like a Machine" and "Poetry Has No Future"); vectorized poems guide the flaneuring across topographies, databases, network topologies, and compositional processes (MARGENTO *Brussels*, Tanasescu "#GraphPoem @ DHSI"); the intra- and inter-lingual translation of poems involves hybridization with other corpora and textual multidimensional expansion and concrete crystallization (MARGENTO *et al. Various Wanted*). In all of these examples, analysis and/as/for creativity outputs or is instrumental in generating and/or expanding poems, databases, community-networks, and/as performances. There is a definitory ethical dimension to and subversive drive behind assembling these techno-ontological constellations, as communities involved in literary computing and intermediality resist control (see [C.] Tanasescu in this collection on the above and the link to Indigenous cultures) while minorities, minoritized literatures, and un(der)represented languages or cultures become pivotal in wider and more "central" contexts by means of analytical creativity and complexity mathematics (MARGENTO *A Computationally Assembled Anthology of Belgian Poetry*). The ethics of algorithms has previously been proven to be intimately if secretly related to major concepts in modern literary history and theory, particularly in terms of post-death-of-the-author authorship and the culture and economics of text primacy and copyright[6] (Amoore). The rise of large language models (LLMs) has recently made this discussion exponentially more complicated and it is again in literature and particularly in digital, analytical-creative or intermedia poetry that some of the culturally and politically relevant aspects can be more easily discerned (Klobucar in this collection; see also MARGENTO *A Computationally Assembled Anthology*). In such contexts, the focus on (inter)media and literary corpus ecologies cogently translates to ecology and sustainability in the widest and most urgent environmental sense as naturally connected with minoritized cultures, languages, and literatures (ibid.).

As we have just seen, there are aspects—and projects—in which hermeneutic modeling and analytical creativity overlap, just as there are also facets, or nuances, at times in the same project, on which they are in contrast. And, as also hinted above and apparent throughout this collection, the same goes for platform intermediality with respect to these two phenomena. The three are, therefore, no orthogonal axes of any comprehensive frame of reference. Rather, contemporary literature can be described as a rainbow in which the three colors can appear from one work or project/ event to the next—in wider or thinner stripes, or percentages, that partly overlap or spill into each other.

How and why did we arrange then the contributions to this collection this way and not another? We (editor and contributors) did that according to, what we thought was, the dominant theme (or "color") in each of them, but the reader is warmly invited to read them differently. Arrange, analyze, and perform them differently. Several ways alternatively, intermedially, across platforms and apps. Include (in automated or HCI manner) other contributions, put together, as poet Dana Gioia was once urging, their own anthologies (Gioia), collections, communities, networks, and/ as performances.

For, in spite of our vision, these are definitely far from being the only colors of the rainbow, or even all the nuances of the colors we are flying here. Creative communities of YouTubers in the Francophone world, for instance, collaborate on and off-line sharing resources and promoting each other's work on SM and beyond (Levoin and Louessard). A one-of-a-kind genre, ambient literature, does *not* exist, in the sense that there are no specific works or instances to analyze, not even as general frameworks or alternative scenarios (Abba *et al.*). It is the reader-viewer-user and their ambience, their specific context that will generate the piece, with always different data and approaches depending on the locales, the mood, the various preferences, and other interfering parameters. A special, unique kind of analytical-creative intermediality? Perhaps, but why not say the latter is a form of ambient literature instead? There are also (always?) antecedents that may slip through the cracks: we speak of (networked textual) "performative relays" in digital space, but compelling arguments were actually made over two decades ago about the "[t]he prospect [...] of having *Ulysses* as a plethora of related and interwoven and yet discrete *textual performances* within a *syncretic space*" (McGann 85, my emphases). Phenomena we are interested in can be even more complex or involve manifestations, for now, beyond our reach. Intermediality, for instance, is to us at at home in performativity, in the process, in digital flux, yet it may also very well be a matter of suspension—between narrative and image, between the novelistic "transcoding" of gaps in official reports (e.g., the one of the 9/11 Commission) and the global circulation of a certain infamous footage (Ganguly on Martin Amis and the contemporary novel as a global form, 43–45). Intermedial literature, in such perspectives, more often than not waits in fact to be (re?)written (or re-performed?) "in the interstices of the digital spectacle with which our mediascapes are engorged" (47–48). Also, while we find the intersection of the computational and the organic of significance and consequence (see Drucker in this collection, also Klobucar's earlier contribution, Klobucar "Vagueness Machines") within a wider framework of biodigitality, and digital ecopoetics and geopoetics, the bigger picture is inevitably much larger and more comprehensive. There is seismic and topogorgical literature, e.g., "planting, composting, and seeding of sonnets as a de(re)generative and de(re)compositional phyto-poetics" (Ryan 103), and thus, writing with, rather than about, flora; writing about/within/as decay, process-based environmental (literary) art, and vegetal subjectivity. The topographical (literary) part of this needs, we think and previously stated, to converge with the networked topological (Tanasescu "#GraphPoem"), but there is so much more to it than just the topographical. Last—in this brief inevitably incomplete enumeration—but not least, there are subjects or themes that are prominent in this collection that have nevertheless been previously addressed from different and/or richer perspectives by one or some of us. Communities, for instance, highlighted here mainly as data-commoning actors and outcomes, thrive in digital poetics in other ways or modalities as well, such as virtual reality (VR) or metagaming deployed in collaborative and interactive writing (Klobucar *The Community and the Algorithm*).

The Chapters in this Collection

In "Dynamical Systems and Interplatform Intermediality. The Case of #GraphPoem," C. Tanasescu discusses platform intermediality from two main angles, dynamical systems and modeling, in the context of possible cross-pollination between intermediality studies and platform studies. Intermediality seen as a complex both algorithmic and improvisational process that spans and combines apps and platforms is most representatively manifest in certain literary projects and performances (case in point, #GraphPoem). The community-networks involved in such events are shaped by data-commoning intermediality and evolve as dynamical systems. The complex mathematics of the latter has significant control-eluding and radical poetics potential, as the specific modeling involved, "intra*model*ity," performatively develops and updates models as emergent phenomena across platforms and apps.

Monjour and Sauret look into a specific case of platform intermediality that they have previously researched under the term *gittérature* (Monjour and Sauret "Pour une gittérature"). Unlike literature on more popular and easier-to-use SM platforms (e.g., twitterature), "giterature" is usually published on GitLab (or GitHub) and therefore requires a specific kind of competence in using the Git protocol. And thus, as is the case with intermediality more generally in the sense foregrounded by the contributions to this collection, it implicates communities-networks in the digital writing process and/as literary performance. *ZAP Rimbaud* was such a communal writing/interactive coding event organized by Abrüpt Press and resulting in a constellation of GitLab repos, a PDF output, and a print book (*enfer.txt, Rimbaud.ZAP* by... ZAP). This networked, performative, and intermedia version of *A Season in Hell* occasions relevant critical distinctions regarding such literature that, given the above-mentioned features, competences, and scenarios involved, cannot be entered under Flores's third generation of e-lit. Moreover, and perhaps even more significantly, it represents an emerging trend with strong ties to both traditional and contemporary avant-garde, "cultural coding:" tech-savvy computational approaches to platforms for (literary) social-political critique and hegemony-subversive purposes.

Raluca Tanasescu examines the treatment of the (poetry) anthology category in literary studies and in the field of translation, which both defined it until very recently in relation to the so-called synthetical forms. She argues that, in trying to offer a holistic perspective on a particular genre or period in literature and showcase a range of works and authors that are deemed representative of a certain literary tradition or school, anthology editing is traditionally based on a very simple (or simplistic?) scaffolding whose inner workings depend almost exclusively on the editor or publisher's subjectivity. The chapter dwells on *"US" Poets Foreign Poets*, a computationally assembled poetry collection in intra- and inter-lingual translation: English to Romanian mainly, but also English to English, to, or from, French, Spanish, Old English, and Old Norse, translations between programming languages and algorithms, etc. The collection offers a reproducible and scalable anthology model with a threefold purpose: to bridge the page-based vs e-poetry gap, to offer models of algorithmic translation, and to reimagine the anthology as a potential literary platform fostering analytical-creative approaches. In discussing this particular case study, the author argues that a postmodern understanding of synthetic forms is more suitable for digital environments and proposes a thorough reconsideration of the category against a complexity thinking backdrop.

In "Hermeneutic Modeling of Detail in Textual Zoom and Literary Texts," Armaselu addresses the challenging issue of detail and its computational treatment within a comprehensive literary meaning framework.

There is a hermeneutic tie-in, argues the author, between the rich semantics and functions of detail in literature and the arts, on the one hand, and the granularity and multilayered architecture of meaning that only computational analysis can foreground, on the other. An erudite tableau of detail-focused theory and criticism is consequently mapped onto the computational method that has informed Armaselu's continued vision of text zoomability. Zooming in on details and out on larger units of literary works either on their own or in nested critically hybridized arrangements can reveal various concurrent levels of semantic specificity. Modeling the latter—mainly by means of topic modeling and fractal theory—hermeneutically circles back to a refined notion of detail, both instructive and ambiguous or contrapuntal.

Galleron, Patras, Arias, Fernández-Cruz, Mélanie-Becquet, and Seminck report on their computational work on prefatory texts in a pan-European novel database, ELTeC, and part of an ongoing research project outputting substantive previous contributions (e.g., on titling practices, Patras *et al.*). The challenge they address is a two-fold one and the contribution thus makes a point, besides its quantitative results, about the complexity of hermeneutic tasks in CLS. On the one hand, the authors comparatively assess the effectiveness of various sentiment analysis algorithms on specific datasets, and, on the other, they offer a critical account of their own efforts to render computationally tractable discriminate literary criticism and theory concepts such as paratext, preface, and others. A more customary DH/CLS approach involving presenting the data, the methods, and the output is thus paired with more traditional literary studies considerations that, nonetheless, feedback themselves into the modeling facet of the research. A discussion of established assessments of prefaces from Genette onwards triggers the theoretical and operational decision to work with a more inclusive genre of "liminal texts," which thus, based on both theoretical and illustrative judgments, becomes instrumental in cleaning the data. The features the authors include in their model are both hermeneutically and technologically challenging: the "pragmatically oriented" *voice* and *engagement,* alongside other (con)textual elements also working as referentiality markers, *topicality, reference to characters, aesthetics,* and *context* per se. As the database is multilingual, another significant challenge was doing sentiment analysis in four (sample) languages, a task that involved several computational tools and foregrounded translation as analytical method.

Stange anticipates Drucker's chapter (see below) by... picking up where she leaves off on issues of interface design. While the latter translates in passing the question of algorithmic speaking and spoken subjects to interfacing environments, the former takes that to the level of reflective-conversation-based modeling. Stange notes the generally rigid and context-agnostic approach to modeling in current DH and CLS and draws on the suppler, more adaptive and dynamic ethos of modern design as he advances the concept and practice of "reflective modeling." He proceeds to reviewing major historical trends in modeling, with insights on concepts as diverse or positively surprising as "epistemic objects" and "agential realism," while also highlighting significant DH contributions to the field from McCarty, Flanders and Jannidis, and Ciula and Eide. Architectural design sketches get then in focus as (evolving) models of (potential final) models that enact a "conversation with the situation" and, in their capacity as epistemic objects, remain adjustable and, more importantly, indeterminate, ambiguous, uncertain. Based on this, Stange advances the notion of "material-related hermeneutics" transferable to computational environments (in quite a similar vein to Armaselu's digital materiality and plasticity) and thus usable in modeling both the data and the user's interaction with the interface. His concept alongside the exemplifying digital tools thus enters itself a reflective conversation with the latest developments in creative technical practice (CTP, see for instance Dieter) and the social-cultural dimension of interface design (e.g., Ratto *et al.*).

Drawing on a couple of previous contributions (e.g., Drucker "Writing like a Machine") and long-standing interest, Drucker asks the question of the "subject position of the algorithm" and explores the particulars of inhabiting that position in procedural mechanical, organic, or conceptual "modes of *poiesis.*" Who speaks in an algorithm (engaged in literary composition and not only), and who is spoken by it? In structural and enunciative linguistics, these two subjects are relatively easy to identify, as the enunciator is the speaking, while the enunciatee is the spoken subject, but the matter becomes much more complicated as we move on to algorithms, and particularly neural ones. And even more so, as the speaker is the one in a poem. Drucker exemplifies with her own work as a poet writing not *like,* but *as* an algorithm, one that analytically creatively applies NLP methods in parsing and (re)writing/condensing texts. A consequential question therefore is then, in what ways, if any, is writing algorithmically "ontologically" different from traditional literary writing that more implicitly follows formal constraints? The author frames the question historically and theoretically (with notable illustrations such as Philomneste's *Amusements Philologiques)* as she also ventriloquizes speakers in various modes and, indeed, ontologies. While the question regarding the latter inevitably remains open, Drucker's working answer relevantly speaks to other contributions to the subject of analytical-creative literary approaches (notably [R.] Tanasescu's): the editor of a collection, particularly one of procedural writing, be it *Amusements Philologiques* or a computationally assembled anthology, is not mechanistic, but emergent.

Klobucar's contribution links timely topics such as general AI (GAI) alongside controversial devices like ChatGPT with applied digital poetics and creativity in literature. By drawing on authors like Foucault, Bert Oliver, and Rancière, Klobucar considers how aesthetic creativity and political subversiveness combine to challenge epistemology, in its turn a site of political power. This opens the possibility for AI to revolutionize control, a preoccupation informing both this contribution and chapter "Dynamical Systems and Interplatform Intermediality," the difference being that Klobucar prefers to refine both AI-human commonalties and distinctions by combining aesthetic and theory-related creativity. Therefore, while, like Drucker, he sets out by noting the deep-running similarity between computer programming and poetry writing, he nevertheless prefers to delve into the history of this relation (from Turing and Strachey in the early 1950s to Scholes and van Dam in the late 1970s) before arriving at more recent poetry works and anthologies, as well as a novel. After a detour through concrete-music listening theories and more recent soundscape art, Klobucar circles back to the question of AI in and versus literary creativity to reach the conclusion that, like poetry, coding is itself experience-driven.

As a closing remark complementing the ones above, none of these contributions seem to worry about any publication-related issues: do such literary projects or events count as, or replace, publishing in more conventional or even traditional terms? Do SM or does digital space work as effectively as more traditional publication "spheres," venues, presses, or platforms? Are they the 'new' publishers (of the postautonomous world, see Vadde) or do they represent actual alternative publishing, as they used to, or still do, for certain Instapoets (Chasar) or twitterature (pornographic and/or intermedia) authors (Monjour and Vitali-Rosatti), as ways to elude mainstream or conservative gatekeepers (Chasar) or effectively challenge the literary establishment and the canon (Monjour and Vitali-Rosatti)? None of the above seem to be a concern any longer, at least definitely not a major or urgent one. While issues of book production and circulation, alongside the place of literary criticism and, actually, more precisely, *the* critic (as "consecrator"), still seemed of the essence just a few years ago in the "digital literary sphere" (Murray), more recent significant contributions aware of platform and SM culture and economics gradually but explicitly departed from such concerns by focusing on literature as online community-relevant phenomenon of a significant inter/multi-media, if still mainly text-based nature (Thomas). This collection continues that trend and also, on certain levels, enhances the emphasis on communities and intermediality, to the extent to which the two get to overlap. In specific ways, literature and community in these contributions are either one and the same, or work as hardly differentiable concerns. They are therefore at home publishing (print) books as well, as part of their intermedial, protean, and arguably uncontrollable fluidity and, at the same time, their assertive, resistant, and subversive ethos. They nonetheless also expand, or spill into, larger environments, forms, or concepts, from interplatform event-communities to performance-book-social-network feedback loops to complex dynamical systems.

Also, if only two contributions discuss translation and multilingualism explicitly ([R.] Tanasescu and Galleron *et al.)*, this is a book in translation. If not necessarily or always in the literal sense, in quite a number of other senses for sure: from modeling, intermediality, or performance as translation to translation of or by means of algorithms to emergence as complex translation, and so on.[7] The collection is in and of itself a database of "performative relays" being translated into a networked event.

Acknowledgments

My gratitude goes to Michelle Salyga for her unparalleled support and guidance in editing this collection, and also to Bryony Reece and Prabhu Chinnasamy for their dedicated expert assistance. Heartiest thanks as well to Karina van Dalen-Oskam, Øyvind Eide, Raluca Tanasescu, and all the other academics and collaborators who preferred to remain anonymous, for their peer-reviewing.

This book would have never been possible without the support, advice, and friendship of Anne O'Connor, Diana Roig-Sanz, and Javier Borge-Holthoefer. A huge thank you from me and the other contributors!

I am endlessly fortunate to have Raluca by my side, the de-facto (co)editor and/or coauthor of everything I publish, and Maria Sophia who has been considerably busy all this time, working all this as I went along, among other things, into a digital song-game; on YouTube Kids and, soon, also GitHub.

Notes

1 In the context one can explore the contemporary cultural trope of "literature *as...*," which, given the wide range of coverage, is relevant to the questions of literature as ubiquitous or literature as *the* space and/or mode of our age. As we will see below, literature as intermediality is part of this paradigm. As briefly touched on in this introduction, the history of (modern) literary genres has been revisited *as the* history of globalization (Habjan and Imlinger). Literature has been also equated with *the* digital (see the discussion in Tanasescu "Literature and/as [the] Digital," 8–13). Digital space (or the Web) has also been, from several perspectives, seen as (a work of) literature (9–10). Approaches in the area can speak to occupying the Web in a "post-Occupy" or "strike art" sense (Tanasescu "Community as Commoning") which is further expanded from a dynamical systems and intermediality-informed angle in the

chapter "Dynamical Systems and Interplatform Intermediality" in this collection. Special mention should also be made of the concept of model(ing)s and/as/of literature (Stierstorfer).

2 A model that is by no means new in literary studies; e.g., Barthes used to read literary texts as networks (see Armaselu's chapter in this collection).

3 Elements and their ensembles in mutual determination and correlated movement/mediation. I have borrowed (Tanasescu "#GraphPoem @ DHSI") the term from Larrue and Vitali-Rosati who, in their turn, imported it from biology, the model being that of a school of fish whose "shape is the outcome of all of the fish's movement but, at the same time, it is also the cause" (Larrue and Vitali-Rosati 53).

4 Writing in digital space has the features of a complex system as it involves multiple and multilayered processes of inscription and also comports emergence (Tanasescu and Tanasescu "Complexity").

5 Just as texts can be seen, in networked (con)textuality and computing environments, as "performative relays" of literary works in digital space (see the discussion above, also Tanasescu and Tanasescu "Complexity"), these more traditional computational analysis approaches can be seen as performative relays of intermediality-based methods in hermeneutic modeling and analytical creativity.

6 An even more complicated issue than one would sometimes expect. Simply copy-pasting or downloading a (literary) text from published files (even if only for research purposes and without sharing it beyond that research) can represent an inevitable infringement (Eve).

7 Translation as convertability is, according to Michael Cronin, at the core of digital humanism (Cronin 131), it is therefore, fundamentally, the digital per se.

Works Cited

Abba, Tom, Jonathan Dovey, and Kate Pullinger, eds. *Ambient Literature. Towards a New Poetics of Situated Writing and Reading Practices*. Palgrave Macmillan, 2021.

Amoore, Louise. *Cloud Ethics: Algorithms and the Attributes of Ourselves and Others*. Duke University Press, 2020.

Andersen, Tore Rye. "'Black Box' in Flux: Locating the Literary Work between Media." *Northern Lights: Film & Media Studies Yearbook*, volume 13, issue 1, Jun. 2015, pp. 121–136.

Armaselu, Florentina. "Genetic Criticism and Analysis of Interface Design. A Case Study." *Digital Studies/Le champ numérique*, volume 12, issue 1, 2022. https://doi.org/10.16995/dscn.8095.

Armaselu, Florentina, and Charles van den Heuvel. "Metaphors in Digital Hermeneutics: Zooming through Literary, Didactic and Historical Representations of Imaginary and Existing Cities." *Digital Humanities Quarterly*, volume 11, issue 3, 2017. http://www.digitalhumanities.org/dhq/vol/11/3/000337/000337.html#calvino1983.

Bodola, Ronja, and Guido Isekenmeier. *Literary Visualities. Visual Descriptions, Readerly Visualisations, Textual Visibilities*. De Gruyter, 2017.

Chasar, Mike. *Poems and New Media from the Magic Lantern to Instagram*. Columbia University Press, 2020.

———. *chinese-poetry*. GitHub, 2018–2023. https://github.com/chinese-poetry.

Ciula, Arianna, Øyvind Eide, Cristina Marras, and Patrick Sahle. "Models and Modelling between Digital and Humanities: Remarks from a Multidisciplinary Perspective." *Historical Social Research*, volume 43, issue 4, 2018, pp. 343–361.

Cramer, Florian. "Post-Digital Literary Studies." *Matlit Revista do Programa de Doutoramento em Materialidades da Literatura*, volume 4, issue 1, 2016, pp. 11–27.

Cronin, Michael. *Translation in the Digital Age*. Routledge, 2012.

Cytter, Keren, Freya Hattenberger, and Magdalena von Rudy. "The Literariness of New Media Art – A Case for Expanding the Domain of Literary Studies." *Journal of Literary Theory*. https://doi.org/10.1515/jlt-2012-0001.

Derrida, Jacques. *De la grammatologie*. Editions de Minuit, 1967.

Dieter, Michael. "Interface Critique at Large." *Convergence: The International Journal of Research into New Media Technologies*, Special Issue: Critical Technical Practice(s) in Digital Research, 2022. https://doi.org/10.1177/13548565221135833.

Drucker, Johanna. "Writing Like a Machine or Becoming an Algorithmic Subject." *Interférences littéraires/Literaire interferenties*, volume 25, guest. ed. Chris Tanasescu, 2021, pp. 26–34. https://www.interferenceslitteraires.be/index.php/illi/article/view/1081.

Drucker, Johanna. "Review of [Poetry Has No Future Unless It Comes to An End, by Davide Balula and Charles Bernstein (Nero, 2023)]" *JD: ABCs*, Aug. 17, 2023. https://johannadrucker.substack.com/p/poetry-has-no-future-unless-it-comes.

Eide, Øyvind. *Media Boundaries and Conceptual Modelling: Between Texts and Maps*. Palgrave Macmillan, 2015.

Emerson, Lori. *Reading Writing Interfaces: From the Digital to the Bookbound*, vol. 44. University of Minnesota Press, 2014.

Eve, Martin Paul. *The Digital Humanities and Literary Studies*. Oxford University Press, 2022.

Flanders, Julia, and Fotis Jannidis. *The Shape of Data in Digital Humanities Modeling Texts and Text-Based Resources*. Routledge, 2019.

Flores, Leonardo. "Third-Generation Electronic Literature." *Electronic Book Review*, Jul. 2019. https://doi.org/10.7273/axyj-3574.

Flores, Leonardo. "Third-Generation Electronic Literature." *Electronic Literature as Digital Humanities: Contexts, Forms, & Practices*, ed. by Dene Gregar and James O'Sullivan, pp. 26–43. Bloomsbury Academic, 2021.

Franklin, Seb. "Cloud Control, or the Network as Medium." *Cultural Politics*, volume 8, issue 3, 2012, pp. 443–464. https://doi.org/10.1215/17432197-1722154.

Funkhouser, Christopher. *Prehistoric Digital Poetry: An Archaeology of Forms, 1959–1995*. University of Alabama Press, 2007.

Funkhouser, Christopher. *New Directions in Digital Poetry*. Bloomsbury, 2012.

Funkhouser, Christopher. "Digital Poetry: A Look at Generative, Visual, and Interconnected Possibilities in its First Four Decades." *A New Companion to Digital Literary Studies*, ed. by Ray Siemens and Susan Schreibman, pp. 318–335. Wiley Blackwell, 2013.

Funkhouser, Christopher. 2019. "'US' Poets Foreign Poets: A Computationally Assembled Anthology." *Asymptote*, Jan. 24, 2019. Web: https://bit.ly/45RuhpR

Ganguly, Debjani. *This Thing Called the World. The Contemporary Novel as Global Form*. Duke University Press, 2016.

Gioia, Dana. "Introduction." *California Poetry. From the Gold Rush to the Present*, ed. by Dana Gioia, Chryss Yost, and Jack Hicks, pp. xix–xxix. Heyday Books, 2004.

Gius, Evelyn, and Janina Jacke. "Are Computational Literary Studies Structuralist?" *Journal of Cultural Analytics*, volume 7, issue 4, 2022. https://doi.org/10.22148/001c.46662

Grigar, Dene, and James O'Sullivan. *E-Literature as Digital Humanities*. Bloomsbury Publishing, 2021.

Habjan, Jernej, and Fabienne Imlinger, eds. *Globalizing Literary Genres. Literature, History, Modernity*. Routledge, 2016.

Hayles, N. Katherine. *Electronic Literature: New Horizons for the Literary*. University of Notre Dame Press, 2008.

Homer. *The Odyssey*, trans. by Robert Fitzgerald. Farrar, Straus and Giroux, 1961.

Hoskins, Andrew. *Digital Memory Studies Media Pasts in Transition*. Routledge, 2017.

Jaramillo, Laura, Michela Cozza, Anette Hallin, Inti Lammi, and Silvia Gherardi. "Readingwriting: becoming-together in a Composition." *Culture and Organization*, 2023. https://doi.org/10.1080/14759551.2023.2206132.

Johnston, David Jhave. *Big-Data-Poetry*. 2015-2016. https://bit.ly/3tVCM5Z.

Johnston, David Jhave. *ReRites*. 12 volumes. Anteism Books, 2017–2018.

Kennedy, Stephen. *Chaos Media: A Sonic Economy of the Digital Space*. Bloomsbury, 2015.

Kirschenbaum, Matthew. "The .txtual Condition: Digital Humanities, Born-Digital Archives, and the Future Literary." *Digital Humanities Quarterly*, volume 7, issue 1, 2013. https://bit.ly/1mCbo2G.

Kirschenbaum, Matthew. *Bitstreams. The Future of Digital Literary Heritage*. University of Pennsylvania Press, 2021.

Kleymann, Rabea, and Jan-Erik Stange. "Towards Hermeneutic Visualization in Digital Literary Studies." *Digital Humanities Quarterly (DHQ)*, volume 15, issue. 2, 2021. http://www.digitalhumanities.org/dhq/vol/15/2/000547/000547.html.

Klobucar, Andrew. "Vagueness Machines: Computational Indeterminacy in the Work of Jen Bervin and Nick Montfort." *Interférences littéraires/Literaire interferenties*, guest ed. Chris Tanasescu, volume 25, 2021, pp. 236–256.

Klobucar, Andrew, ed. *The Community and the Algorithm: A Digital Interactive Poetics*. Vernon Press, 2021.

Krämer, Sybille. "Should We Really 'Hermeneutise' the Digital Humanities? A Plea for the Epistemic Productivity of a 'Cultural Technique of Flattening' in the Humanities." *Journal of Cultural Analytics*, vol. 7, no. 4, Jan. 2023, https://doi.org/10.22148/001c.55592.

Lagerkvist, Amanda. *Existential Media. A Media Theory of the Limit Situation*. Oxford University Press, 2022.

Larrue, Jean-Marc, and Marcello Vitali-Rosati. *Media Do Not Exist. Performativity and Mediating Conjunctions*. Institute of Network Cultures, 2019.

Leithauser, Brad. *Rhyme's Rooms: The Architecture of Poetry*. Knopf, 2022.

Levoin, Xavier, and Bastien Louessard. "Le déplacement de l'incertitude au cœur de la (re)configuration d'une filière. Le cas de la fiction sur YouTube." *La Découverte*,

"Réseaux" special issue 213, 2019, pp. 83–110. https://www.cairn.info/revue-reseaux-2019-1-page-83.htm.

Li, Yucheng, Shun Wang, Chenghua Lin, Frank Guerin. "Metaphor Detection via Explicit Basic Meanings Modelling." *ACL*, 2023. https://aclanthology.org/2023.acl-short.9/.

Lievrouw, Leah A., and Loader, Brian D. "Introduction." *Digital Media and Communication Handbook*, ed. by Leah A. Lievrouw and Brian D. Loader, pp. 1–5. Routledge, 2021.

MARGENTO. *"US" Poets Foreign Poets. A Computationally Assembled Poetry Anthology*. Fractalia, 2018.

MARGENTO. *BrusselsHyperSonnet*, 2021. https://github.com/Margento/BrusselsHyperSonnet

MARGENTO, Steve Rushton, and Taner Murat. *Various Wanted/Se caută diversuri: An (almost) Missing Original and Five—Literary, Computational and Visual—Translations*. Timpul, 2021.

MARGENTO. *A Computationally Assembled Anthology of Belgian Poetry*. Peter Lang, 2024.

McCarty, Willard. "Modeling: A Study in Words and Meanings." *A Companion to Digital Humanities*, ed. by Susan Schriebman, Ray Siemens, and John Unsworth. Wiley Blackwell, 2004.

McGann, Jerome. *Radiant Textuality. Literary Studies after the World Wide Web*. Palgrave Macmillan, 2001.

Monjour, Servanne, and Nicolas Sauret. "Pour une gittérature. L'autorité à l'épreuve du hack." *Reconnaissances littéraires*, issue 2, 2021, pp. 237–252.

Monjour, Servanne, and Marcello Vitali-Rosati. « Pour une redéfinition pornographique du champ littéraire. Une exploration des marges de la littérature numérique avec les travailleuses du texte. » *Interférences littéraires/Literaire interferenties*, guest ed. Chris Tanasescu, volume 25, 2021, pp. 51–67.

Murray, Simone. "Charting the Digital Literary Sphere." *Contemporary Literature*, volume 56, issue 2, 2015, pp. 311–339.

Navas, Edward, Owen Gallager, and xtine burrough eds. *The Routledge Handbook of Remix Studies and Digital Humanities*. Routledge, 2021.

Noble, Safiya Umoja. Algorithms of Oppression. *How Search Engines Reinforce Racism*. NYU Press, 2018.

Paget, Brian, Diana Inkpen, and Chris Tanasescu. "Automatic Classification of Poetry by Meter and Rhyme." *Proceedings of The Wenty-Ninth International Florida Artificial Intelligence Research Society Conference (FLAIRS-29)*, 2016 https://cdn.aaai.org/ocs/12923/12923-60593-1-PB.pdf.

Patras, Roxana, et al. "Thresholds to the 'Great Unread': Titling Practices in Eleven ELTeC Collections." *Interférences littéraires/Literaire interferenties*, guest ed. Chris Tanasescu, volume 25, 2021, pp. 163–187.

Perloff, Marjorie and Craig Dworkin. *The Sound of Poetry/The Poetry of Sound*. The Chicago University Press, 2009.

Plato. *Cratylus*, translated by Benjamin Jowett, 1999 [2022]. https://www.gutenberg.org/files/1616/1616-h/1616-h.htm.

Pold, Søren Bro, and Malthe Stavning Erslev. "Data-Realism: Reading and Writing Datafied Text." *Electronic Book Review*, 2020. https://doi.org/10.7273/n381-mk15.

Primorac, A., Arias, R., Francois, P., Schoch, C., Herrmann, B., Kristsone, E. E., van Dalen, K., & Patras, R. "Distant reading two decades on: Reflections on the digital turn in the study of literature." *Digital Studies/Le Champ Numerique*, 2023. https://bit.ly/3QfPtzU.

Ramsay, Stephen. "Algorithmic Criticism." *A Companion to Digital Literary Studies*, ed. by Ray Siemens and Susan Schreibman. Wiley Blackwell, 2013. https://onlinelibrary.wiley.com/doi/abs/10.1002/9781405177504.ch26.

Ramsay, Stephen. *Reading Machines: Toward an Algorithmic Criticism*. University of Illinois Press, 2011.

Raposo, José, António Rito Silva, and Manuel Portela. "LdoD Visual—A Visual Reader for Fernando Pessoa's *Book of Disquiet*: An In-Out-In Metaphor." *DHQ*, volume 15, issue. 3, 2021. http://digitalhumanities.org/dhq/vol/15/3/000569/000569.html.

Ratto, Matt. "Interfaces and Affordances." *Routledge Handbook of Digital Media and Communication*, pp. 63–74. Routledge, 2020.

Rettberg, Scott. "Electronic Literature as Digital Humanities." *A New Companion to Digital Humanities*, ed. by Susan Schreibman, Ray Siemens, and John Unsworth, pp. 127–136. Wiley Blackwell, 2015.

Rettberg, Scott. *Electronic Literature*. Polity, 2019.

Rippl, Gabriele. "Intermediality and Remediation." *Handbook of Anglophone World Literatures*. De Gruyter, 2020.

Roig-Sanz, Diana, and Neus Rotger. *Global Literary Studies. Key Concepts*. De Gruyter, 2023. https://doi.org/10.1515/9783110740301

Ryan, John Charles. "Seismic, or Topogorgical, Poetry." *Geopoetics in Practice*, ed. by Eric Magrane, Linda Russo, and Sarah de Leeuw, pp. 101–116. Routledge, 2020.

Sadowski, Jathan. "When Data Is Capital: Datafication, accumulation, and extraction." *Big Data & Society*, volume 6, issue 1, 2019. https://doi.org/10.1177/2053951718820549.

Schaefer, Heike. "Poetry in Transmedial Perspective: Rethinking Intermedial Literary Studies in the Digital Age." *Acta Univ. Sapientiae, Film and Media Studies*, volume 10, 2015, pp. 169–182.

Shutova, Ekaterina, Beata Beigman Klebanov, Joel Tetreault, and Zornitsa Kozareva eds. *Proceedings of the First Workshop on Metaphor in NLP*, 2013. https://aclanthology.org/volumes/W13-09/

Simanowski, Roberto. *Digital Art and Meaning: Reading Kinetic Poetry, Text Machines, Mapping Art, and Interactive Installations*. University of Minnesota Press, 2011.

Sondheim, Alan, Brian Kim Stefans, Johanna Drucker, John Cayley, and MARGENTO. "Our Shared World of Language: Reflections on 'US' Poets Foreign Poets." *Asymptote*, "Essays" section of the journal's blog, 2019. https://www.asymptotejournal.com/blog/2019/05/30/our-shared-world-of-language-reflections-on-us-poets-foreign-poets/.

Stefans, Brian Kim. *Word Toys: Poetry and Technics*. University of Alabama Press, 2017.

Stierstorfer, Klaus. "Models and/as/of Literature." *Anglia*, vol. 138, no. 4, 2020, pp. 673–698. https://doi.org/10.1515/ang-2020-0053.

Tanasescu, Chris. "#GraphPoem @ DHSI: A Poetics of Network Walks, Stigmergy, and Accident in Performance." *IDEAH* volume 3, issue 1, 2022. https://doi.org/10.21428/f1f23564.e6beae69.

Tanasescu, Chris. "Collection Computing, Computational Collections. Data as Performative Knowledge and Live Heritage." Talk at KBR. *Auditing Digitalization Outputs in the Cultural Heritage Sector*, 2021. Slides available at https://adochs.be/wp-content/uploads/2021/09/ChrisTanasescu_CollectionComputing.pdf.

Tanasescu, Chris. "Literature and/as (the) Digital. An Introduction." *Interférences littéraires/Literaire interferenties*, volume 25, guest. ed. Chris Tanasescu, 2021, pp. 1–25. http://www.interferenceslitteraires.be/index.php/illi/article/view/1078/937.

Tanasescu, Chris, and Raluca Tanasescu. "#GraphPoem: Holisme analytique-créatif, le genre D(H) et la performance informatique subversive." 2021. https://journals.openedition.org/recherchestravaux/4900

Tanasescu, Chris, and Raluca Tanasescu. "Complexity and Analytical-creative Approaches at Scale. Iconicity, Monstrosity, and #GraphPoem." *Zoomland. Exploring Scale in Digital History and Humanities*, ed. by Florentina Armaselu and Andreas Fickers, pp. 237–260. De Gruyter, 2023.

Tanasescu, Chris, Vhaibhav Kesarwani, and Diana Inkpen. "Metaphor Detection by Deep Learning and the Place of Poetic Metaphor in Digital Humanities." *Proceedings of The Thirty-First International Florida Artificial Intelligence Research Society Conference (FLAIRS-31)*, 2018, pp. 122–127. https://aaai.org/papers/122-flairs-2018-17704/.

Tanasescu, Chris, Vaibhav Kesarwani, Diana Inkpen, and Prasadith Kirinde Gamaarachchige. "A-poetic Technology. #GraphPoem and the Social Function of Computational Performance." *DH Benelux Journal*, volume 2, 2020. https://journal.dhbenelux.org/journal/issues/002/article-39-tanasescu/article-39-tanasescu.html.

Thomas, Bronwen. *Literature and Social Media*. Routledge, 2020.

Vadde, Aarthi. "Platform or Publisher." *PMLA : Publications of the Modern Language Association of America*, Vol.136 (3), May 2021, pp.455–462.

Vauthier, Bénédicte. "The. txtual Condition, .txtual Criticism and. txtual Scholarly Editing in Spanish Philology." *International Journal of Digital Humanities*, volume 1, issue 1, 2019, pp. 29–46.

Part I
Platform Intermediality

1 Dynamical Systems and Interplatform Intermediality

The Case of #GraphPoem @ DHSI

Chris Tanasescu

This chapter studies a specific type of intermediality as related to a specific kind of evolving community and the complex model that best describes it. In events like #GraphPoem, the platform intermediality involved is the one that combines not only modes of mediation but also multiple platforms. Data are collectively assembled, expanded, and analyzed across platforms as a way of assembling an online community in/as performance, a phenomenon described in previous publications as data commoning (e.g., Tanasescu *et al.* "A-poetic Technology"). While this special case of intermediality requires an updated approach revisiting and putting in dialog the areas of intermediality studies and platform studies, the most suitable model for the related data commoning appears to be dynamical systems. The latter present remarkable mathematical complexity and computational challenges, which renders such projects and events relevant from a digital-culture and cross-disciplinary perspective, and, at the same time, potentially elusive, at scale, to the hegemonic culture of control informing platform society and economy. Dynamical systems, as a model of resistance and subversion in this case, are complemented by another type of modeling, one of free performativity, unrestricted synergy, and iterative metamorphic consistency. I term the latter inter*model*ity and illustrate it below with an episode part of the latest #GraphPoem installment.

Intermediality and Platforms—Preliminary Notes

Intermediality and digital platform studies are two areas that closely examine our contemporary culture in potentially relevantly related ways and topics, and yet the confluences between the two are not really that frequent. Platform studies acquired various acceptances over time, but in recent years, work on digital platforms has come to mean researching the political, cultural, and most saliently, economic and ethical aspects of what has been called "platform capitalism" (Srnicek). It specifically refers therefore to the complex infrastructure-based economics of websites (even

DOI: 10.4324/9781003320838-3

the term "platform" has been seen as problematic if not manipulative) such as those managed by giants like Google, Facebook, Amazon, Twitter (meanwhile X), and Apple.[1]

Intermediality, on the other hand, emerged as a notion coming from the world of traditional and contemporary avant-garde—the term itself was (most likely) coined in the 1960s by Dick Higgins, leader of Fluxus (Higgins)—and has to this day focused mainly on inter-art hybridization and fusion. While often purporting to speak to media studies in general terms, it largely addresses specific issues in cross-artform criticism and theory such as (the) music(alization) of/and/in literature, inter/multi/hyper-mediality in cinema, theater, and performance art, and media combinations in traditional and modern religious discourse.

Yet there are realities, phenomena, and initiatives that cannot be fully critically addressed by either of the areas above while combining the two could indeed prove beneficial. Interactive coding events organized by publishers on GitLab and resulting in both text-and-code repositories and crowd-authored books of *gittérature* (see the chapter by Monjour and Sauret in this collection), GitHub-based archives involving corpora and communities, data-commoning interplatform performances (see below), social-media-based communities of women writers contesting/reformulating the literary canon and reshaping (inter)media technology at the same time (Monjour and Vitali-Rosati), big-data (and) coding used in both partici-patory poetry-writing events and "A.I. + human"-authored book series (Johnston's *Big Data Poetry*, *ReRites*), etc., are examples of such phenomena that need an updated critical paradigm. Neither of the two above-mentioned academic areas are likely—in their current state and prevailing focus—to be able to fully tackle the related complexity since although intermedia and platformization are of the essence and essentially inter-woven in cases such as those enumerated above, not many current critical approaches cover them as such.

Moreover, in researching these phenomena one can locate facets of the two areas that need to be critically revisited and possibly reformulated in ways conducive to synergies heretofore hardly explored. While studies in intermediality, for instance, do not usually take into account pervasive contemporary cultural phenomena like platformization alongside their societal and "onto-formative" (Armano *et al.* 3) functions and impact—on a wide range of realities and aspects, including intermediality—digital platform studies in their turn would also benefit from symmetrical inter-disciplinary exchanges. The modes in which various media interact and combine and thus performatively inform a platform's infrastructure and operation—in short, the very intermediality always at play in the context—can shed significant light on its economics and its political bearing, which are core issues in the subject.

Combining the two aspects and concerns therefore in exploring *platform intermediality* can help to both delve deeper into the specificity of our contemporary cultures and build bridges between academic areas that are already at the forefront of the relevant research and would nevertheless gain further insight and relevance themselves in that respect from the cross-pollination. As literature has always been (a consistent reflection) about its own medium or media—and traditionally about the "surface(s)" on which it was "inscribed" (see, for instance, Tanasescu's "Poetry and Poetics of DH")—contemporary literature is inevitably linked to platforms in intermedial ways. I will analyze below one such project in a wider comparative framework that can prove instrumental in reaching the cultural insight and academic cross-pollination mentioned above, but before doing that I will have a closer look at the two subjects at hand.

Intermediality Studies versus/plus Platform Studies

Intermediality has been generally and conventionally understood as the combination/fusion of, or "intersection between," different media (Chandler and Munday, *Dictionary*). It has been seen as a definitory feature of phenomena "crossing their [i.e., media's] borders" (idem) and therefore belongs in a rich constellation of terms including "transmedia(lity)" or "transmediation," "multimedia," "multiplatform," "convergence," "hybridization," "remediation," and "multimodality," some of which will inevitably occur and be contextually discussed below as well. The fuzziness if not mere paradoxicality of the concept and its related plethoric terminology[2] mainly stem from the difficulty of the concept of media per se. In certain ways, media are in fact already intermedial in and of themselves, as they cannot exist in isolation (from each other, from other media) but are always interrelated and functionally located in networks, in networked media, or mediating networks. Therefore, intermediality is at times seen as an inherent "in-betweenness" of media (and, originally, the arts, see Higgins) or, moreover, a philosophically non-essentialist concept foregrounding the performativity of mediation and thus rendering the very notion of media irrelevant (see Larrue and Vitali-Rosati and their concept of "mediating conjunctures").

As the very term and concept of intermediality, and earliest actual approaches, originated in literary (interdisciplinary) studies and inter-art crossovers (e.g., literature and music or painting, see, e.g., Townsend), much of the relevant literature deals to this day with issues of art form combination, fusion, or contamination. Contributions usually treat artforms or genres as interchangeable with media, and therefore concepts elucidating and refining intermediality are steeped in cross-artform considerations and illustrations. Wolf, for instance, details *extracompositional intermediality*—intermediality going beyond the confines of a certain specific work—into *transmediality* and *intermedial transposition*. The former defines phenomena that involve various media without being specific to, or having the origin in, any of those media, while the latter pertains to types of mediality or mediation specific to a certain medium transposed or transferred or translated (in)to another medium or media (Wolf 461–2). Detailing and exemplifying these concepts involve the arts only as in, for instance, the occurrence of certain motifs in both literature and music or even "metareference" in either independently (e.g., the various literary styles in "Oxen of the Sun" in Joyce's *Ulysses*, 461).

There is a twofold consequence to the above. First, intermediality studies are for the most part paradoxically forgetful of the very medium-related side of things. Issues of mediality, modality, mediation, situatedness or embeddedness, and, consequently, the societal-political regularly elude such approaches as they consistently understand the "inter" in intermediality mainly as the "in-between" of arts and genres. The latter thus inevitably tend to be at least implicitly essentialized. While there are indeed authors in the field emphasizing the importance of historizing intermedia(lity) (see Townsend who, nevertheless, perpetuates the medium-as-artform reduction), others, typically absorbed by how intermediality bridges art forms, make theoretically shrewd distinctions but still adopt a rather atemporal—medium and reception-indifferent—stance (Wolf, for instance, even terms certain transmedial formal devices "ahistorical," Wolf 461).

Second, if media or artforms are fixed or essentialized, then the abovementioned in-between will also have to act as, or involve/include, a go-between. This third element instrumental in relations between media, that is, in "transmedial reference," has been named the *tertium comparationis* by Jens Schröter whose example of choice was narrativity (Neitzel 587). Neitzel (584, 592–8) adapts this concept to video games by significantly shifting the focus from media's materiality and sign systems to performance practices and the ways in which the ludic can act as tertium comparationis in those practices. I find such conceptual adjustment relevant as it points to intermediality as performativity and process and also foregrounds the utility of performance per se in illustrating, exploring, and understanding intermediality. As we will see below, these third elements are present in intermediality not only as media connectors and not necessarily as transversal or comparative concepts only. They can in fact be movements—literally, as in "gestures" or "routines," and also, more metaphorically, "stages" or "evolutions"—in a performance spanning and connecting platforms and applications.

If contributions in intermediality do not in most of the cases discuss the digital and its relevance to the subject in general or that of digital media specifically, one may be quite surprised to discover that in platform studies the situation is not necessarily strikingly different either. Contributions in the field are so focused on the economics and politics of digital platforms that they barely ever discuss digital technologies per se, let alone their forms and modes of media(tion). They will at times analyze the ethos informing—and, consequently, the political, historical, and cultural bearing of such technologies on—platform capitalism and digital cultures (see, for instance, Uluorta and Quill). Yet they will nevertheless refrain from addressing the medial ins and outs of those technologies and the ways in which they factually (infra)structure platforms and, consequently, online communities.[3]

The latter are significantly and specifically better covered by contributions to the subject of digital media, a topic, concept—and term, to begin with—almost inexistent in platform studies. Digital media studies do focus on the specifics—and once in a while, specific algorithmics—of platform infrastructures, mediality/ies, and, consequently, sociality/ies. Particularly the focus in the field on artifacts, practices, and arrangements as the "three co-determining elements of new media infrastructure" (Lievrouw and Loader 2) is what makes the approaches to the relevant issues more effective. The "new media infrastructure" is none other than platform(ization) infrastructure, and the above-enumerated three constitutive elements deeply inform the ways in which platform-based cultures, identities, and communities are shaped, interact, and evolve. Topics such as the relationship between digital—platform and therefore "occult"—infrastructure and (individual assimilation into) communities of practice (Slota *et al.*), decentralized social network management (Bortoli *et al.*), hacking and the "sharing of tools, machines, communities, and systems" (Brunton) or also hacking and its multiple upsides (Munro), and infrastructural open-access and commoning (Brunton, Tanasescu and Tanasescu "#GraphPoem: Holisme analytique-créatif") among others are relevant to platform culture(s) and economics and could significantly refine the existing approaches and insights in platform studies. Platform capitalism relies, for instance, on specific artifacts and affordances that users can work with in diverse ways that are consequential to their negotiated or "artificial" plural/segmented identities and the resulting communities and complex practices thereof. These aspects in turn have an impact on the specifics and diversity of platform-based labor and value or surplus production, issues at the heart of (digital) platform studies that more often than not are not examined in the field within such frameworks.

While preoccupied with issues related to algorithmically shaped identities (see Armano *et al.*), contributions in platform studies are unfortunately not fully aware of the performative nature of online identity and the complex ways in which this is related to community shaping. Identities are far from atomic or univocal in digital space (and not only), and the specific way in which they are created—or, in fact, *performed*—draws on remix and digital storytelling practices deeply embedded in digital participatory culture (Chayko 181 et infra). But that is also closely interlinked with the complex ways in which platform capitalism socially and economically operates at the intersection of entertainment, self-assertion/performance, and subjection. This complex interdependence between identity or persona performance and online community shaping is informed by the digital-media-specific transition from masses to networks (Lievrouw and Loader),[4] the simultaneous form and formlessness of the latter and their role in the emergence of hybrid communities (Ganesh and Stohl). Without exhausting the ways in which platforms—and platform capitalism—work, all of the elements above have a sizable impact on the imbrication of hegemony and resistance in digital environments. Most significantly perhaps, complex theory approaches in social science can account for the multilayered interdependence and mutual shaping of systemic micro- and macrolevels (e.g., individuals versus encompassing social systems, see Byrne and Callaghan, 36 et infra) and thus look at platform-based networked communities and identity performance from a both shrewd and inclusive angle.

Intermediality studies would also benefit from such refined and/or updated perspectives on the societal and community-relevant dimensions of (inter)mediation. Since, as already noted, the field is pervasively dominated by studies in literature and the arts, plentiful resources would have been available in, for instance, literary studies to draw on in terms of the involvement and/or shaping of communities in/by the literary (see, for example, Biggs and Travlou). Yet, as mentioned above, the consistent concern with cross-artform or genre (extra)compositionality precluded contributions from taking advantage of (and critically revisiting) such resources or addressing the relevant issue afresh, with the notable (and, one may say, non-accidental) exceptions of certain approaches in video games or performance studies (Neitzel, Ljungberg). Just like in the case of platform studies, revisiting such existent substantive precedents would require updating and possibly refining the approach by drawing on the above-cited advances in social science, media studies, and, last but not least, platform studies.[5]

One cannot but notice that, symmetrically, platform studies and even studies in digital media would have significantly to gain from considering and perhaps examining closely relevant phenomena and aspects related to intermediality. Expectations to the contrary—and even if reference resources (e.g., *A Dictionary of Media and Communication*, Chandler and Munday) state that intermediality is present "typically in the context of digital media" (Chandler and Munday, web)—publications in the area hardly ever mention the term, let alone approach the concept. Intermediality, in its more simplified acceptances such as a combination of media but also in the more sophisticated ones involving, for instance, mediating conjunctures (Larrue and Vitali-Rosati)—would make a significant difference in teasing out the multiple aspects, contexts, modalities, and, yes, medialities informing platform capitalism and the cultures thriving around and by means of digital media.

Contemporary literature, with its characteristic platform intermediality, may represent a propitious site for such a dialog, and after a few related general considerations, I will focus below on a case in point and the ways in which it illustrates such conduciveness.

Notes on Literature and Its Relevance in the Context

A post on Facebook, a tweet on Twitter, or a search and click on Google is a typical imbrication of social causality, algorithmic and participatory culture, and alphabets or vocabularies. The latter may refer to more conventional meanings of intermedia—e.g., combinations of text and image or sound/video—but also to combinations or fusions of platform-specific ways of expression, such as share and comment/response, comment and post, and accept and share. Intermediality can fulfill in these contexts a range of interrelated functions, from asserting belonging to, and/or prominence in, a certain social network to complying with and/or resisting platform policy and hegemony to "creating," meming, and remixing data. Platforms are the venues where such interrelations are perhaps most apparent and where consequently, social life, politics, economics, mediation, and signification are themselves made manifest as interrelated complex systems (Newman, see also Byrne and Callaghan) whose interactions and evolutions are non-linear, whose demarcations, overlapping, and nesting are fluctuating, and the observation and analysis of which are inextricably entangled with the observer's both general and platform-specific situatedness.

Intermediality is, moreover, so much at home on platforms, and platforms in their turn so infrastructurally conducive to intermediality that their cohabitation can spill into further forms of manifestation beyond conventional scenarios and delimitations. That is specifically where literature—particularly literary performance—can step in in a potentially relevant way. It is mainly in the context of literature performances or community-involving literary events that intermediality evolves in such ways that it eventually involves media(tions) and forms beyond the initial platforms. Case studies presented and analyzed, for instance, by Monjour and Vitali-Rosati or Monjour and Sauret in this volume involve tapping into the kind of experimentalism that both innovated new media technology and undermined patriarchal and conservative literary canons and practices, and, respectively, publications expanding the platform's potential and thus turning the latter into an actor within a more complex intermediality network. Performances such as those presented by Jhave (David Johnston) implicate the audience in making choices regarding revising/rewriting/interacting with certain poems, which triggers the execution of the GitHub-based coding script that generated those poems in the first place. The texts outputted at that intersection of live crowdsourcing and the automated sampling and mixing of online poetry "big data" are then collected in a poetry book series. And, the case in point of this chapter, the #GraphPoem events presented at Digital Humanities Summer Institute (DHSI)[6]—annually since 2019—interoperationally combine a number of platforms, including JupyterHub, Twitter, Facebook, and GitHub into collective data assemblage ("data commoning," Tanasescu "#GraphPoem @ DHSI," also see below) and web-based coding performances ("webformances," Tanasescu *et al.* "A-poetic Technology") into a specific and more ample type of intermediality (interplatform intermediality, see below). In all of these examples, intermediality involves forms of media(tion) beyond the conventional boundaries or infrastructural confines of a single platform or a number of infrastructurally networked platforms.

Literature is more than ready to take advantage of such affordances, and there are historical and formal reasons for that. It generally, even traditionally tends to absorb the various forms of mediation of its contextual culture (see, for instance, Grøtta) and manifest various, arguably inherent, ways of intermediality (see the discussion in the introduction to this volume on "literature as..."), most recently as *the* remix artform (Frosio). Yet it is not only the art's conduciveness or suitability to the culture's dominant modes of mediation that is at stake here. Online social life inherently involves a push-and-pull kind of relationship between users—and particularly the way they form communities—and the platform algorithms they find various ways to resist. Literature and literary performance in these environments and contexts are fundamentally about such resistance as they lay bare the hegemonic neoliberal ideology informing those algorithms, and, in cases including those discussed in this section of the volume, most explicitly pursue the latter's subversion (see Monjour and Sauret in this collection; also Tanasescu "#GraphPoem @ DHSI"). As such issues are among the most sensitive ones in platform studies, studying these relevant cases within the wider framework of contemporary literature can relevantly (and finally) bridge the two fields of intermediality and platform studies while opening new avenues in understanding contemporary cultures. As we will see below, the already mentioned interplatform intermediality, while playing a major role in the phenomenon, is only one of these new potentially significant concepts and aspects.

#GraphPoem Communities as Dynamical Systems

#GraphPoem is a series of literary events taking place at DHSI on an annual basis since 2019. Participants (in the institute) are invited to register for the event—and the vast majority have done so since 2020—and are subsequently given access to a JupyterHub repo where they can contribute files live to a data folder and/or run a Python script analyzing those data. The latter are thus represented as an evolving network that is analyzed for topological features and the consequently significant nodes (files in the dataset) are sampled by a Twitter bot, @GraphPoem. This whole process is fed into a Facebook livestream (@Margento.official) that can be watched by anybody anywhere online or on screens around the University of Victoria campus and is also recorded and uploaded onto YouTube and featured on the DHSI website.

As already mentioned, one of the concepts advanced for these events is "data commoning" (Tanasescu "Community as Commoning," Tanasescu "A-Poetic Technology") referring to the ways in which collectively assembling and analyzing datasets map onto the emergence of an active community in/as performance (Tanasescu and Tanasescu "#GraphPoem: Holisme analytique-créatif," Tanasescu "#GraphPoem @ DHSI"). This community is much larger than that of the participants in the event, attracting viewers and social media (SM) users on various platforms that interact with, or are impacted by, #GraphPoem in various ways and that sometimes continue to do so even after the event per se and/or between editions.

Modeling and computationally learning the communities and interactions—generated and/or augmented by events like #GraphPoem—are both mathematically and computationally speaking, significantly complex tasks. Users "get together" (on, and sometimes also, off-line) for such events in various scenarios, either by connecting on certain platform(s) for the first time, or (re)connecting for the event after having already been "friends" or (mutual) "followers" within other, (ir)relevantly related groups or platforms. They sometimes reunite for a new edition while also interacting (or not) on the relevant platform(s) in between editions of the event (or related events). We are dealing with entities and configurations or (in terms of the above-referenced digital media studies terminology) "arrangements" (Lievrouw and Loader) evolving over time, the likely most suitable mathematical framework for, which being as I will detail below, dynamical systems.

Dynamical systems involve, in simplest terms, two sets and a mapping (or function) from the combination (or "product") of those sets to one of them. It is not just any kind of sets or any kind of mapping, but that is already beyond the scope of this chapter (see, for instance, Holmgren). The concept becomes intuitively more graspable though when one of those sets is considered to be the time axis, and the other one space (a Euclidian space, in mathematical terms, or locally Euclidian, that is, a "manifold"). A certain point x in that space becomes (or gets to), after a time t, another point, and the latter represents the value of the above-mentioned mapping (f) applied to both x and t. Later on (after a time $t1$), this new point $x1$ becomes, or arrives at, a new point, $x2$ representing the application of f to $x1$ and $t1$, which (in a way definitory of a dynamical system) is the same as f applied to the initial x and the amount of time $t + t1$, i.e.,

$$[f(x1, t1) =]\, f\big(f(x), t1\big) = f(x, t + t1).$$

The mapping f is the system's solution describing its dynamics (and therefore named at times *flow)*, and the succession of the points x above make up the *solution path*. If a point x is in its own "future," that is, if it appears on the path once again after its first occurrence, then the path is an *orbit* (Akin). The vocabulary is obviously redolent of the branch's traditional and formative applications in physics and particularly in celestial mechanics (as well as fluid mechanics) among other fields, but the science is applicable to any such system whatsoever.

The main relevant facets of dynamical systems, extensively tackled in the literature, are their topological dynamics and their ergodicity. Topological dynamics, as already hinted and in even simpler terms, deals with how close or how distant certain points (i.e., states of the system) stay or become to each other as the system evolves in time. It therefore implicates concepts and formulaic ways to simplify such developments. Key terms are, in the context, the system's dimension and mean dimension referring to the minimum number of subsets of its state space needed to "cover" its evolution (Coornaert) and, respectively, the average of this number when the iterations (the sequence of moments in time) tend to infinity (Lindenstrauss and Weiss). The latter is particularly relevant as it speaks univocally to the entropy—and, therefore, degree of complexity—of the system: if the entropy is finite, then the mean dimension is zero, and if it is infinite, then the mean dimension is greater than zero (Coornaert). And, to return to the two facets stated above, ergodicity, once again in roughly simplified terms, refers to the capacity of a system to evolve in such a way that it infiltrates, percolates into, and/or "takes over" an entire relevant environment (while more strictly mathematically speaking it refers to the congruence between the temporal and spatial evolution of the system, see, for instance, Walters).

In our particular case, each of the points on our solution path, each x, represents a specific state of the group of users involved in a platform-based literary event (or series of events and/or projects). We can consider x to be either the entire group(s)—all the users and (certain parts of) their neighborhoods—or just a user (and therefore consider a number of x, y, z ... points simultaneously and comparatively in their evolution). In the first scenario, x would be a matrix quantifying the platform-based links between the users in the group(s) and the distance between x and $x1$ would represent the distance (or difference) between the matrix at moment $t0$ and $t1$. In the second, x and y would be two users at moment $t0$, and the system would be described by the distance—the length of the path across nodes—between x and y at $t0$ and then again at $t1$. In the specific case of #*GraphPoem*, there will be multiple paths and therefore manifold distances between x and y as there are multiple platforms involved. Or, in the first scenario, x would be a matrix representing the links between users within the complex network represented by the multiple platforms in which they may (or may not) be connected throughout the (series of) event(s) and, possibly, afterward.

In its initial stages, such a dynamical system—the users participating in certain or consecutive editions of #*GraphPoem*, for instance—most likely has a finite topological entropy (or zero mean dimension, see above). Yet given the remarkable complexity of the setup (the overall system, that is), with users having multiple neighborhoods in multiple platforms with non-linear evolution (particularly across multiple editions of the event, but not only), its infinity-limit entropy is in fact most likely infinite itself. Even before reaching that threshold, the system is considerably difficult to learn (its above-mentioned function f remarkably hard to identify) since informed by two dominant apparently antagonistic forces. As the distance between certain users—e.g., directly involved in a particular edition of the event—can become remarkably short and stay that way for a certain time span—a centrifugal tendency will become manifest as well. These users' involvement in the event will directly or indirectly impact over time their various neighborhoods in sections of the network(s) (initially) not participating in the event, thus bringing into focus users at a(n increasing) distance whose evolution may nevertheless be relevant to the phenomenon and therefore the dynamical system per se. Such evolution is particularly encouraged by the intermediality and interplatformity of the event per se, with users being present and active in multiple networks in(ter)dependently and their intermediality operating in multilayered and non-linear ways. A phenomenon is also amplified by the various temporalities of involvement in and interaction within different editions of the event as well as the multiple forms of remix those are informed or made to clash by. As a consequence, the complexity of the system will be manifold itself in its evolution, with distances between users decreasing on certain platforms and increasing in others and with non-linear, multiple, and mostly unpredictable (non-) causal correlations between users' evolution in terms of both distance and connectivity in various communities and across, again, various platforms.

Given the fact that the systemic control (see, for instance, Tanasescu and Tanasescu "Complexity") informing platform capitalism and algorithmic culture (Franklin, Armano) relies, among its main directions, on data extraction, user profiling, and monitoring value production (Miconi), the related tasks will present truly remarkable computational complexity as well as machine-learning-relevant difficulty when dealing with dynamical systems of users such as the ones described above. Extracting user data fundamentally deals with platform (as network) topology which, as already shown, in the context of literary platform intermediality in general and #*GraphPoem* events in particular, can be rendered unusually complex by multiple factors and actors. Among the former, interplatformity is just one major element, as extracting data across multiple platforms is hardly feasible when they have different owners and, thus, inevitably, different infrastructures, algorithmics, and, of course, control-related privileges. Among the latter (the "actors"), users initially not involved or directly influenced by the events under discussion are a particularly significant challenge in terms of running the above-mentioned tasks (for the reasons outlined in the previous paragraphs in this section).

And so are the data and algorithms involved in and/or shaping the course of those events; as objects and at times agents of commoning, they are particularly difficult to access and/or parse by (single-)platform algorithms. Specifically speaking, collectively assembling and sharing data and running analytical algorithms on those data on JupyterHub as part of #*GraphPoem,* makes the entire process opaque to the other platforms affected by that commoning activity, namely, Twitter and Facebook. Moreover, given the above-mentioned particular tasks for the platform algorithms, the mathematics of the relevant dynamical systems will most likely have to be tweaked to even further levels of complexity. Since, as already speculated, the evolving entropy will gradually involve more and more users whose data and profiles may non-linearly be influenced by significantly hard-to-track multiple (interplatform) factors and actors relevant to the events, the defining metric of the dynamical system will have to better reflect that kind of complex evolution itself. Besides measuring distances between users, it will also have to quantify their connectivity, the evolving number of neighbors as well as the evolutions of the nature and weight of the links to those old or new neighbors on various levels, on multiple platforms, and as possibly intersecting across or in-between various editions of the events.

What is more, not only the metric but also the number of users initially considered to be involved in the dynamical system to analyze will have to be increased. As the state of the system is defined at various moments by participants' neighborhoods on various platforms, (portions) of these—actual and potential—neighborhoods will also have to be included. Such augmented complexity invites a potential tie-in between the two main dynamical-system-related aspects relevant to our discussion, topological dynamics and ergodicity: it is not only the intra-relational evolution of the system that is at stake but also its expansion over time within the (metrical) space that contains it. While this tie-in needs to be mathematically validated and seems, at least at first glance, problematic both in this respect as well as in terms of a foreseeable probability of a sizeable expansion of event-related communities that so far have not gone beyond scales of hundreds or, at most, thousands of users (more on that from a speculative future perspective below), the issue of needing to consider potentially progressively wider contexts and neighborhoods than just the actual participants in developing model for such events is obvious.

For somebody studying these and other similar dynamical systems for extraction and control purposes in particular, the task of computationally solving the system is, as already hinted, in quite a number of respects and for all the reasons above, significantly complex. As has been shown (Vidyasagar), mathematically speaking, dynamical systems are generally speaking identifiable, and they are also computationally learnable, as the identification problem can be translated into a learning one (Vidyasagar, 932 *et infra*). Yet all the above-mentioned features make formalizing the system extremely difficult since, paradoxically, the task of (user) data extraction and profiling, for instance, seems potentially severely impeded by the very lack of sufficient data. The intermediality and interplatformity of such events as well as the relevant communities' alternative, non-conformist, disruptive, and/or radical *modi operandi*, among other parameters, can obscure data and data flows and thus dramatically increase the difficulty of an already, as briefly outlined above, significantly complex task.

Complexity beyond Complexity. The Complexity of Resistance

The issue of mathematical and computational task complexity is further enhanced in contexts such as those under discussion by the presence and interaction of, in fact, two main complexities. The complexity of user data extraction, profiling, and control, on the one hand, and the complexity of data commoning, on the other. While operating with assumptions of stark differentiability between users' assembly initiatives and hegemonically pre-established frameworks of activity, between working against and (in compliance) with platform-based algorithms, and consequently between resistance and adaptability/conformity would be questionable on multiple levels, there are *certain* activities and forms of association (Lievrouw) in which the platform-algorithm-resistant algorithmics is more evident—if not prevailing—by comparison to others. Instances of data commoning can, particularly in interplatform environments, represent such specific situations.

In the case of #*GraphPoem,* the ways in which commoning renders extraction even more complex as a task include, most saliently, first, involving the analysis of the dynamical system in the event, and, thus, in the system's evolution per se, and, second, developing a particular kind of networked modeling informed by intermediality/performativity and heterogeneity in such ways that it works and keeps developing and branching out across multiple applications and platforms, which I will term inter-*modelity.* In this section, I will develop these two main features and the relevant poetics and technics particularly from a complexity perspective and thus look into their potential platform-intermediality and resistance-culture significance.

The ongoing analysis of the data-commoning[7] involved in the event as a network graph is an implicit analysis of the involvement of the participants and the evolving connections between them within the emerging community and on various platforms (in short, of the already described dynamical system they make up). The outputs of these analyses are further used in the performance, being highlighted on two of the platforms, as part of a tweet from the event bot and, also, the Facebook livestream; which, inevitably, impacts the specific involvement of each participant as well as the interactions between them, and thus, the evolution of the dynamical system. This evolution and the multiple parameters impacting it make the task of identifying and learning the system indeed even more complex than the already challenging above-described general scenario.

Yet, what I think is even more relevant here is the complexity-specific nature of such data analysis as involved in data commoning and, thus, data creation. It is, to begin with, a performative kind of analysis, analysis within, for, as, and by means of performance. As the text network analysis algorithm creates SM content, the involved social network evolves itself accordingly yet in hardly predictable non-linear ways. Certain users thus gain sudden prominence, agency, and/or activeness, which can, and in most cases will, impact the evolution of the text network, which in turn, by means of a continued feedback loop will impact the social network back again. The analysis thus simultaneously informs, turns into a driving force of, and is absorbed by, the analyzed phenomenon per se. As such, the consistent pursuit of analysis as collective performative and creative impetus is more than a question of emergence, a matter of complexity-in-the-process: it speaks to the kind of complexity at stake. The mathematics of analysis as recurrently submerged in the analyzed process paradoxically goes beyond mathematics, by "incorporat[ing] both narratives and mathematics" (Cilliers quoted in Byrne and Callaghan 29) and taking the complexity level from "restricted" to "general" (Morin).

In #*GraphPoem* there are indeed, to reiterate Cilliers's above-quoted phrase, "both narratives and mathematics," and the narratives refer to how the mathematics—of the *graph*, the commoning networks, and thus the community per se—are digitally written, that is, performed. It is the story of the community generated by data commoning and the way it performs the network-analysis algorithms, contributes to the data, runs the code, plays related videos as part of the performance commoning, navigates the designated platforms as well as other platforms and websites, and so on and so forth. By doing all of the above and more, the community refashions itself and tells the (analytical) story of its own evolution—as a network, a dynamical system informed by the defining network mathematics—and, thus, the story of the event-performance, the "ourstory" (Tanasescu "#GraphPoem @ DHSI").

Unlike the established digital genre of the "mystory," which still relies on a notion of the "self" expressed by the narrative in oblique ways involving multiple media and "cultural lenses" to foreground a dialectics of the "me," "not me," and "not not me" (Gratch 55–56 and 61, Tanasescu "#GraphPoem @ DHSI") an "ourstory" is plural on multiple levels (Tanasescu "#GraphPoem @ DHSI"). As a commoning story, it involves networks of SM users, data, and AI that are made to operationally overlap while being performed as ontologically imbricated (Tanasescu *et al.* "A-poetic"). The approach consequently renders the issue of "self" close to irrelevant as it potentially reaches further than "not [not] me" in its networked heterogeneity and topological dynamics. These two latter features are fused into a three-pronged "poetics of network walks" (Tanasescu "#GraphPoem @ DHSI")—consisting of distance-based (centrality) network analyses (informing the performance), pathfinding across the graphs representing (specific sections of) the datasets involved, as well as flaneuring across various networked data (including scripts, platforms, and other [un]correlated windows involved in the performance, see below). By intermedially pushing the mathematics beyond itself, this poetics instills a specific paradox into the characteristic "narrative-and-mathematics" "ourstory," i.e., in the project's complexity.

The concept of distance in its various acceptances, e.g., the above-detailed metric distance defining the dynamical system and the distance across the graph(s) representing the data commoning, brings a pervasive discreteness to the event(s) under discussion. A mathematical discreteness that nevertheless comports amassing and agglutination to the point of—as hinted above, performative and therefore ontological—indistinguishability. This paradoxical manifestation speaks to the modes in which intermediality informs an ourstory in, as already alluded, using *maths to go beyond maths* and to distance oneself from the very metrical distance towards a form of *immediate complexity* (see MARGENTO, *A Computationally*

Assembled Anthology of Belgian Poetry). The related poetics of network walks not only means to reach into the social and cultural situatedness of data and data-commoners but to also engage that in a translation of the Western traditional Platonism regarding mathematics as a deep or ideal, remote code, or model of reality (see, for instance, Linnebo) into a reflective hegemony-resistant commoning opportunity.

In spite of the widely purported assumption of objectivity and universality, there is of course nothing amazing nowadays to state that mathematics, like science in general in fact, is culturally, historically, and politically situated (see, for instance, Williams). In a complexity paradigm such as the one under discussion, that becomes programmatically apparent as the data-analysis-and/as-expansion component of the performance, the complex network analysis algorithmics, is extended into, and submerged under the related SM ramifications. As mentioned above, the poetics of network walks make it possible to bridge the mathematics and the narrative(s) involved—the data analysis and/into the data commoning—within a comprehensive complexity paradigm (see, for instance, Byrne and Callaghan 3 *et infra).* The latter places its own mathematics in perspective as it also factors in the observer(s) as far from independent, objective, or abstractly distant, but striving to account for a (sequence of) scenario(s) in which they are actively involved in or even co-construct, and are, at the same time, constructed by.

Yet in the case of data-commoning projects or events such as #*Graph-Poem,* the complexity of those scenarios goes beyond questioning—and exposing the fallacy of—the observer's privileged ("objective") vantage point. They possibly even go beyond actively engaging both the observer and the observed in synergy, multilayered or nested contexts, and enhanced awareness. There is, in these cases, a still more complex relationship between the observer and the observed as they start to gradually and procedurally overlap, and consequently open new perspectives and opportunities. As *the* form of remix *par excellence* (and, therefore, of creativity, Tanasescu and Tanasescu "Complexity," Tanasescu "#GraphPoem @ DHSI") analysis transforms and helps to expand data as part of the data commoning, and, in doing so, also transforms the networks of participants alongside their various neighborhoods. These networks thus learn and transform themselves as data—in/as intermediality—carrying out the data commoning. And as agents and neighbors within those networks learn each other as data—relationally and intermedially—they do so not by means of or for the purpose of data extraction, but data commoning. Data contributed, analyzed, and expanded together perform—i.e., digitally write (see below), learn, celebrate, and refine—togetherness. As all of the above take place on closely surveilled, more often than not giant corporate platforms, where resistance can only be enacted by "playing by the rules" (Tanasescu "Poetry and Poetics of DH"), idyllic complacency could hardly ever color such vision though.

Control, as a systemic ubiquitous phenomenon informing the very medium (Franklin, Tanasescu "Poetry and Poetics of DH"), inevitably shades any digital-space-based activity and initiative. Yet while thus inextricably entangled, it is their different kinds of specific complexity that consequentially differentiate between data commoning and data extraction. The differences arise mainly from their discrepant mathematics, mathematical philosophy, and the notion of otherness, and thus crack open an unexpected gap between control and resistance, rooted in complexity. The observed, since the object of surveillance and control, will inevitably stay rigidly separated from an algorithmic data-extracting observer whose analysis will have to be 'objective' and output 'universally' valid (i.e., commercially solid) qualitative and quantitative features and values. While such setup and approach confine platform-based algorithmics to a restricted type (Morin, see above), in the case of data commoning, as already alluded, there is general and, in fact, a special type of general complexity: one in which the observers become themselves the object of their own mathematical inquiry as the latter is further complexified by their narrative situatedness, specifically for *#GraphPoem*, by a poetics of network walks.

The gap is therefore indeed mathematical, but not only. Besides the above-mentioned paradox of data extraction tasks that can get severely hindered by the very lack and, at the same time, complexity of data, there is mathematically speaking the problematic issue of identifying the dynamical system representing the evolution of communities of users involved in or impacted by events such as *#GraphPoem*. As has been demonstrated in the literature and already briefly referenced above (Vidyasagar), the problem of system identification can be, under certain conditions, indeed translated into a (statistical and computational) learning one. The conditions refer, roughly, to the possibility of replacing an infinity with a limited number of measurements, as the former is characteristic of dynamical systems, and the latter of statistical learning problems. This is usually done by imposing certain "fairly reasonable conditions" (Vidyasagar 934) on the system, such as BIBO (bounded input, bounded output) (Vidyasagar 934), a questionable simplification given that the field is still in its inception with regards to metrical-distance-based solution assessments (of obvious relevance to the examples in this chapter). The mathematical and computational aspects are rendered even more challenging by the recent advances in theoretical computer science regarding learnability in general, and the decidability of learnability and (the impossibility of) predicting machine learnability in particular (Ben-David *et al.*, Sterkenburg).

In spite of all these difficulties, the above-mentioned gap between data extraction and the types of data commoning under discussion is not only mathematical. Moreover, it is not mainly mathematical. Given its restricted complexity, multiple social, cultural, and political realities, interactions, or nuances elude data extraction's scope and horizon. Analyzing, for instance, the relationships between users as the combination of their manifold interactions in various social layers (e.g., family and professional) and SM platforms, even if already a complex task will get even more complex when considering the same relationships from an overall and multiple (multilayer) network angle. Such an angle would place users and their connections in a holistic, multiple-system, and large-scale perspective which remains largely inaccessible as long as the analysis is carried out from supposedly beyond that all-engulfing environment. This is the paradoxical—and perhaps, also paradoxically, inevitable—vantage point of hegemonic actors that, in order to exercise their hegemony, need to place themselves outside the medium they "own" and control. And the paradox runs even deeper as such a stance can only render its main purpose, commercially oriented data extraction and user control, less effective than the one pursued in a general complexity scenario. It is literary projects and events like *#GraphPoem,* and not only (see below) besides other alternative or activist new media (Lievrouw) that can make that paradox apparent.

Yet, taken out of context, and in most everyday contexts, the notion that there is more, or a superior level of, complexity in a few literary projects and performances than in the ways in which giant-platform algorithms extract user data (and then profile and target users based on those data), may of course sound intriguing, even amusing. Still, would it be for the first time that hegemonic power acts in a blunt and leveling but perhaps effective way (we actually just saw exactly how effective), while the resistant, the underdog, the indigenous community is nuanced, subtle, and sophisticated? Another question would nevertheless be, why would platform giants care about networks of hundreds or thousands of users when they have pools of millions and, in certain cases, billions to make profits off of? While the subject of speculative or creative futures—and their intersection with literary studies ("literary futures," see, for example, Braun)—is beyond the scope of this chapter, one cannot help but wonder what the future would look like as such communities keep scaling.

Intermodelity. The Complexity of Assertion

As we have seen in the case of the complexity model informing data commoning in intermedia interplatform literary performances such as *#Graph-Poem,* the formal separation between observer and the observed, between users themselves, as well as between analysis and creativity, becomes a really thin line. These actors, entities, and methods get to overlap on multiple levels and in multiple ways—procedural, technical, philosophical, etc. (Tanasescu *et al.* "A-poetic")—while still not fully coinciding, not becoming one and the same thing altogether. A similar kind of dialectics is definitory of interfaces; it is just that in this case the interface is itself performed and mediated. Within a wider framework of complexity and performativity in digital writing, what "happens" thus on the "screen" turns out quite relevant in terms of how intermediality—particularly with its stigmergy and accident-related facets (Tanasescu "#GraphPoem @ DHSI")—can occasion a performative kind of modeling, termed below inter*mode*lity.

Intermediality has been, as detailed above, particularly researched in relation to the arts, and it is in that context that theater has been considered to be the *hypermedium*, the medium that can incorporate all other media, or, the art that can absorb and represent all other arts while remaining the same itself (Kattenbelt "Theatre" 37, Tanasescu "#GraphPoem @ DHSI," Larrue and Vitali-Rosati 25; see also a more specialized intermediality-studies-based discussion in Georgi). The metaphor of theater as a window to both *look at* and *look through* has been extended into the digital where, for instance, a webpage featuring other windows is a look-at hypermedium in its own turn (Richard Lanham qtd. in Larrue and Vitali-Rosati 25). An even more particular type of hypermedium is the computer screen broadcasting the livestream and being shared within the livestream involved by an event like *#GraphPoem*. As it goes beyond the look-at/look-through binary, and, through the interplatform intermediality, it engages in and actually livestreams itself, such particular computer screen proves to be not, as it may initially seem, a shared interface but an instance of interfacing mediation (Tanasescu "#GraphPoem @ DHSI"), not performance, but performed venue, and therefore, a locus and agent of inter*mode*lity.

While the *#GraphPoem* events involve several platforms in correlation, and participants can be active on either or all of them both on their own and in coordination—and viewers can follow what happens on all of these platforms except one (JupyterHub)—the concourse of all processes and platforms is the Facebook livestream. The latter simply broadcasts what happens on the *#GraphPoem* event chair's computer screen and, as it is the livestream that is shown on large screens and digital displays for DHSI in-person audiences to watch in certain spots on the University of Victoria campus, it is that broadcast that is usually perceived to be the event per se and the streamed/streaming computer screen its actual performance venue. On the featured computer screen, a mouse arrow keeps navigating—and thus displaying—the relevant platforms and the processes taking place on them while performing actions contributing to, and impacting alongside the other participants, those processes. The mouse also executes a number of other related algorithms or coding scripts for various purposes, such as pairing certain poems (or other data items) highlighted by the above-mentioned processes with (mostly YouTube) musical or movie scene videos and playing the latter. It also (alongside the keyboard in fact) once in a while gets engaged in other more mundane, everyday activities such as browsing Google search results and other websites, texting or emailing people, and opening various files, e.g., e-books, and making highlights or annotations.

While all of the above seem to be just one person's actions on their own computer as visible or recorded on its interface, they are in fact (also) determined or impacted by, or responding to, the actions of the other participants in the event. Participant's actions are in their turn impacting each other and impacted by what is shown on the screen. The latter, as an apparent event venue, "shows" "what is happening," but in doing so, it refers to, it is a window to look at, what is not shown: the multiple multilayered and interplatform interactions between the participants (and between the latter and other SM users) and the complex ways in which they shape what is indeed shown, or, rather, performed as being shown. There are data inputted into such "interfacing mediation" by the participants' data commoning but, as we will see, there is data modeling involved as well, a specific one also made possible by such collective involvement and its integration into the activities of the mouse and keyboard mentioned above.

The example I want to give here is *The Tree$ of $cience Feed* presented as part of the event *#GraphPoem @ DHSI 2023*. It is a recent and suitably illustrative case in point as it implicates inter*model*ity both in this initial elaboration and its incorporation into the #GraphPoem performance. The poem had to work with two main features manifest as simultaneously compositional and existential challenges. First, there was the in-person experience of spending two nights alone as a guest at somebody's place in a neighborhood and city I hardly knew. Second, the computational need to go through, and make sense of, the piles of books in that apartment and the ways in which they, alongside other (variously) related data, spoke to a number of things going on at the time—not least of which the kind of job I had in the city while actually living thousands of miles away.

The owner had purchased the apartment just before leaving on a trip with her two children and leaving the keys with me, so there was hardly any furniture in it or anything else except books stacked up everywhere, a couple of stickers the girl and boy had hurriedly put up on the walls to just mark for now what would later on become their rooms, and an old piano in a nook off the night hall overlooking an air well. There was a tall fern-like tropical plant in there as well, and a Wi-Fi modem, blinking and dimly flashing across the piano's ivory keys. An already fully equipped kitchen right across, with a fridge I stuck a Xibeca 6-pack and a few bottles of Ladrón de Manzanas in as soon as I got there. That was no vacation though, a push notification reminds me while I surf Google Maps to locate the police department that I need to stop by tomorrow first thing to get my legal status and work permit in order. A narrow traditional *balcó* with wavy and ornate wrought-iron railing all along the western side; cool breeze blowing in from the steep *putxet* towering the city with its dark woodlands and incessant birdsongs slowly resurfacing now that the invisible-traffic roar seems to start to die down.... I realize the place is not rectangular, and neither are a couple of the rooms; tree-like, arborescent, as I leaf through *El árbol de la ciencia;* dim-mazy, creaky-mumbly—as I dive into *Vuelo ciego.* The milky radiance hovering on the other side, rising off the sightless ever-calm sounds lined up by the ravines down in Poblenou and floating up La Rambla, shapeless, fathomless, city-light-flooding foliage-like-rustle floating-stone-ramose-mast-and-spire bustle now turning then roaming tirelessly touchlessly and ever thirsty for more, perhaps down Avinguda Diagonal. It's not Tibidabo, it's Antonio Machado, the *aparcament,* and the view from my car, the view is you... you.... Need to spot the network and then guess the passcode from a number of possible permutations.... The people, the rooms, the sights and sounds, the books, the communications. The architecture as inhabited, as habitation and traffic, the topography as (unknown) encoded poetry, the topology as a dialog between (suddenly culturally topographic) masses of poems. The algorithm walks across networks of place/people/poem-databases.

I needed a method that reunited the relevant datasets and drew on their coincidental numbers (rooms, people, books, etc.) while performing the place and its politics, and the affective-intellectual experience of navigating them. That is how I arrived at the Fibonacci regression tree, the six-tier version that decomposes eight into a sequence of Fibonacci additions of gradually smaller numbers (down to zeros and ones). This worked well in establishing from the very first step a correspondence between the three people living in the house and the five main rooms as well as the eight most representative books while using natural language processing (NLP) to formalize those correspondences and make them evolve through the subsequent stages and within wider (con)textual formations or arrangements. The poem thus fared from the very start as a complexity modeling journey, branching out into several related processes, applications, and/or platforms simultaneously. A literal journey, as it went live and was realized as a poem as part of a particular graph poem, that is, in performance (MARGENTO's #GraphPoem, 7:09–7:27).

There were several windows on the screen (and part of the above-mentioned interfacing mediation) that were directly involved in *The Tree$ of $cience Feed* during #GraphPoem @ DHSI 2023, most relevantly a Keynote file structured as a talk PowerPoint, a Microsoft Word document, and a Jupyter Notebook, being alternated with other ones more generally relevant to the overall performance and yet once in a while (suddenly) speaking to the poem under discussion too (see below). The Keynote slide-show titled *The Tree$ of $cience Feed* and having the subtitle *The Data and the Algorithm* presented the various data involved (from the place architecture to the books and their authors) and algorithms (plural, in fact), and then took the tiers of the Fibonacci tree one at a time dedicat-ing at least a slide to each one of them, the ways in which books, people, and places were interrelated and how these connections evolved one step of the algorithm to the next, and how lines of verse from the books and other voices were correlated and then distributed to populate the nodes (the "leaves") of the regression tree. The Word document went by the same title (of the poem and each of its mediating components), but the subtitle was different—(*the textual performative relay*)—and consisted of only two landscape-formatted pages, the first one arranging the book titles in two columns, one on the left-hand side and the other on the right-hand side of the page, each title split in two, the first half appearing in the first column and the second one in the second column (e.g., *Vuelo... ciego*, *Color... humano*, and *El árbol... de la ciencia*). On the second page, what looked like a concrete poem featured the tiers of the tree made of lines of text obtained by means of the algorithms described in the Keynote file, each leaf having the number of lines equal to its value in the regression sequence, 8, then 3 and 5, then 1, 2, and 2, 3, etc., and font sizes decreas-ing gradually from one tier to the next to the extent to which the lines on the bottom tier were hardly visible. And finally, the Jupyter Notebook, which contained the script sequentially following the same order of tiers and leaves, with certain lines of verse in the Word doc every now and then appearing as outputs of various cells containing the relevant line(s) of code (MARGENTO's *#GraphPoem @ DHSI 2023*, 17:36–18:43).

Such a combination of modes of mediation and apps or platforms may, in certain contexts, be described as transmedia, transmediality, or (a par-ticular case of) transmedia forms. Yet the ways these concepts are defined in either media and communication studies or intermediality studies do not really fit the bill. In the former field, the entry in the already cited lat-est edition of the *Dictionary of Media and Communication* is "Integrated media content employing multiple platforms and formats, typically in-volving interactivity (see also interactive media). Often distinguished from cross-media forms" (Chandler and Munday web). In intermedial-ity studies, this is the topic where, as previously mentioned, qualifiers like "ahistorical" can occur as the question at hand refers to the "extra-compositional" circulation of themes, motifs, "framing structures," or "metareference" across art forms or genres of a certain historical/stylis-tic period or not only (Wolf 461). Those elements, trends, or (stylistic) approaches, once initiated or adopted ("extracompositionally"), evolve within the work ("intracompositinally") as if in a self-contained autonomous and/or organic space of aesthetic development. #GraphPoem practice and platform-based literary intermediality in general do not observe such a paradigm though and cannot operate with such binaries anymore. Transmediality—just as "intermedial transposition" or the transfer/translation of modes from one medium or, in our case, platform or app, to another (see Wolf 462 and below)—is part and parcel of a compositional process that straddles the frame of an individual, clearcut, and/or static work. A rather stigmergetic kind of composition develops *The Tree$ of $cience Feed*, for instance, while developing the #GraphPoem it is part of, as a processual segment whose evolution both impacts and is impacted by that of the larger work and of its habitation in multiple digital environments simultaneously. While the *trans* in Rajewsky as well as Wolf's transmediality has fundamentally to do with a mediatic "beyond" or even "meta" (as in the above-cited "metareference"), the one in our case is closer to a kind of transfer, circulation, or flow within and beyond at the same time or, more precisely, the inner goings of a within that is also a beyond.

For the media studies definition of transmedia forms then, the multiplicity of platforms it involves most typically implies items created on or embedded in each of those platforms adding up to the overall work or piece of information per se. From whence, the prominence of the term "content" in the definition. The term refers in the field to either text as quantitatively analyzable or to specific "media content" such as photographs, videos, and audio files. In our particular case, the content is simply the interaction and interrelation between the above-mentioned platforms and apps in intermediality, the content is the form of that synergy, its process, methods, and procedures. As a consequence, the text in the Word doc is not the "content" of the work (to be further analyzed), but one of the, or one of the many possible, outputs of the analysis and associated modeling of the data at hand. The analysis as performance alongside the modeling (e.g., the Fibonacci regression tree) is also responsible for the typography of the text in the document, another important feature of the poem's *form as* content. It is a kind of formalism in mediation that tries to steer clear of any essentialism in either artforms/genres or platforms/media (such as the ones informing the above-referenced definitions of transmedia forms and transmediality). As a consequence, the poem is (in) none of the enumerated files, apps, platforms, or models, but in their ongoing interaction and, most importantly, their specific intermediality, their stigmergetic performative interaction with and integration into the digital environment they are embedded in. As we will see in a bit, such embedding combined with the event's intermedia poetics recurrently elaborates on the poem as a performative act and, as such, continues the complexification of its modeling—its inter*modelity*—in sometimes surprising ways.

While the poem can be seen therefore as a conglomerate or unusual combination of certain more or less usual models or ways of modeling—among the arguably more usual, vectorizing texts, among the less, correlating such vectors with voices and walks in charting places—such a view would not really cover the entire range of specifics within a project like that. A more accurate account (or, indeed modeling) of the model would start at the above-mentioned correlation, at the intermediality level, and foreground the component (sub)models—alongside their apps and platforms—as interrelated. Not as preexistent, but as discovered, (re)generated, and modeled by the poem's stigmergetic movement. It is the walk-through, the walk with, and the performance of places/people/books that establish these elements as processual and interrelated. In the process, established models are redefined. Vectorization, for instance, becomes a poetic form termed "vector prosody" or "computational prosody" (see, for instance, MARGENTO's *BilingualCorpusJourney*).[8]

Modeling in science refers to representing, simplifying, and/or finding a "metaphor" (see, e.g., Byrne and Callaghan 13) for, a phenomenon in order to render it more easily tractable. The above-referenced dynamical systems, for instance, are mathematical and physical models of relevance and applicability, and the challenge often is, as also mentioned, to identify (if possible) the specific system best fitting and representing a certain event or reality. In the humanities, modeling is a relatively recent concern that has gained more significant traction with the advent of digital humanities (DH), although such remarkable development paradoxically entailed in certain cases an obfuscation of the underlying principles and complexities in favor of a mostly illusory and at times even misleading transparency of dedicated tools and affordances (Flanders and Janidis). Just as the overall subject per se, modeling in DH has had a strong text-based focus from its earliest inception—its paradigmatic model being the digital edition—flourishing around text encoding (and the text encoding initiative or TEI), text analysis, and relevant NLP applications but also popular developments such as network analysis or geographic information system (GIS)-based applications that are not (necessarily) text-related. Among the relevant theoretical conundrums, formalization is a major one (Flanders and Janidis): modeling data in/for the humanities can perhaps never attain the formal crystallization of mathematics or logics, but then would one really want it to? Quantification inevitably informs such modeling and thus contributes to its remarkable upsides, but there are also some potentially large question marks hovering over it as well. What about aspects that cannot be quantified (Stierstorfer), or that are quantitatively unremarkable but potentially significant otherwise (e.g., Drucker's "Writing Like a Machine")?

Once again, enter literature. As Stierstorfer has shown, modeling has a much longer and richer history in literature than is usually acknowledged and a generous inter and trans-disciplinary potential (Stierstorfer). While the *model* obviously dates back to ancient paragons or the recently unearthed poetics of William Scott, it has evolved from idiosyncratic acceptances in Shakespeare's universe to etymologies relevant to this discussion (e.g., models as water-flow-controlling pipes, Stierstorfer 674) to sophisticated approaches that can shed a useful light on modeling in literature and beyond. A distinctive feature, as foregrounded by Lotman (qtd in Stierstorfer), for instance, is the literary model's two-faceted nature informing both the work at hand and the writer's comprehensive "world view" or philosophy of life (Stierstorfer 678), which can gain fresh relevance in the present context as well as in light of the metamodeling and cross/trans-disciplinary applicability of literary models, particularly the narrative ones. Lotman's vision (qtd in Stierstorfer) speaks both to the above-mentioned "simultaneously compositional and existential challenges" informing works like *The Tree$ of $cience Feed* (and not only, see below) and the cultural trope of "literature as," which, in multiple contexts, has been instrumental in advancing a representative, comprehensive, and/or (potentially all) inclusive status of literature in global, (post)digital, and/or intermedial contexts (see the introduction to this collection, particularly the note on "literature *as...*"). Both the "poet's world view" in such a case and the magnitude (if not totality) of what literature could involve or absorb in our culture(s) converge to being embedded in digital space, intermedia, and operating systems or computing environments more generally. They consequently both grapple with the porous and actually progressively blurred line between "the work" and its digital embedding (a phenomenon I will exemplify in a bit), as well as between individual "physical" and communal (or even commoning) computational existence.[9]

This is complemented quite conveniently by Stierstorfer's speculations about the metamodeling and cross-disciplinary modeling potential of literature and the examples he gives pertaining to the "literary turn" and specifically related to the role narratives can play in modeling across fields and subjects (Stierstorfer 692–4). The author draws on recent contributions from authors such as Scott Fortmann-Roe and Gene Bellinger to emphasize the pervasive role played by narratives in contemporary culture and specifically the ways in which even "[n]umbers and mathematics are just another way of telling a story" (Fortmann-Roe and Bellinger qtd. in Stierstorfer 693). There is here an evident possible tie-in with the discussion in the previous section dedicated to the narrative(s) that, when added to the mathematics, can bestow complexity on a certain model thus accounting for multiple systems, for richer and more nuanced and comprehensive layers of reality (the situatedness of the observer included). As stated above, when the narrative is, moreover, an "ourstory" foregrounding the observer as both a collective (interplatform intermedia data-commoning) "mathematician" and an object of their own mathematics, the resulting dynamics represent a specific kind of complexity particularly subversive of hegemonic platform algorithmics. From this new speculative (futures) perspective, the overall narrative of our culture and mathematics becomes a (meta)modeling vision originating in literature.

The case in point of *The Tree$ of $cience Feed*—corroborated with the other examples below—can help to further detail this possible future applicability and extrapolation of narrative-based (meta)modeling as already, in certain particular aspects, in actuality. As part of is above-mentioned embedding in the overall #GraphPoem event and, together with the latter, in/as the relevant dynamical system(s), the SM, computing, and other digital-space-based environments, the already referenced network walks, etc., the poem is performed and navigated simultaneously with other windows and web-based apps or projects. Among the latter, *Wealth shown to scale*, presented during *#GraphPoem @ DHSI 2023*, a project designed and created by Mike Korostoff as an interactive and comparative way to expose the incredible magnitude of the wealth of certain people, particularly the founder and executive chairman of Amazon, Jeff Bezos, against the (quantified) backdrop of increasing world poverty and hunger, Covid pandemic, climate change, migration, other contemporary major crises, ailments, and challenges, and the incomes of underprivileged, average, or even relatively rich but comparatively poorer individuals or categories. The website displays a strip almost as wide as the height of the web browser and scrollable to the right representing Bezos's wealth and, as one scrolled, smaller or larger patches in different colors on top of the strip with captions detailing the amount of money and whose income it symbolized or the world issue it would take care (in most cases, for good) of, if donated for that cause ("Annual cost of health care for a family of four," a tiny literal dot, or larger squares still incredibly small in the context, e.g., "Annual cost of chemotherapy for all cancer patients [\$9 billion]," to which another caption soon pops up in response, "On July 20th 2020 Jeff Bezos made \$13 billion in a single day," etc. [idem]). While one keeps scrolling and scrolling and seems to never get to the end of the magnate's wealth, some of the patches are simply meant to stress even further the hugeness of what is represented there at scale: "Every 10 pixels you scroll is \$5 million," or "We rarely see wealth inequality represented to scale. This is part of the reason Americans consistently underestimate the relative wealth of the super rich" (idem).

Wealth, shown to scale became part of the resources for, and was shown during, *#GraphPoem @ DHSI 2023* after being added to the event data pool by one of the participants (R. Tanasescu). It was presented as part of the livestream in combination, and alternation with, other windows, including those making up *The Tree$ of $cience Feed* (MARGENTO's *#Graph-Poem @DHSI 2023*, 1:08:04–1:08:18). When showing the relevant Word doc (containing "The Tree$ of $cience Feed [the textual performative relay]"), the livestream involved zooming in on it to the extent to which the above-mentioned gap between the columns containing the split titles of the books got to occupy the entire screen (1:08:30). The mouse arrow navigating the screen and performing the interfacing mediation kept switching, mostly to the beat of the music played at the time, between various windows and tabs, and, whenever it retuned to *Wealth, shown to scale,* it (or more likely the gestures made on the touchpad) continued scrolling to the right. At a certain point though, while alternating mainly between the two windows under discussion, the scrolling movement performed on the *Wealth...* website was replicated on the Word document as well. As a consequence, the wide white gap within *The Tree$* file started being scrolled across almost identically as the apparently endless ochre strip representing Bezos's fortune on the other app (1:08:18–1:08:44), in a sort of textbook illustration of the "tertium comparationis" in intermediality studies (Schröter qtd. in Neitzel, see above). The two windows were then both demonstrated this way alternatively for a while (1:09:45–1:12:09) before the performance moved on to its next stage.

The literal—and potentially metaphorical—parallel thus drawn between the two windows and what they represented can of course be read in more than just one way. Among these possible meanings, one may very well be formulated along the rather obvious lines of "there is at least as much richness between just two words in (the title of) a poem or poetry collection by Idea Vilariño, García Lorca, or Salvadora Medina Onrubia as it is in the bank accounts of the richest business owner on the planet." Such romantic reading will perhaps have to be qualified, or at least nuanced, by the $ symbol in the poem's "Tree$" and "$cience," and maybe also by the fact that "science" represents a potential mistranslation or inadequate word choice in rendering Pío Baroja's title: "knowledge" would have been a more suitable solution. And in fact, what interests us more here is how such already existing elements or features were further augmented or contrasted by the surprising development in the presentation; the continuation of the modeling in and by means of performance.

For while involving, as already stated, established computational or DH modeling strategies such as vectorization and regression trees, the compositional method employed in *The Tree$...* also comported elements that can be indeed revisited as modeling in light of the above-referenced narrative-turn paradigm. Algorithms are obviously recountable as narratives, which comes in handy, as is the case with such events, when presenting them sequentially in/as performance. Yet the experience of pacing around an apartment and/as roaming the hardly discovered city it is located in and/as being submerged in foreign noises/barely heard or remembered voices/overwhelming readings, is not exactly one's customarily modeled data.[10] Grappling with them though can become a way of modeling in this new integrated narrative-turn-informed perspective, one that can cohere with more traditional or applied-science-based modeling methods.

As already anticipated, this predictive "metamodeling" vision is nevertheless, in certain respects, already realized in the case of projects and events like those under discussion. Far from being congealed definitive systems or configurations, models are, in those contexts, dynamic, processual, open-ended, and performative; they are ongoing narratives. As certain features and potentialities lurking within these models are suddenly highlighted, developed, and/or contrasted by the various evolutions in the performance, the latter itself becomes the iterative narrative of modeling... the ongoing modeling narrative. What makes such iterative modeling possible is the previously articulated poetics of network walks (Tanasescu "#GraphPoem @ DHSI," see also the synthetic recapitulation above) enacted within a comprehensive intermediality-informed conceptual framework of digital writing (Tanasescu and Tanasescu "Complexity"). The latter consists of two mutually feeding features, performative relays and (re)performance, where performative relays are records—e.g., networked texts, recordings, and the above-mentioned ongoing narratives— that propagate, reiterate, and/or reformulate the event over time. Any instance of digital writing is also an event, an instance of intermediality, a performance that is always a reperformance (Widrich; see also the concept of Re-Play, Jahrmann) as it inevitably comes with a record, the relay iteratively bringing its history into its future (Tanasescu and Tanasescu "Complexity"). It is these two synergetic components that make the "iterative narrative of modeling the ongoing modeling narrative" above possible, which became apparent in the *The Tree$ of $cience Feed* continued modeling example. One of the poem's performative relays, which actually goes by that very subtitle, "the textual performative relay," was being (re)performed when the ongoing—participant-shared, and thus, data-commoning—network walks reached the *Wealth, shown to scale* website and scrolling application. The evental, intermediality component of the digital writing at work translated the scrolling movement from one of the apps to the other, thus (re)performing the poem by reiterating and re-writing its relay within a wider, continuously modeling environment. This type of iterative, interplatform, multilayered intermediality modeling— inter*modelity*—is informed by stigmergy (Tanasescu "#GraphPoem," see also above), a poetics of inter-related and mutually shaping wholes and of ever wider and ever more complex integrating contexts. A poetics of complexity, therefore, which engenders emergence modeling (see Stierstorfer too for literary modeling as emergence in complex systems, 690).

Without embracing an explicit poetics of network walks and stigmergy, Jhave does practice a distinct kind of inter*model*ity in his *ReRites/Big Data Poetry* events. His GitHub repository *Big Data Poetry* involves a computational model of reading, sampling, and reassembling verse data of indeed remarkable scale (collected from the Poetry Foundation website where short of 50,000 have been archived to date). The code was programmed to output poems on a regular basis for a year, which the poet edited and published as the "AI + human" authored series *ReRites*. As these poems alongside the GitHub code can be, in terms of the above-mentioned poetics, seen as the performative relays of the overall project, they are indeed intermedially (re)performed at public events in an audience-involving manner that can be described as a special kind of data commoning. At the performance presented at ELO 2018 in Montreal, for instance, Jhave demonstrated the code and rolled the poems on a big screen, both representing, in fact, automated processes that he interfered with by asking the audience out loud to suggest edits that he entered live as the presentation went along. As changes were thus being made to the poems, the updated "big data" kept being fed back to the code, which resulted in new output poems which, in their turn, were edited by Jhave as directed by the audience, and so on and so forth. This kind of continued modeling represents itself an instance of interplatform intermediality and data-commoning involving GitHub, previously output and collected poems (see [R.] Tanasescu's chapter in this collection, particularly her reflections on anthologies as platforms) alongside their Poetry Foundation data source, and live input from the audience, constitutes the very inter*model*ity representative of Jhave's project and performances.

Conclusion

Data commoning—collectively assembling and working computationally on data as a way of forming and manifesting communities in/as performance—has a significant resistance and subversion-related component in platform intermedia literature. In projects and events such as #GraphPoem, that component is enhanced by correlating several platforms within the data commoning, a strategy termed interplatform intermediality. In the process, the interdependence and overlapping of the various data implicated (the literary computing included) and the community evolve into a system of two-fold complexity. On the one hand, there is the complexity of resistance, described by specific mathematical models—namely, dynamical systems—and the complexity of assertion, a special type of modeling—inter*modeli*ty—employing mathematics to get beyond mathematics and to turn existing intermediality models into further branching-out, performative, and communal networks.

Notes

1 A.k.a. GAFTA, which has in fact evolved to various listings and also came to include secondary platforms, that is, platforms dependent on the infrastructure of mainstream ones.
2 The *Oxford Dictionary of Film Studies* provides for the "intermediality" entry not so much a definition as an enumeration of other related terms and entries such as "digital cinema," "media studies and film," and "post-cinema" (Kuhn and Westwell).
3 For notable exceptions see, for instance, Bigot *et al.*, relevantly focusing on platformization as a societal techno-semiotic process.
4 Platform studies inevitably focus on issues of community from a pregnantly political and historical perspective, as in, assessing the relevance of evolutionary models, e.g., from masses to classes to multitudes in Hardt and Negri (qtd. In Miconi) from an updated platform-capitalism-critique and post-connectivity-culture standpoint (Miconi), but they are still in need of updated approaches and methods such as the ones in complex science (e.g., applied in social sciences, Byrne and Callaghan) or digital humanities (Tanasescu *et al.* "A-poetic Technology," Monberg).
5 The monumental *Palgrave Handbook of Intermediality* that came out as of this writing passes a critical milestone in that respect, and thus fortunately invalidates part of the criticism articulated in this paragraph. (Bruhn et al.)
6 www.dhsi.org
7 Collectively assembling and sharing data in control-free or subversive ways and environments (see Brunton for a comprehensive definition of "commoning").
8 A poem's meter in vector, or computational, prosody is the average of all the vectors of its lines (see MARGENTO *BilingualCorpusJourney* and *GooglePageRankPoems*).
9 I am far from generally equating the individual with the physical and the communal with the digital beyond these very specific considerations (for further useful distinctions see for instance the research on hybrid communities by Ganesh and Stohl).
10 See for instance Lagerkvist (*8 et infra*) for a discussion of the literature on existential aspects that are, or are not, easily digital(ized).

Works Cited

Akin, Ethan. "Topological Dynamics." *Mathematics of Complexity and Dynamical Systems*, ed. Robert A. Meyers, pp. 1728–1747. Springer, 2011.
Armano, Emiliana, Marco Briziarelli, Joseph Flores, and Elisabetta Risi. "Platforms, Algorithms and Subjectivities: Active Combination and the Extracting Value Process – An Introductory Essay." *Digital Platforms and Algorithmic Subjectivities*, ed. Emiliana Armano, Marco Briziarelli, Elisabetta Risi, pp. 1–18. University of Westminster Press, 2022.

Ben-David, Shai, Pavel Hrubeš, Shay Moran, Amir Shpilka, and Amir Yehudayoff. "Learnability Can Be Undecidable." *Nature Machine Intelligence*, volume 1, Jan. 2019, pp. 44–48.

Biggs, Simon, and Penny Travlou. "Distributed Authorship and Creative Communities." *Dichtung Digital. Journal für Kunst und Kultur digitaler Medien*, volume. 41, issue 1, 2012, pp. 1–17. http://dx.doi.org/10.2596.

Bigot, Jean-Édouard, Édouard Bouté, Cléo Collomb, and Clément Mabi. "Platforms to the Test of the Dynamics of Platformization." *Questions de communication*, volume 40, issue 2, 2021, pp. 9–22.

Bortoli, Stefano, Themis Palpanas, and Paolo Bouquet. "Pulling Down the Walled Garden: Towards a Paradigm for Decentralized Social Network Management." Proceedings of the IADIS International Conference on Web Based Communities, June 2009, pp. 35–42.

Braun, Rebecca. "World Author: On Exploding Canons and Writing towards More Equitable Literary Futures." *Globalization and Literary Studies*, ed. Joel Evans, pp. 226–244. Cambridge University Press, 2022.

Bruhn, Asunción López-Varela, and Miriam de Paiva Vieira, eds. *The Palgrave Handbook of Intermediality*. Palgrave Macmillan, 2023.

Brunton, Finn. "Hacking." *Digital Media and Communication Handbook*, eds. Leah A. Lievrouw and Brian D. Loader, pp. 75–86. Routledge, 2021.

Byrne, David and Gillian Callaghan. *Complexity Theory and the Social Sciences: The State of the Art*, 2nd edition. Routledge, 2023.

Chandler, Daniel, and Rod Munday. *A Dictionary of Media and Communication*, 3rd edition. Oxford University Press, 2020.

Chayko, Mary. "The Practice of Identity. Development, Expression, Performance, Form." *Digital Media and Communication Handbook*, eds. Leah A. Lievrouw and Brian D. Loader, pp. 115–125. Routledge, 2021.

Coornaert, Michel. *Topological Dimension and Dynamical Systems*. Springer, 2015.

Drucker, Johanna. "Writing Like a Machine or Becoming an Algorithmic Subject." *Interférences littéraires/Literaire Interferenties*, volume 25, guest. ed. Chris Tanasescu, pp. 26–34. 2021. https://www.interferenceslitteraires.be/index.php/illi/article/view/1081.

Flanders, Julia, and Fotis Jannidis. *The Shape of Data in Digital Humanities Modeling Texts and Text-Based Resources*. Routledge, 2019.

Franklin, Seb. "Cloud Control, or the Network as Medium." *Cultural Politics*, volume 8, issue 3, 2012, pp. 443–464. https://doi.org/10.1215/17432197-1722154.

Frosio, Giancarlo. "A Brief History of Remix: From Caves to Networks." *The Routledge Handbook of Remix Studies and Digital Humanities*, eds. Edward Navas, Owen Gallager, and xtine burrough, pp. 19–35. Routledge, 2021.

Ganesh, Shiv, and Cynthia Stohl. "Fluid Hybridity. Organizational Form and Formlessness in the Digital Age." *Digital Media and Communication Handbook*, eds. Leah A. Lievrouw and Brian D. Loader, pp. 258–280. Routledge, 2021.

Georgi, Claudia. "Contemporary British Theatre and Intermediality." *The Handbook of Intermediality*, ed. Gabriele Rippl, pp. 530–546. De Gruyter, 2015.

Gratch, Lindsay Michalik. "Experiments in Performance, Identity, and Digital Space: 48 Mystory Remixes, Remixed." *The Routledge Handbook of Remix*

Studies and Digital Humanities, eds. Eduardo Navas, Owen Gallagher, and xtine burrough, pp. 53–69. Routledge, 2021.

Grøtta, Marit. *Baudelaire's Media Aesthetics. The Gaze of the Flâneur and 19th-Century Media*. Bloomsbury Academic, 2015.

Higgins, Dick. "Synesthesia and Intersenses: Intermedia." *Ubuweb*, (1965). https://www.ubu.com/papers/higgins_intermedia.html.

Holmgren, Richard A. *A First Course in Discrete Dynamical Systems*. Springer, 1996.

Jahrmann, Margarete. "The Big Urban Game, Re-Play and Full City Tags: Art Game Conceptions in Activism and Performance." *Performing the Digital*, eds. Martina Leeker, Imanuel Schipper, and Timon Beyes, pp. 171–190. Transcript Verlag, 2017.

Johnston, David Jhave. *Big-Data-Poetry*. GitHub, 2016. https://github.com/jhave/Big-Data-Poetry.

Johnston, David Jhave. *ReRites*, 12 volumes. Anteism Books, 2017–2018.

Kattenbelt, Chiel. "Theatre as the Art of the Performer and the Stage of Intermediality." *Intermediality in Theatre and Performance*, eds. Freda Chapple and Chiel Kattenbelt, pp. 29–39. Rodopi, 2006.

Korostoff, Mike. *Wealth Shown to Scale*, 2021. https://mkorostoff.github.io/1-pixel-wealth/

Kuhn, Annette, and Guy Westwell. *Dictionary of Film Studies*, 2nd edition. Oxford University Press, 2020.

Lagerkvist, Amanda. "Digital Existence. An Introduction." *Digital Existence. Ontology, Ethics and Transcendence in Digital Culture*, ed. Amanda Lagerkvist, pp. 1–25. Routledge, 2019.

Larrue, Jean-Marc, and Marcello Vitali-Rosati. *Media Do Not Exist. Performativity and Mediating Conjunctions*. Institute of Network Cultures, 2019.

Lievrouw, Leah A., and Brian D Loader. "Introduction." *Digital Media and Communication Handbook*, eds. Leah A. Lievrouw and Brian D. Loader, pp. 1–5. Routledge, 2021.

Lievrouw, Leah A. *Alternative and Activist New Media*. Polity Press, 2023.

Lindenstrauss, Elon, and Benjamin Weiss. "Mean Topological Dimension." *Israel Journal of Mathematics*, volume 115, 2000, pp. 1–24.

Linnebo, Øystein. "Platonism in the Philosophy of Mathematics." *Stanford Encyclopedia of Philosophy*, 2023. https://plato.stanford.edu/entries/platonism-mathematics/.

Ljungberg, Christina. "Intermediality and Performance Art." *The Handbook of Intermediality*, ed. Gabriele Rippl, pp. 547–561. De Gruyter, 2015.

Margento. *BilingualCorpusJourney*. GitHub, 2022. https://github.com/Margento/BilingualCorpusJourney.

Margento. *GooglePageRankPoems*. GitHub, 2022. https://github.com/Margento/GooglePageRankPoems.

Margento. *#GraphPoem @ DHSI 2023*. YouTube, uploaded by Chris Tanasescu, Jun 14 2023. https://www.youtube.com/watch?v=7LufQLkAqtQ&t=1254s.

Margento. *A Computationally Assembled Anthology of Belgian Poetry*. Peter Lang, 2024.

Miconi, Andrea. "On Value and Labour in the Age of Platforms." *Digital Platforms and Algorithmic Subjectivities*, eds. Emiliana Armano, Marco Briziarelli, and Elisabetta Risi, pp. 107–119. University of Westminster Press, 2022.

Monberg, John. "Building Urban Publics." *Making Sense of Digital Humanities: Transformations and Interventions in Technocultures*, eds. Julian Chambliss and Ellen Moll, Michigan State University Libraries, 2022. https://openbooks.lib.msu.edu/makingsensedh/chapter/building-urban-publics/.

Monjour, Servanne, and Marcello Vitali-Rosati. "Pour une redéfinition pornographique du champ littéraire. Une exploration des marges de la littérature numérique avec les travailleuses du texte." *Interférences littéraires/Literaire Interferenties*, guest ed. Chris Tanasescu, volume 25, 2021, pp. 51–67. https://interferenceslitteraires.be/index.php/illi/article/view/1087/946.

Morin, Edgar. *On Complexity*. Hampton Press, 2008.

Munro, Aaron. *Hacking in the Humanities. Cybersecurity, Speculative Fiction, and Navigating a Digital Future*. Bloomsbury Academic, 2022.

Neitzel, Britta. "Performing Games: Intermediality and Videogames." *The Handbook of Intermediality*, ed. Gabriele Rippl, pp. 584–601. De Gruyter, 2015.

Newman, Mark E. J. "Complex Systems. A Survey." 2011. https://arxiv.org/abs/1112.1440

Rajewsky, Irina. "Transmedial Passages. Remarks on the Heuristic Potential of a Transmedial Research Perspective in the Wider Field of Comparative Literature." *Between*, volume 8, issue 16, "Screens. Representations, Images, Transmediality," 2018. https://doi.org/10.13125/2039-6597/3526.

Slota, Stephen C., Aubrey Slaughter, and Geoffrey C. Bowker. "The Hearth of Darkness. Living within Occult Infrastructures." *Digital Media and Communication Handbook*, eds. Leah A. Lievrouw and Brian D. Loader, pp. 9–31, Routledge, 2021.

Srnicek, Nick. *Platform Capitalism*. Polity Press, 2016.

Sterkenburg, Tom F. "On Characterizations of Learnability with Computational Learners." *Proceedings of Thirty Fifth Conference on Learning Theory (COLT 2022)*, PMLR 178, 2022, pp. 3365–3379. https://arxiv.org/abs/2202.05041.

Stierstorfer, Klaus. "Models and/as/of Literature." *Anglia*, volume 138, issue 4, 2020, pp. 673–698. https://doi.org/10.1515/ang-2020-0053

Tanasescu, Chris. "#GraphPoem @ DHSI: A Poetics of Network Walks, Stigmergy, and Accident in Performance." *Interdisciplinary Digital Engagement in Arts & Humanities*, volume 3, issue 1, 2022. https://doi.org/10.21428/f1f23564.e6beae69.

Tanasescu, Chris. "The Poetry and Poetics of Digital Humanities." *Digital Humanities Quarterly (DHQ)*, forthcoming.

Tanasescu, Chris, Vaibhav Kesarwani, Diana Inkpen, and Prasadith Kirinde Gamaarachchige. "A-poetic Technology. #GraphPoem and the Social Function of Computational Performance." *DH Benelux Journal*, volume 2, 2020.

Tanasescu, Chris, and Raluca Tanasescu. "#GraphPoem: Holisme analytique-créatif, le genre D(H) et la performance informatique subversive." *Recherches & Travaux*, volume 100, 2022. Shttps://doi.org/10.4000/recherchestravaux.4900.

Tanasescu, Raluca. "Subject: Re: Quick Question [as in, heeeeelp please ;))]." Private correspondence with the author, 12 Oct. 2022.

Townsend, Christopher. "From the Periphery to the Interstices: Avant-Garde Film, Medium Specificity and Intermediality, 1970–2015." *Cinematic Intermediality. Theory and Practice*, ed. Kim Knowles and Marion Schmid, pp. 73–87. Oxford Academic, 2021.

Uluorta, Hasmet M., and Lawrence Quill. "The Californian Ideology Revisited." *Digital Platforms and Algorithmic Subjectivities*, ed Emiliana Armano, Marco Briziarelli, Elisabetta Risi, pp. 21–31. University of Westminster Press, 2022.

Vidyasagar, Mathukumalli. "Learning, System Identification, and Complexity." *Mathematics of Complexity and Dynamical Systems*, ed. Robert A. Meyers, pp. 924–936. Springer, 2011.

Walters, Peters. *Introduction to Ergodic Theory*. Springer-Verlag, 2000.

Widrich, Mechtild. *Performative Monuments: The Rematerialisation of Public Art*. Manchester University Press, 2016.

Williams, Travis D. "Procrustean Marxism and Subjective Rigor: Early Modern Arithmetic and Its Readers." *"Raw Data" Is an Oxymoron*, ed. Lisa Gitelman, pp. 41–59. MIT Press, 2013.

Wolf, Werner. "Literature and Music: Theory." *The Handbook of Intermediality*, ed. Gabriele Rippl, pp. 459–474. De Gruyter, 2015.

2 Platform Intermediality

Giterature and the Anti-book

Servanne Monjour and Nicolas Sauret

Introduction

At the turn of the 21st century, the advent of Web 2.0 resulted in a massive supply of digital technologies, with the combined effect of better access to devices (less expensive, more compact, and designed for individual uses), to the Web (with its wider, cheaper, and faster coverage), as well as to publishing tools (thanks to the emergence of CMS[1] and social media requiring minimal technical skills). This marked a shift toward a full-fledged digital *culture* which, beyond the technological, involves a host of conceptual mutations as well (Doueihi). In the field of electronic literature, where authority is partly based on computer skills, the development of writing platforms raises many questions. What credit can be given to a work conceived on popular platforms which, like WattPad, have developed their promotional discourse around an ideal of emancipation from computer skills?[2] What about literary writing published on social media (Twitter, YouTube…) whose primary function is neither aesthetic nor poetic? Last but not least, should we beware of the "platformization effect" generally described as going beyond the literary (Poell et al.; Bullich; Gillespie)? Could it be considered as a new form of publishing monopoly, even though some platforms have already given their name to forms of literary writing—*twitterature, literatureTube, auto-blography*? Are these practices still part of electronic literature in the strict sense of the word,[3] or do they belong to the broader field of what has been widely called in French criticism *"littérature numérique"* (digital literature) (Bouchardon; Gervais; Guilet)?

In this chapter, we will analyze the main conceptual and aesthetic issues of what we call "platform-literature" also identified by Leonardo Flores as a third generation (also called "third wave") of electronic literature—after a first generation marked by hypertextual practices that preceded web-based writing and then a second generation of writings favoring multimedia and interactivity.[4] First presented at the 2018 ELO conference in

DOI: 10.4324/9781003320838-4

Montreal, Flores's approach has gone deeper and deeper into the relevant phenomena ever since. In 2019, Flores summarizes the difference between the second and third generations as follows:

> The 2nd generation seeks originality and formal innovation while 3rd generation is exploring existing forms, established platforms, and interfaces. In 2nd generation works readers must learn how to operate them—to the extent that many works feature instructions and many books about electronic literature, feature explanations on how to read works of e-lit (such as Funkhouser's *New Directions in Digital Poetry*). In 3rd generation works, readers are already familiar with the interface and genres and the works don't usually seek to challenge that established training because it reduces readership. This is why works from the 2nd generation are published in websites and that readers must go visit with their computer frequently needing plugins to access the work, while 3rd generation works seek to reach audiences where they already are with computationally simpler works. Perhaps the most significant difference is in the line between digital modernism and postmodernism and their respective affinity to (highbrow) literary culture and (lowbrow) popular culture.
>
> (Flores)

In this chapter, we wish to examine more closely this "3rd generation" of e-lit where platforms and their *dispositifs*[5] are brought to play an essential role in the construction of the narratives and their poetics. Departing from Flores's work, we propose to examine the distinctive features of this new generation through the concept of intermediality (Larrue and Vitali-Rosati; Méchoulan; Rajewsky; Müller), which covers both a theoretical and a methodological approach. By breaking away from the canonical definitions of electronic literature, we will study the stakes of this platform-based writings through the lens of a (inter)media-turn in literature, underpinned in its turn by the *contemporary paradigm* established in the field of visual arts (Goldsmith). Our approach attempts to go beyond the traditional opposition between modernity and post-modernity, and it concurs with a theoretical trend that is increasingly gaining traction in French literary studies, where the "contemporary paradigm" of literature knows a growing interest (largely influenced by Anglo-Saxon criticism). Like the corpora we are going to present in this chapter, our theoretical and methodological tools have been developed over the last 20 years in French-speaking criticism (especially in France, Quebec, and Belgium), where they have allowed literary studies to renew themselves, by surveying new territories beyond those of the printed book (Mougin; Ruffel; Nachtergael; Gefen and Perez; Gervais).

Therefore, from now on, we will strictly distinguish e-lit and digital literature.

Indeed, the concept of electronic literature hasn't been successfully used in French theory, which prefers the expression "digital literature" (*littérature numérique*). This choice can be explained by two reasons at least. First, very few French writers or artists claim to practice e-lit. We can, of course, mention the very important work of Jean-Pierre Balpe, Philippe Bootz, Serge Bouchardon, or even Alexandra Saemmer, but there's not a French e-lit community: more exactly, there are French writers and artists who belong to the international e-lit community. Secondly, in French, the adjective "numérique" (traduced by digital) massively occupied both the field of French theory and common usage. Thus, when Serge Bouchardon published one of the first books written in French dedicated to digital literature (in which he talks about e-lit), he entitled it *La valeur heuristique de la littérature numérique (Heuristic value of digital literature)*.

But we can also argue, with Marcello Vitali-Rosati, that the expression "digital literature" comes with a normalization of digital tools and emphasizes a cultural shift:

A few years ago, the definition of electronic literature focused on the tools used to produce literary works, and critical analyses concentrated on objects produced with new technologies. The shift to the adjective "digital" [numérique] has brought about a change in perception: nowadays, we refer more to a cultural phenomenon than to technological tools and, from this perspective, the challenge is no longer to study literary works, but to understand the new status of literature in the digital age.

(Vitali-Rosati "La Littérature Numérique, Existe-t-Elle?,"
n.p., our translation; all translations in
the chapter are ours)

In other words, the concept of digital literature shifts the focus from computer literacy to digital literacy, understood as an expertise in the (digital) contemporary culture. Therefore, digital literature stands inclusively for the digitally produced and published literary practices. It does include e-lit practices, yet proposes another perspective on its three generations.

The first corpus we will study is called *twitterature*. As its name indicates, twitterature includes all the writings (poetic, autobiographical, fictional...) produced and published on the social media platform Twitter—now renamed X. Broadly speaking, twitterature belongs in what we have previously called "profile-writing," a term coined to designate literary practices that question social platforms (Monjour "Le Profil Numérique"), whether in formal ways (through a game played with the writing constraints of the platform) and/or in critical terms (self-mediation, personal data, digital identity, etc.). We will show how much these instances of "profile-writings," whose legitimacy is still debated in the field of electronic literature, engage digital expertise that is probably more cultural and social than truly computer-based. Whereas literary value has long been played out at the level of coding mastery as a form of poetic writing in electronic literature (eliciting critical approaches such as the ones in critical code studies), these new writing practices pave the way for a literarity informed by a more complex literacy, one involving a more comprehensive cultural and even political awareness. We will then focus on a second corpus, which will allow us to present a new "genre" of digital literature: *giterature*, named for the software and protocol Git shared by several platforms (GitLab, GitHub, etc.) traditionally occupied by communities of programmers, but recently sought for by literary communities as well. While Flores calls at the end of his article to think about the relationship between the third generation and its predecessors,[6] our analysis of giterature envisages for its part to draw a link between platform-based writing and a sharp kind of digital literacy involving the mastery of many if not all layers of digital writing (Petit and Bouchardon), from the one of the code to the one of the interface.

Could "Non-e-lit(ist)" Practices Be the Future of Digital Literature? For an Alternative Conceptual Framework

Could we consider "(non-)e-lit" practices as the future of digital literature? Far from mere quipping, such probing aims first of all at questioning the criteria of literariness that have been formulated since the 1990s in institutionalizing electronic literature, notably in academia. It will also occasion stating the field in which we are operating, as the matters at hand relate more to *digital* literature rather than *electronic* literature. But before detailing that distinction, let us elucidate the epistemological stakes of our research question.

Questioning the value of digital writings constitutes a somewhat risky challenge: why indeed run the risk of falling into the essentialist trap set by the concept of "literariness"[7] whose criteria seem so difficult to define? First of all, we must recognize the topicality of a problem that has caused tension in the field of contemporary literature, more specifically digital literature, as the latter is still seeking legitimization despite several decades of existence. For a researcher looking into experimental poetics, publishing, and transmedia experiments of the digital era, the question of literariness cannot be framed by an epistemological reflection to begin with. Indeed in the print paradigm, traditional authority plays a fundamental role in legitimating writings, even long before a work gets to be analyzed by academics. Quite on the contrary, in digital environments, many of those instances of authority are no longer relevant. Therefore, our work on contemporary corpora strongly contributes to its institutionalization—just as we seek, for ourselves, a form of legitimization in an academic context whose borders are still, despite everything, relatively strict. This corpus is quite ephemeral and fragile. We regularly lose whole sections of it for very diverse reasons: technical obsolescence, a writer's oversight who did not renew a domain… This phenomenon has repercussions on our own work, as we focus on contemporary literature, significant portions of which can turn out quite short-lived.

Researchers, librarians, and cultural institutions are well aware of the need to find appropriate solutions to archive and index this literary heritage from the early days of the digital age. But what will be the validity of this heritage in 50 or 100 years? Will it be studied for its literary qualities, or will it bear witness to a moment of technological transition and media exploration? How many of us have actually read Michael Joyce's *afternoon, a story*? Such questions plead for an epistemological work on the methodological, theoretical, and critical approaches of digital literature and even e-lit. An essential part of the relevant epistemological debate refers in fact to the influence of the technical medium, or more precisely the value that we—researchers or researchers-creators—assign to a literary work's technical facet. The latter has garnished substantial attention in digital—and particularly electronic—literature criticism and theory via approaches whose very names embody this preoccupation: critical code studies, software studies, and platform studies. These approaches, by focusing on what is obviously one of the most salient features of these literary practices, namely, a fundamentally computerized form of writing, tend however to draw the reader's attention to the technical aspects of such literary works—to the point of closely equating literarity with technicality. The bias is regularly underlined by the authors themselves, as we can see for instance in the following excerpt from "Digital Literature Is Dead," by the French writer Thierry Crouzet:

> In the nineteenth century, did we organize symposia on "the author in the age of the carved quill," or "in the age of the Sergent-Major quill" (1856) or the typewriter (1872)? No one had such a crazy idea. To speak of authors in the digital age, of digital authors or digital literature locks us up, suffocates us, tears us away from the field of literature. We exclude ourselves from it, and for good reasons we almost never mix with those who are not of our parish. This self-enclosure, of which I cannot accuse the academics since we are ourselves the first culprits, leads the analysts to speak about our status as authors, our publishing and promotion strategies, and at times even the way we work, but almost never about our texts.

It seems that we don't write, it seems that those who talk about our work never read us.

(Crouzet, n.p.)

The approach we propose, grounded in intermedial studies, does not oppose this technical perspective, it simply recalibrates it, by adopting a radically anti-essentialist view on technology, and on any medium in general. The intermedial approach could be literally defined as thinking the *in-between* that imposes to de-essentialize media and to understand them as dynamic feeding off technical modalities of previous and contemporary media as well as of publishing, writing, social, and community practices, be they ancient or contemporary. This idea is in particular at the origin of the concept of "mediating conjunctures" forged by Jean-Marc Larrue and Marcello Vitali-Rosati as breaking free from "an essentialized vision of the phenomenon of mediation" (Larrue and Vitali-Rosati, 52) and foregrounding mediations as "moving combinations" conjunct with mediatic interrelations.

For the technical aspect is undoubtedly not the only one to raise issues in defining digital literary writing. The use of the term "literature" and, to a greater extent perhaps, the established disciplinary term "literary studies," may also prove problematic. The main difficulty is likely first and foremost purely institutional. As far as we are concerned, it is primarily a question of advocating openness, both of the literary phenomenon and of its study. The very choice of the expression "literary phenomenon" is indicative of a will to understand the diversity of literary productions in a transversal way, by binding together features as heterogeneous as the stylistic, the mediatic, the semiotic, the technical, the sociological, the economic, and so on and so forth. It is therefore a question of taking into account the "énonciation éditoriale"[8] of literary objects, and particularly their mediatic enunciation.

A first reframing (or "breaking open") of the concept of literature therefore, revisited as literary phenomenon, would invite adopting the current theoretical and methodological purviews sensitive to the various (sociological, mediatic, semiotic, etc.) conditions of existence and production of texts over those advocating an immanent approach to corpora (seen as text only). The opposition is obviously somewhat caricatural: in the history of literary criticism, the dividing line is far from being that clear.[9] One needs nevertheless to take into account the notable influence exerted by the formalist and then post-structuralist heritage in literary studies, where we note a tendency to over-value the text, even in the very definition of literature and the practice of the discipline. And if one pleads for a transitive concept[10] of literary phenomena, the latter still remains quite often cloistered in the domain of language, seen as works of language and style only, and impervious to other—e.g., material or institutional—elements. At the same time, we cannot but notice a related partitioning—that also needs to be surmounted, "broken open"—in an established definition of electronic literature. In a foundational theoretical contribution to the field of hypermedia studies, that Flores draws on to introduce his concept of a third generation of e-lit, Katherine Hayles defines electronic literature by its capacity to be performed by the machine. If the *dispositif*-related dimension of literary objects gets in the focus then the formalist influence may actually not be that far behind, and we agree on this issue with Philippe Bootz who has noted the relevant transition "from a textual structural literarity to a literarity bound to the device of communication:"

> We can also examine them from the angle of the device of communication and look at the new situations of communication that these productions propose. This aspect is particularly instructive because the fundamental specificity of computer literature does not reside in its screen or multimedia character, a character that video or opera have explored elsewhere, but in the singularity of the device of creation/reading that it establishes. Asking such question implies a displacement of the status of literature. Starting from a structuralist approach focusing on the forms of the text, literature, now understood as *dispositif,* has moved to a systemic approach.
>
> (Bootz, 13)

While presupposing a *dispositif*-based definition of electronic literature, this conception, widely shared by the e-lit research community, has paradoxically tended to replace the critical discourse on text with one on code, at the risk of instituting a new formalism. Indeed, pointing at a "displacement" of literature then became necessary in demarcating these new writing practices from other more "traditional" literary outputs, disseminated in print. The latter has in fact become a largely transparent medium, whose poetic potential is hardly explored anymore. Flores himself, in his argument regarding the third generation, operates with such a definition:

> I define electronic literature as a writing-centered art that engages the expressive potential of electronic and digital media. Even though it has origins in oral culture, particularly poetry, literature as an artistic tradition and field of study has been shaped for centuries by writing and print technologies.
>
> (Flores, n.p.)

In a recent article, Marcello Vitali-Rosati underlines the problem posed by these first definitions of electronic literature which function at first by exclusion. He thus pleads for an opening of "electronic" literature, which must already be requalified as "digital" literature, and even reintegrated into "literature" as a whole:

> By agreeing with Dylan Kinnett and Paul LaFarge, Gefen asserts that it is not possible to define digital literature in opposition to the rest of literature, but rather that it must be understood by inserting it into the continuity of literary practices. In this sense, rather than talking about "digital literature," focusing on the technological tools used for the production and reception of literary works, we should talk about "literature in the digital age." This very inclusive approach has the advantage of making it possible to take into account a whole series of literary practices that do not fit into the more exclusive definition of the electronic literature organization, but which nevertheless have a growing presence and impact within the contemporary literary panorama. In particular, all forms of writing that could be defined as "homothetic" to paper, such as short stories published on blogs or other online platforms, or novels that circulate exclusively in digital form, but which, because of their format, could just as easily be distributed in printed form without losing any of their specificity.
> (Vitali-Rosati, "La littérature numérique francophone," 211)

Marcello Vitali-Rosati's proposal thus encourages a third "breaking open:" that of the definition of the *digital*, whose cultural and not-only-technological facets need to be highlighted. This acknowledgment of a "cultural" dimension of the digital, which Vitali-Rosati borrows from Milad Doueihi, is of essential relevance to the demonstration that follows. Digital literary practices require a *dispositif*-based critical approach, by taking into account digital culture, that is to say, the overall conditions of the process of production, distribution, and also legitimization of those literary works. Such conditions include the technical features of the writing tool, its cultural or economic connotations, the institutional conditions of dissemination of the literary works, their legal classification, etc. The next step will involve the intermedial analysis whereby one will first dwell on the relevant—mediatic—dimension of the digital literary work at hand; once again, media in a resolutely anti-essentialist acceptance, as a conjuncture of technical, esthetic, and political aspects, practices, and know-how, as well as the individual and collective imaginary.

Twitterature, LiteraTube, AutoBlography: Questioning the Platformization of E-lit

Thinking within a digital-culture framework can help to grasp what is really at stake in the platformization phenomenon pointed out by Flores.

Social media have been widely used and explored over the past 20 years by established authors of electronic literature and other writers alike, within as well as outside the e-lit community. While some of them already had writing and publishing backgrounds (mostly in rather traditional settings), digital writing platforms also gave birth to numerous new voices; and Flores does indeed underline the importance of amateur communities within this third wave. Although the explicit purpose and utility of social media are obviously more informational and communicational rather than literary, they have been widely frequented by such writers for their simplified writing, publishing, and broadcasting features. This phenomenon, marking a significant evolution in literary practices, requires a different critical approach than the one usually deployed in tackling previous chapters of e-lit. More often than not, these new practices involve no computer programming.[11] While coding literacy (instrumental for instance in automatic text and multimedia generation or web-based creativity) was a mainstay of first- and second-generation e-lit, it is no longer a prerogative of these writers who in the meantime rely on the above-mentioned platform interfaces and the in-built algorithms thereof. These new forms necessitate new literariness assessment criteria, and it is the critic's job to come up with the latter.

The best example of this shift is the Wattpad platform, designed for amateur writers, which has built its reputation and its communication strategy on the already mentioned promise of technical simplification: "don't think, just write." This slogan echoes previous discourse in the history of technology, notably in photography, as Kodak once urged users to "press the button, we do the rest." Such a catchline had the merit of implicitly advocating opening up photography to a mass audience, but that came at a significant cost for photography, since it had already been suspected for decades of being an artless technique requiring no particular skill. As a response to such concerns with authority and legitimation, typically related to significant media transition, most digital platforms attach algorithmic or community-based evaluation and recommendation to their writing and publication spaces. These features contribute largely to the construction of users' authority or social capital. In this context, the academic work of description and analysis of those emerging literary practices can propose a critical alternative to these *dispositifs* of authority, and legitimate authors who take the risk of exploring forms and spaces miles away from institutionalized canons.

Several neologisms have been coined in the last decade to designate these hybrid literary practices. Many of them draw on the very platform names: e.g., twitterature (poetry, fiction, autobiographical pieces posted on Twitter), literaTube (literature filmed and broadcast via a Youtube channel (Bonnet)), autoBlography (self-narrative published on a blogging or microblogging platform), etc.[12]

These diverse and formally inventive practices call for several remarks. Giving up programming skills—since no longer necessary—does not imply giving up esthetics, but rather challenging literarity. Whereas Philippe Bootz has identified a new literarity in the code and the programming informing the works of the first and second e-lit generations, in the case of platform writing, one can speak of a certain kind of cultural literariness. The latter refers to having a deep familiarity with digital culture, particularly the ability to tap into, and play with, the cultural patterns of these platforms and their recommender systems and algorithms more generally. Since fundamentally social, these platforms require "écranvains"[13] to be particularly knowledgeable of, and able to put to use, their new digital social realities and their relevance to aspects such as the dynamics of legitimation or performativity's impact on writing and the textual output per se.

Formally internalizing such realities and modalities in writing presupposes a knowledge of the technical, semiological, and epistemological dimensions of these platforms seen as a new literary space. In spite of the promised simplicity, platforms cannot claim to have the mediatic transparency that new media and media theories often boast (Bolter and Grusin). The authors-artists willingly adopt (or rather play along with) that simplicity/transparency to just immediately twist the platform's social and cultural codes as part of their creative endeavor. An estrangement effect is at stake, whose subversiveness invites questioning the platform and its algorithmic governance in particular. We could thus characterize the 3rd e-lit generation by a dislocation of literariness toward a reflection on the social, political, and cultural implications of the "general public" digital tools.[14]

How does this platform-literature manifest itself in concrete terms? Let's examine for instance the case of twitterature, understood, evidently, as writings produced and disseminated on (and for) Twitter.

In his publication, Flores[15] devotes a long passage to the bots currently swarming on Twitter. This example however, as relevant as it may be, still speaks to earlier e-lit practices and, specifically, definitions of the field involving computer programming carried out by the author(s) as an integral part of the writing per se.

> The techniques for creating them are not very different from bots in earlier generations, but rather than creating custom datasets, programmers are pulling or processing content from API services or using

user-friendly platforms like the Twinery-powered Cheap Bots Done Quick! Rather than being standalone custom experiences, these bots leverage social media networks as contexts and spaces to develop audiences. For example, when you're on Twitter, a bot might re-act artistically to something you posted, such as @HaikuD2 or @Pentametron, which detect tweets that could be cut into haiku or happen to be written in iambic pentameter, respectively. While there are more people with the programming skills necessary for bot-making, services like CBDQ and Zach Whalen's SSBot tool have lowered the barrier to entry, which magnifies the production of works in this vein.

(Flores, n.p.)

As we can see, programming skills remain at the heart of the practice presented by Flores, for whom the interest of the platform resides first of all in the new economic and distribution paradigm specific to Web 2.0:

Third generation works respond to new markets, platforms, and monetization possibilities and have developed without the need for academia and its validation. [...] An aesthetic of difficulty would undermine the very spreadability and commercialization paradigms that help 3rd generation works thrive. And as Kirschenbaum pro-vocatively stated in his keynote, "maybe what matters is the contin-ued growth and diversification of an e-lit that is not dependent on whatever contradictions or complications attend its status in relation to an academic valuation of the avant-garde" (Kirschenbaum 7).

(Flores, n.p.)

It appears to us, however, that twitterature is not necessarily computa-tional, in the sense that the text is not necessarily generated by a computer program. Its most interesting productions are realized by means of a more classical if technically savvy kind of writing that conforms to the platform's practices and forms, while nevertheless disrupting their established usage. There lies in fact the main relevance of platform-literature: like a Trojan horse, or, moreover, by following in the footsteps of *tactical media* (Garcia and Lovink), it embraces the uses prescribed by the platform to just advance alternative practices, thus occasioning a critical reflection on the relevant new modes of communication and contemporary media culture. Another signifi-cant aspect of this literature is its formal relatedness to literary genres beyond e-lit: on a poetic level, the compulsory conciseness invites practicing forms like the haiku, the aphorism, the epigram; at the same time, given the importance of Twitter profiles, the platform also offers a new space for autobiography or autofiction; finally, as a microblogging tool, it reconnects with the tradition of the *feuilleton* and thus becomes a timely venue for serialized fiction.

The example we will next be looking into is that of Guillaume Vissac's *Accident de personne* (Vissac). The title alludes to the expression used in railway contexts to designate a collision between a train and a pedestrian: it is usually translated as train-pedestrian fatality (which reveals the extent to which the French have chosen a euphemism to refer to what, in most cases, represents an instance of suicide).

> For almost two years, I spent between two and three hours a day on public transport (RER, metro). All that time, put together, made me a bit dizzy. I've had my fill of personal accidents, I haven't counted them, but there's always a special atmosphere on the train when the driver announces it, or on the platforms when the screens flash. One day, one of them made me arrive two hours late for my job at the time. That day, I had the idea of doing something about it, taking notes, and writing the very first one.
>
> I took notes for a year and a half. All (or most) of these notes were written straight while in transit, either in a train car or on a platform, on a classic cell phone, then an iPhone. [...] At the end of 2010, I had over 200 fragments of writing, all under 140 characters, so I created the account @personne/, and cleaned up my text. I kept about 160 fragments. This way, I was able to post 5 fragments a day for just one month. It was November, so I chose December, and the timing was perfect, with Christmas and New Year's Eve as the climax. The idea had been there from the very beginning, to be able to schedule the tweets at a fixed time, every day at 7am, 9am, 12am, 6pm and 8pm, so that the tweets could be read at peak times, on the transport system to be precise. And then there was the soap opera aspect: followers began to know that it was "soon @personne time."[16]

As Guillaume Vissac tells us, *Accident de personne* was put together to fit on the Twitter platform and simultaneously distort it: the news feed is used to publish fictional stories, involving fictitious victims. Adopting the platform's most salient constraint (no more than 140 characters per tweet at the time), Vissac works with a short form that reminds one of the funeral epigram. But he also appropriates the media support: the smartphone, used as a writing support (like a digital version of Oulipian "subway poems"), and which is precisely the first expected reading support. Smartphone is indeed the medium that the reader has at her disposal on the subway, connecting and gathering all the readers at the same time to follow the feuilleton.

> all of them bent over their touchscreens, screens, pocket scanners: how many can see the executioner behind them & the raised axe?[17]

But *Accident de personne* is also representative of a platform-literature which, by doing away with e-lit's specific computationality—whereby a work can only be "read" (or rather viewed) when the underlying code and/ or data are instantiated—becomes amenable to multiple inscriptions and forms. It will obviously be hosted on the platform on which it was initially inscribed, but it can also end up on other platforms or websites where it gets redistributed and/or remediated, possibly even into book format (epub or print). Thus, since its first publication on Twitter, *Accident de personne* has been published in e-pub format (publie.net) and even as a printed book (Nouvel Attila). Certain aspects of, or elements in, that first performance were obviously lost in remediation, but others were gained— such as the editing, arrangement, and reorganization of the initial contents into the form of a lexicon—bringing new meaning to the story:

By the end of December, I had put it all together in an alphabet book. Originally, I hadn't planned for any figures to emerge, but then characters popped up by themselves, for instance the one who searches for an ideal song to play while committing suicide, the one who kills herself several times in a row, as every attempt actually fails, the traffic controllers I saw twice a day, and so on. So classifying them into characters was an idea. The footnotes came about during this phase, for getting people to communicate, so all the notes are previously unreleased, never posted on twitter, and some are longer than 140 characters.[18]

This curation into book form, both digital and printed, allows for the creation of more individualized characters than the publication on Twitter would encourage, as the footnote apparatus can help to build a more complex narrative structure. The book form appears to be crucially impactful by comparison to Twitter's non-chronological publication format which makes the performance hard to revisit as such.

He or she who… speaks
    I pace the platforms in search of information to feature: timetable, delay or suicide [160]: I shout them to the shadows till they burst
    due to a train-pedestrian accident [161] at station X, train Z to Y has been cancelled, our alphabetical apologies…,
    SNCF voice bug: endless vain announcements murderous train not coming: still waiting for it[19]

This last excerpt is indeed quite illustrative of one of intermediality's most salient outcomes: the de-essentialization of platform(-based) digital performance and, at the same time, the closely intertwined de-essentialization of the book. The work's various inscriptions—describable in fact as sequential "states" of the text or stages of the literary project—thus prove to operate certain media translations, from digital to print and vice versa. Yet it is, as argued before, in book form that the potential of *twittérature* is fully realized... This in no way disconsiders the poetic relevance of the work as published-performed on the platform but actually further highlights the latter's relevance as a work-in-progress.

Giterature: Preliminary Definitions

To the already long list of digital-literature-related neologisms, we would like to append the term *giterature*, a fusion of Git—the computer protocol—and literary writing. Advancing the concept, and formulating (below) a definition, of giterature was largely inspired by Abrüpt's significant projects. Abrüpt has indeed promoted an alternative form of platform-literature well beyond the framework of third-generation e-lit as described by Flores. But let us first propose a definition of giterature as a literary phenomenon combining, on the one hand, the writing and publishing affordances of a certain platform (the collaborative software forge GitLab), and computer skills—specifically writing with(in) protocols—geared toward literary creativity and poetic innovation, on the other. Giterature also inherits features from single-source publishing and emerging publishing processes and practices as it breaks up with traditional workflows and fosters collaborative environments informed by Web standards, formats, and platforms.

The study of the third generation has rather focused on (mis)appropriation and the platform-adapted dissemination strategies (tackled from a platform studies perspective), whereas giterature requires revisiting the concurrence of two writing modes: literary writing and computer code writing, reunited in the same writing space through the Git protocol and the GitLab platform. While such a question would perhaps be most often relegated to a critical-code-studies-based approach, we will once again prefer the intermedial perspective, which, nevertheless, will not prevent one from addressing the poetics of code either.

Giterature has already been defined by the Swiss digital publishing house Abrüpt, which has been also illustrating the concept through its various activities over the past several years.

Let us linger a while on the very name, "Abrüpt," an entity that describes itself as an "us," thus maintaining a certain equivalence between "human" actors (publishers, authors, developers, designers, all of whom are *tinkerers* of sorts), "techniques" (formats, tools), and "institutions" (protocols, distribution circuits). More than a collective, Abrüpt seems to enact the fusion of these actors into a new kind of publishing ecology, where traditional authority becomes dismantled.

It is abrüpt. The word scatters in the dark, and all we are left with is books to cast into the world and voice dreams and howls. We organize around texts that agitate and revolt, that morph into anti-books that unravel by sharing. We engage in transdialectics and tamper with paper, we take note of a cyberpoetics whose verb foments the error in the heart of the real. It sounds. We listen.

(« Antilivre », n.p.)

Abrüpt's "we" is in and of itself an attempt to redefine publishing as embodiment into a new publication object: the "anti-livre" (anti-book). According to Abrüpt, anti-books do not necessarily rule out the more traditional book-in-print scenario but aim to deconstruct the traditional print-medium paradigm guaranteeing the immutability of text and the institution of the author (of a legal and economic nature rather than an aesthetic one). In a way, the anti-book represents a new *media* book concept whose definitory features emerge to be modularity—each title is made available in print form (for sale) as well as HTML and PDF (free)—and open source/open access: the texts and the code are uploaded into a Git repository for free reuse or appropriation. The definition of the anti-book lies at the heart of Abrüpt's manifesto:

The anti-book is a metamorphosis, is its disorder, is the affirmation of a literature of short-circuits, of its joyful circulation, against the era, against the book and its grammar, against its chain and its humming, for a future of alterations, for free and reticular information, for a multitude enlightened by it.

The anti-book has no form, its impermanence disposes of all forms, it transforms itself ceaselessly, and its raw information knows no fixity, no border, it fragments its essence, distributes the common, deploys its freedom in front of our cybernetic singularities.

The anti-book has for enemy all culture. Culture does not fight, it holds the baton, it entertains, then knocks out.

(« Antilivre », n.p.)

In Abrüpt's anti-book manifesto, poetics and politics are inseparable. The reference to the commons movement is accompanied by a call to shake up the world, the language, and more broadly culture. The manifesto, just like the catalog, echoes with both classics of 20th-century humanities and social science thought (Simone Weil, Pierre Kropotkin) and contemporary authors that one can come across on well-known literary platforms (e.g.,

Pierre Ménard and Christine Jeanney, regular contributors to publie.net). Heteroclite in terms of genres and artforms (essay, poetry, narrative, or visual arts such as photography, drawing, collage) as well as format and appearance (every HTML anti-book comes with a new design), the catalog is nevertheless consistent in terms of editing and publishing, both carried out exclusively on one single platform, GitLab. Thus, Abrüpt's editorial and publication protocol is fundamentally one and the same as the Git protocol informing the platform. It is the latter, as we will further detail below, that occasions a redefinition of the concept of literature in the context, both poetically and politically speaking.

Abrüpt's anti-book project relies on the platform GitLab, which was named for Git, a file versioning and synchronization protocol. Thanks to its versioning system, Git allows developers to generate, share, and update code by means of contribution, exchanges, and collaboration. The free software GitLab integrates this protocol, to which it adds, on a dedicated interface, collaborative affordances such as a wiki, a bug tracking and communication system, and, last but not least, a social media platform for sharing code and other kinds of digital text. In other words, GitLab is what has been called in computer science a "forge:" a collaborative text and code development, maintenance, and management system.[20]

GitLab can probably be considered more of a geek's rather than a writer's tool. Unlike the above-mentioned writing platforms (Wattpad or social media platforms like Twitter), GitLab requires certain technical skills: one needs to have a minimal coding background, be able to use the command line and be comfortable with branch management and versioning. This is no longer simply a matter of digital cultural literacy, but of acquiring writing and scripting skills that are not confined to software development solely any longer. In fact, these skills are far from being shared by everyone, and the literature practiced by Abrüpt is first of all a publishing endeavor rather than a genuine instance of co-writing factually involving other co-authors. Throughout the catalog, Abrüpt is more often than not the only actual contributor to its own repositories. The well-known *ZAP Rimbaud* project, of which more in a bit, is, in fact, just an exception.

What could appear to be a technical deadlock is however compensated by an explicit lack of any formal authority, as the modus operandi involves co-authoring and (re)source sharing. More fundamentally, mastering or acquiring the necessary technical competence is seen as a way of political and formal emancipation—since literary and artistic forms ultimately tend to be as overdetermined by the hegemonic proprietary dimension of the platform as they used to be in the apparently more uniformizing ecosystem of traditional/print media—and therefore of esthetic creativity.

Is GitLab a "niche" platform? With its over 30 million developers, let us say that it addresses a category of writers particularly aware of the wide range of contemporary digital cultures, who have complemented their literary expertise with digital-tool and computer-programming literacy and thus opened up a whole new world of possibilities to themselves. As current approaches in critical code studies have argued, one would be wrong to consider code writing as a purely technical activity (Marino). Giterature represents, moreover, an opportunity to challenge established literature practices by means of another writing model borrowed from code developers and the field of software engineering. Such synergy is instrumental in shaking up long-standing traditional literary concepts not the least of which is the one of authority.

Computer writing is indeed deeply informed by a *hack spirit* whose origin goes back to the very emergence of computer science as a discipline (Coleman; Mauro). As we will show below, that spirit can also be traced back to the 20th-century avant-gardes as recently critically revisited within a contemporary paradigm (Nachtergael; Mougin; Ruffel).

From Hack Politics to the Poetics of Uncreative Writing

Over the past few years, mainstream media, cinema, and, to an even greater extent, TV series, have shaped a *hack* imaginary largely fantasized and contradictory: at best, the hacker evokes a romantic outlaw figure, at worst, he appears to be a shrewd criminal bent on stealing our personal data and hacking into our bank accounts. In reality, hacking is part of the history of computer science (Mauro) and, to the present day, arguably, common computer practice. Computer writing, generally speaking, in both its methodology and overall philosophy, has something to do with it: hacking can definitely, in more prosaic terms, help one become a better programmer.

Anthropologist Gabriella Coleman has specialized in the study of hacker communities. Her book, *Coding freedom*, helps us to understand the philosophy of hacking, in its political as well as ethical and even esthetic dimensions:

> Although hackers hold multiple motivations for producing their software, collectively they are committed to productive freedom. This term designates the institutions, legal devices, and moral codes that hackers have built in order to autonomously improve on their peers' work, refine their technical skills, and extend craft-like engineering traditions. This ethnography is centrally concerned with how hackers have built a dense ethical and technical practice that sustains their productive freedom, and in so doing, how they extend as well as reformulate key liberal ideals such as

access, free speech, transparency, equal opportunity, publicity, and meritocracy.

(Coleman)

The *hacker* is a tinkerer, provided with a compulsive taste for observing and understanding what lies *under* "the hood of" our machines and their software interfaces. Hacking means also appropriating and altering code. In fact, in programming, one generally never does coding "from scratch" or on a "blank page" but recycles existing (scraps or blocks of) code by adapting, amending, or improving it (or them). If we draw a comparison, writing code can be seen as similar to writing on palimpsests. From such an angle, hacking proves to be a form of playful writing—not quite un-related to traditional literary genres such as parody, pastiche, and more recently, Oulipian experimentalism.

As hack can be seen as related to the above-mentioned 20th-century avant-garde traditions (Bootz; Perloff; Funkhouser), it naturally also speaks to the more recent or updated relevant paradigms such as the one a theo-retician like Kenneth Goldsmith is most representative of in literature. His theory of *uncreative writing* (Goldsmith) is in certain ways a theory of the modern palimpsest. According to Goldsmith, a writer's authority in this age cannot be measured anymore by the singularity of the style or the original-ity of her story. Writers always tell more or less the same story, with similar tools: language, grammar, and syntax. Drawing on the specific paradigm that has governed the visual arts for over a century now, Goldsmith adopts a performative point of view: originality is *making*. Creating new works mat-ters less than continuing a dialog with the forms of the past, and thus play-ing with recontextualization, reformulation, copy-paste, mash-up, or remix:

How I make my way through this thicket of information—how I manage it, how I parse it, how I organize and distribute it—is what distinguishes my writing from yours.

(Goldsmith)

Slipping Shakespeare's tirades into .JPEG files converted into .txt (in order to question the becoming-text of photography in the digital age); asking a hundred students to copy the same edition of the NYTimes (and finding that no copy will be exactly the same as another); printing the Web (ten tons of paper won't be enough) ... these are the kind of experiments Goldsmith engages in.

Some would likely say that is conceptual art, but one can also describe it as publishing art; a kind of art involving the "upstream" and "downstream" (re-)appropriation of the work at hand through media displacement, where hacking eventually appears to be an intermedial practice.

The Register of the Forge: The Commit as Editorial Metatext

Obviously, such a writing paradigm could not work without a toolbox for disassembling and reassembling code. Enter GitLab... GitLab can be first described as a particular kind of library, one where code, or snippets of code, are stored; therefore not a coding, but a code, library. Yet the metaphor of the library needs to be complemented with another, even more suitable, image: that of the "accounting register." A register is a private or public notebook, book, ledger, or directory for recording data, transactions, names, and/or figures for later (accurate) reference. The Git protocol thus determines how all the actions, i.e., the instances of writing, carried out in the files of a given directory are *recorded*. But why speak of forges? The register only keeps track of the differences between one state of the text and another. Thus, it is by re-reading the register step by step, by sequentially adding and deleting strings from each record in the register that the text—or computer code—can be *forged*. The forge is therefore about the merging of all contributions together.

Let us briefly explain how that works. The user "clones" a local code repository onto her/his computer and manipulates the files as s/he pleases (by writing, editing, and/or coding), until s/he obtains a satisfactory "state,"[21] which s/he must then "declare," i.e., register. Once registered in the register, the user pushes this registration onto the server in order to synchronize her/his local register with the online one, so that each contributor can synchronize her/his local register in their turn.

Each of these records must be documented and justified: this is called a *commit*. These commits can be seen as edits and as a form of meta-writing at the same time. Indeed, a project's list of *commits* represents a history of its progress—the corrections, amendments, additions, etc.—as well as, for each of the listed records, the "author's" (user)name. Writing (or rather, committing) by the Git protocol does not mean giving up one's auctoriality: quite on the contrary, it actually allows for a better recognition or valorization of each contribution, however small. In the case of a digital literary work making use of the poetic-technical potential of the digital *medium*, this recognition is capital: it will render evident the IT/software developer's own involvement in the composition/construction of the work. GitLab thus relevantly provides, as a forge, an account of all the editing involved in the making of a work of digital literature.

The question therefore arises in the context, of whether we are transitioning to a shared or collective form of auctoriality or not. It is a potentially sensitive matter particularly in the case of literary writing, as the related economics alongside symbolic capital continue to gravitate to forms and methods of publication still informed by the print tradition. The singularization of authors and authorship has represented a major trend in that tradition, an issue which, in the specific case of Abrüpt, requires a politically militant stance:

> Our works are hidden behind the abbreviations CC-BY-NC-SA 4.0, in other words, they are made available under the terms of the Creative Commons Attribution-NonCommercial-ShareAlike 4.0 International License.
> Behind these abstruse names lies an equally abstruse will, that of taking a step aside from the sacrosanct intellectual property. Free license, open license, free distribution license, free software, open source, open data, open access, open data and open sources, copyleft, from commons to commons, and free culture, and free art, and the terms that float senselessly, drunk with their metamorphic power.
> (Abrüpt, "Partage," n.p.)

The editors argue at length on their website in favor of what they term the "scalpel-like treatment of copyright," all in the name of freedom of data and information. A pragmatic choice involving actual steps toward the voluntary public domain. Surprising as such a choice may sound coming from a publisher, it may, in fact, seem even bothersome to other players in the world of literary publishing more widely speaking. Intellectual property is not only an economic issue out there—how will authors as well as book production and distribution workers be remunerated?—but also an aesthetic one—how will one handle, after releasing one's work into the public domain, its possible distortion, corruption, or, worse, "destruction." While the first question is beyond the scope of this chapter, we will try to address the second one by means of a concrete case study.

ZAP Rimbaud, Anti-Publishing Experiment

For all our already quite numerous theoretical considerations, navigating between forges and protocols, hack spirit, and contemporary paradigm, our concept of giterature still seems at best utopian, at worst impracticable. One must admit that, even in the case of Abrüpt, whose editorial model is based on this concept, most of the anti-books deposited on Git-Lab are rarely reedited. The anti-books await their reappropriation in repositories whose sole contributor is Abrüpt. The writers, in other words, do not write directly in the files uploaded onto the server, which means that Git is most likely not deployed until the very last stage of the editing and production process. Among these repositories, the recent project *ZAP Rimbaud,* initiated and realized entirely on GitLab, appears however to stand out.

ZAP means "Zone Autonome à Poétiser." The project was born in May 2020, when an important part of the world was already in lockdown, or was about to be. In compliance with the established practice of the *book sprint*,[22] the ZAP was conceived as a collective and festive event organized as part of the *Open Publishing Fest*.[23] On that occasion, Abrüpt sent out a call "to set up a squat in the Rimbaud monument and to launch a frenetic and collective rewriting of his *Season in Hell*." The M.O. is quite straightforward: people are invited to collectively write *over* Rimbaud's original poem and thus emerge a new literary object, whose genre Abrüpt calls "cyberpoetry." As a collective enterprise, ZAP imposes on its contributors a short chapter of rules among which the renunciation of auctoriality (the outcome will be deposited into the public domain) and the use of free or open-source computational tools only.

Technically speaking, each participant must "clone" the repository onto her own machines, rewrite parts of the texts her personal "branch," then submit the resulting file via a *merge request* for inclusion into the main branch maintained by the editors. On the server, those multiple versions accumulate in the register, and, when merging, they materialize live into the progressive hack of Rimbaud's text. In the repository, a set of HTML, CSS, and JS files edit, organize, and structure on-the-fly the evolving collective poem through Gitlab's continuous deployment on a dedicated website.[24] The editors' specific editorial work consists of making sure the unaltered parts from Rimbaud's original poems and those rewritten by the participants are printed out in different colors on the "palimpsest" website. In the same way, Abrüpt has named its artifacts "anti-livre," we can consider Abrüpt's radical approach as "anti-publishing," which is fully realized in the ZAP Rimbaud experiment. Its radicality lies precisely in the fact that it overturns the established publishing model and its associated concepts of author, editor, book, artwork, writing, or editing.

Indeed, in the particular case of *ZAP Rimbaud*, the *giterary* comes specifically from a virtuous cycle combining literary and computational writing. That's what cyberpoetics is all about. The latter involves in this instance "hacking" a classical work, that is, specifically writing over, "writing through," or in any way modifying *A Season in Hell*, the consistent input or starting line of the cyberpoetic process. Between and over Rimbaud's original terms and syntax, between and over literary and computational practices, this "writing over" experiment precisely instantiates the very intermediality by calling on a conjunction of technological and cultural-political elements and processes. Figures of stylistics and rhetoric are thus grafted onto code hacking (or, at times, improvement) procedures. For example, code refactoring (the computer science term for restructuring or "reformulating" existing code) is paralleled by poetic repetitions, anaphors, or epiphoras:[25]

> Ma langue vide les lacs de Cervoise la langue inculte ma langue venue du fond des âges ma langue Wisigothe ma langue Attila ma langue ma langue luisante c'est une guillotine ma langue ma langue velue ma langue barbare maltraite ma langue cou-cou-coupe l'amour par le milieu.[26]
>
> (Collectif, n.p.)

Where the code constructs, calls, and/or iterates through variables, the poetics deploys polyptoton, pre/suffixing, and/or other types of word variation, even when such figures implicate ventriloquizing the *bug*:

> La parascience, notre nouvelle noblesse! La croissance de la décroissance. Le progrès déprogresse. Les âmes de bien déprogressent. Salvatio for the Pachamama. Nous, êtres du mal, nous l'accélération. Contre le monde en marche. Le globe sur la tête. Marquage au fer. Pourquoi ne révolutionnerait-il pas, à l'envers? Décentré, décuplé en caniveaux de billets inventés, de cours adescendants. La science, la nouvelle noblesse! Le progrès. Le monde marche! Pourquoi ne tournerait-il pas? La science, la nouvelle noblesse! Le progrès. Le monde marche! Pourquoi ne tournerait-il pas? La science, la nouvelle noblesse! Le progrès. Le monde marche! Pourquoi ne tournerait-il pas? La science, la nouvelle noblesse! Le progrès. Le monde marche! Pourquoi ne tournerait-il pas? La science, la nouvelle noblesse! Le progrès. Le monde marche![27]
>
> (Collectif, n.p.)

Such re-appropriation, one may note, translates or even teleports the Rimbaldian poem to the 21st century and, in the process, makes new themes emerge, particularly the one of the computer. Words get replaced in the context (the "witches" or "sorcières" in the original, for instance, become in the new poem "hackeuses," the French feminine for hackers), whereas inserts or inserted characters get to literally dialogue with(in) the work of the poet whose name is now appropriately transposed from Rimbaud to "rim-bot:"

> Ah! Le réseau à l'estomac! #NOFILTER! Ne jeter pas vos yeux derrière nos difformités. Et ce poison, ce baiser mille fois maudit! #JETEBAISE. Ce baiser mille fois baisé! Ma faiblesse, la cruauté du monde! #JETEBAISE. Mon Dieu, pitié, cachez-moi, hackez-moi, je me tiens trop mal! #JELESBAISETOUS. — Je suis caché et je ne vis plus. Selfie! #NOFILTER + #JETEBAISE = <3! Je suis haché et je ne sais plus.[28]
>
> (Collectif, n.p.)

All those linguistic and (typo)graphic games impact the materiality of the digital text by accommodating, for instance, machine code in its most elemental form, e.g., sequences of 0s and 1s incorporated into Rimbaud's poem where they replace the letters "o" and "i:"

> [quel-que-f01s-je-v01s-au-c1el][des-pla-ges-sans-f1n][c0u-ver-tes-de-blan-ches-na-t10ns][en-j01e][un-grand-va1s-seau-d'0r] [au-des-sus-de-m01][a-g1-te-ses-pa-v1l-l0ns][mul-t1-c0-l0-res][s0us-les-br1-ses-du-ma-t1n][j'a1-cré-é-t0u-tes-les-fê-tes][t0us-les-tr1-0m-phes][t0us-les-dra-mes][29]
>
> (Collectif, n.p.)

An already epitomizing work of a still emergent genre, giterature, *ZAP Rimbaud* fully realizes and, moreover, performs the anti-book concept as formulated by Abrüpt. It implements all its required features: it creates conditions for the appropriation of an existing text, it delivers an editing protocol that enables free collective writing, and it uses Git, first, as formal constraint (to rewrite only what has not been rewritten—"*no toying*") and, second, as submission mechanism (via the *pull request*). Last but not least, Abrüpt releases an actual publication, namely a more tangible (anti-)book, featuring both poems in distinctive colors (Rimbaud's versus the collective's). This seamless convergence of the Git and editing protocols is illustrative of the degree to which literature in general is inextricably linked to the editorial, mediating, and publishing strategies at play, while giterature in particular emerges itself as the intermedial fusion of literary and computational writing. More specifically, rendering the differences between the original and the collective text visible—by means of the *git diff* function—amounts to an overarching metaphor binding the Git protocol to the kind of continuous and collective writing it has catalyzed.

What is there left of Rimbaud, of his *Season in Hell*, once this cyberpoetic hack is completed? Nothing, apparently, or, one may very well add, probably everything. Picking a work of the "poète voyant" for this experiment was certainly no accident: the ZAP concludes with a syllepsis celebrating the collective adventure: "Ci-GIT je" (Here lies I). If the poet used to say "je est un autre" ("I is another"), Abrüpt makes a point that all of us are, or can become, Rimbaud.

Conclusion

Particularly when in digital forms, modes, and environments, literature does not cease to "overflow:" it overflows the book, the institution, the genre, etc. Case in point, giterature and the ways in which, by importing techniques and technics from, by and large, non-literary medialities, it overflows the very meaning of writing. The appropriation of the relevant tools and affordances implies indeed adopting, at least to a certain extent, the philosophies and the epistemic models that inform them.

Giterature is thus part of a larger trend in contemporary cultures to the effect of de-essentializing literature and artforms as such. By means of its text and/as code versioning and anti-books, it embraces the (inter)media turn in literature. Given its (digital or analog) temporal and spatial open-endedness, it marks the transition from a definitive-text paradigm to a process-based performative approach to editing and publishing. And, last but not least, through its collective dimension, it ushers in a new reformulation of the author's status.

Notes

1 Content Management System is computer software used to manage the creation and modification of digital content (content management).
2 One of Wattpad's slogans is "Don't think, just write."
3 A literature in which literary writing is closely associated with a poetics of code, as we will see below.
4 Flores returns to this first categorization effort that we owe to Katherine Hayles: "When she [Hayles] established the concept of first-generation electronic literature, she defined it as pre-web, text-heavy, link driven, mostly hypertext, that still operated with many paradigms established in print. She defined the second generation from 1995 onward, as Web based and incorporating multimedia and interactivity. After some of the critical conversation around her notion of generations, she renamed the first generation as classic and the second as contemporary electronic literature." (Flores)
5 We refer to the concept of "dispositif" proposed by Michel Foucault, which "implies a field of forces acting upon a technological, social, legal etc. context or environment" (Kessler).
6 "We need to build bridges between e-lit generations so they can learn from us as we learn from them. Nothing less than the future of the field is at stake" (Flores).
7 Introduced by Jakobson (who talked about "literaturnost"), the concept of literarity refers to all aspects that make a text literary. It has been then discussed by many French theoreticians, such as Jacques Rancière or even Gérard Genette.
8 The concept "énonciation éditoriale" has been proposed by Emmanuel Souchier. It "refers to the plural elaboration of the textual object. It heralds a theory of the polyphonic enunciation of text produced or uttered by any instance likely to intervene in the conception, realization or production of the book, and more generally of the written word. Beyond that, it is of interest to any medium combining text, image and sound, notably computer screens – it being understood that any text is seen as well as read" (Souchier).
9 The impact of cultural studies and the host of interrelated trends usually entered under the label "French theory" in North America has strongly contributed to blurring the line between the literary and the non-literary. From the 1970s onwards, by following in the footsteps of authors like Barthes, Eco, Kristeva, and others, the canon has been considered to be the offspring of certain power mechanisms, always (re)constructable in alternative fashions. The porosity of the frontier between the literary and the non-literary, in such contexts, has thus become a given.

10 The concept of transitivity opposes Roland Barthes' "intransitive writing," considering that literature is not a pure act of stylistic speech, but has something to say about *and to* the world.

11 Note should be made however that even if Flores bases his third-generation argument particularly on the Twitter-based literary bots, the most striking user content on such social media do not come from bots but from humans whose writings are "arranged" on, and by, the platform. We will develop on this below.

12 We borrow most of these neologisms from Gilles Bonnet, whose book *Pour une poétique numérique* abounds in ingenious and playful neologisms (Bonnet)

13 This French term, also used by Gilles Bonnet, is a play on words involving "écrit" (writing) and "écran" (screen) in distorting the term "écrivain" (writer).

14 This is what Flores himself seems to suggest when he says "Most 3rd generation e-lit writers are a younger generation who have naturalized what was experimental to us, and even though the work they create may be naïve and disconnected from the artistic and literary traditions of the past, they were more directly formed by digital culture." (Flores) Our aim here is to demonstrate that digital culture can engender complex works that are not necessarily disconnected from the past—quite on the contrary, as we will see below, they even relate to forms that predate e-lit.

15 Note that Flores does not use the term twitterature, but explicitly mentions bots on Twitter and its counterparts (mastodon, etc.)

16 In the original text: «Pendant presque deux ans, je passais entre deux et trois heures par jour en transport en commun (RER, métros). Tout ce temps-là, mis bout à bout, ça fout la lourde comme on dit par chez moi, le vertige. J'ai donc eu mon compte d'accidents de personne, je ne les ai pas comptés, mais toujours une atmosphère particulière dans le wagon lorsque le conducteur l'annonce, ou sur les quais quand les écrans clignotent. Un jour l'un d'entre eux m'a fait arriver deux heures en retard dans mon boulot de l'époque. Ce jour-là, l'idée d'en faire quelque chose, de prendre des notes, et l'écriture de la toute première. La prise de notes a duré un an et demi. Toutes ces notes (ou la plupart) ont été écrites directement embarqué soit dans les wagons, soit sur les quais, au téléphone portable classique, ensuite via l'iPhone. [...] Fin 2010, j'avais plus de 200 fragments d'écrits, tous de moins de 140 caractères, alors j'ai créé le compte @personne, j'ai épuré mon texte. J'en ai gardé environ 160. De cette façon, j'ai pu mettre en ligne 5 fragments par jour pendant un mois tout juste. C'était novembre, j'ai choisi décembre, et ça tombait bien avec Noël et réveillon à la fin comme acmé. L'idée était là depuis le tout début, de pouvoir programmer les twitts à heure fixe, tous les jours 7h, 9h, 12h, 18h et 20h, afin que les twitts puissent être lus aux heures de pointe, dans les transports précisément. Et puis ça avait un côté feuilleton: les followers ont commencé à savoir que c'était "bientôt l'heure d'@personne" ».

17 In the original text: « Tous penchés sur leurs tactiles, écrans, scanners de poche: combien pour voir derrière eux le bourreau & au dessus la hache? »

18 In the original text: « Passé fin décembre, j'ai mis au propre, rassemblé le tout dans un abécédaire. A l'origine il n'était pas prévu que des figures émergent, et puis des personnages sont apparus d'eux mêmes, par exemple celui qui cherche une chanson idéale pour la passer au moment de mourir, celle qui se tue mais plusieurs fois, car ça marche pas, les régulateurs de flux que je voyais tous les jours deux fois par jour, etc. Alors les classer par personnages, c'était une idée. Les notes de bas de page, c'est venu pendant cette phase là, histoire de faire dialoguer tout le monde, du coup toutes les notes sont inédites, jamais apparues sur twitter, plus de 140 caractères pour certaines. »

19 In the original text: « Celui ou celle qui... parle. J'arpente les quais en quête d'infos à donner: horaire, retard ou suicide [160]: je les gueule pour les ombres jusqu'à ce qu'elles éclatent en raison d'un accident de personne [161] survenu en gare de X, le train Z à destination de Y a été supprimé, toutes nos excuses alphabétiques... bug sur voix SNCF: annonce en vain sans fin train meurtrier qui ne vient pas: quand même l'attendre. »

20 According to Violaine Louvet: "The objective of a forge is to offer a space of permanent exchange and online collaboration to software developers, and a space of distribution (public versions of developed software: source packages, web pages) for users (for everyone if the forge is public). It thus makes it possible to gather projects and developers, but also other people working on these projects (users, translators...)" (Source: PLUME – https://hnlab.huma-num.fr/hnso/ouvrage-in/proposition-fonctionnalites.html)

21 The term *state* is preferable to that of *output,* as the digital forge operates under the sign of processual publication rather than the one of mere editing.

22 A book sprint is a method of creating a book collaboratively in a short period of time (three to five days), completing both the writing and the publishing at the end of the sprint period. Books are made available immediately at the end of the sprint as e-books and/or print-on-demand publications (source: https://en.wikipedia.org/wiki/Book_sprint).

23 As we can read on the website initiative, "Open Publishing Fest is a decentralized public event that brings together communities supporting open source software, open content, and open publishing models." (source: https://openpublishingfest.org/).

24 See also Fauchié on GitLab's platform-related relevant functions.

25 We chose not to translate the ZAP Rimbaud excerpts for several reasons: first, they already represent translations (palimpsests of Rimbaud's work), they are multilingual, and they have salient visual and typography-related features. We have nevertheless provided the "originals" in the subsequent endnotes.

26 In the section « mauvais sang » of the original text, Rimbaud asks the question: « sais! qui a fait ma langue perfide tellement, qu'elle ait guidé et sauvegardé jusqu'ici ma paresse? »

27 In the original text: « La science, la nouvelle noblesse! Le progrès. Le monde marche! Pourquoi ne tournerait-il pas? »

28 In the original: « Ah! remonter à la vie ! jeter les yeux sur nos difformités. Et ce poison, ce baiser mille fois maudit! Ma faiblesse, la cruauté du monde! Mon Dieu, pitié, cachez-moi, je me tiens trop mal! — Je suis caché et je ne le suis pas. »

29 In the original text: « Quelquefois je vois au ciel des plages sans fin couvertes de blanches nations en joie. Un grand vaisseau d'or, au-dessus de moi, agite ses pavillons multicolores sous les brises du matin. J'ai créé toutes les fêtes, tous les triomphes, tous les drames. »

Works Cited

Abrüpt. https://abrupt.cc/. Accessed 3 June 2021.

Abrüpt. "Partage." https://abrupt.cc/partage/. Accessed 3 June 2021.

Antilivre. https://www.antilivre.org/. Accessed 3 June 2021.

Bolter, J. David, and Richard A. Grusin. *Remediation: Understanding New Media.* MIT Press, 2000.

Bonnet, Gilles. "Fabula, Atelier Littéraire: LitteraTube." *https://www.fabula.org,* 2018, http://www.fabula.org/atelier.php?LitteraTube#_ftnref2.

———. *Pour Une Poétique Numérique: Littérature Et Internet.* Hermann, 2017.

Bootz, Philippe. "La Littérature Déplacée." *Littérature Numérique Et Caetera, Formules/Revue Des Littérature à Contrainte*, edited by Serge Bouchardon et al., 2006.

Bouchardon, Serge. *La Valeur Heuristique de La Littérature Numérique.* Hermann, 2014.

Bullich, Vincent. *Industrialisation, Marchandisation Et Médiatisation Des Expressions: Le Modèle Des Plateformes Numériques.* 2019. Grenoble Alpes, habilitation à diriger des recherches.

Candel, Étienne, and Gustavo Gomez-Mejia. "Écrire l'auteur: La Pratique Éditoriale Comme Construction Socioculturelle de La Littérarité Des Textes Sur Le Web." *L'auteur En Réseau, Les Réseaux de l'auteur*, edited by Oriane Deseilligny and Sylvie Ducas, Presses universitaires de Paris Nanterre, 2013.

Coleman, E. Gabriella. *Coding Freedom: The Ethics and Aesthetics of Hacking.* Princeton University Press, 2013.

Collectif. *RIMBAUD.ZAP.* https://antilivre.gitlab.io/rimbaud.zap/. Accessed 3 June 2021.

Crouzet, Thierry. "La Littérature Numérique Est Morte." *Tcrouzet.com*, 2018, http://tcrouzet.com/2018/03/30/la-litterature-numerique-est-morte/

Doueihi, Milad. *Digital Cultures.* Harvard University Press, 2011.

———. *Pour Un Humanisme Numérique.* Seuil, 2011.

Fauchié, Antoine. *Déployer Le Livre.* 2021, https://deployer.quaternum.net.

Flores, Leonardo. "Third Generation Electronic Literature." *Electronic Book Review*, Apr. 2019, https://electronicbookreview.com/essay/third-generation-electronic-literature/

Funkhouser, Chris T. *New directions in Digital Poetry.* Bloomsbury, 2012.

Garcia, David, and Geert Lovink. "The ABC of tactical media." *posting to Nettime mailing list* 16, 1997.

Gefen, Alexandre, and Claude Perez. "Extension Du Domaine de La Littérature." *Elfe XX-XXI. Études de La Littérature Française Des XXe Et XXIe Siècles*, vol. 8, 2019, https://doi.org/10.4000/elfe.736.

Gervais, Bertrand. "Naviguer Entre Le Texte Et l'écran. Penser La Lecture à l'ère de l'hypertextualité." *Les Défis de La Publication Sur Le Web: Hyperlectures, Cybertextes Et Méta-Éditions*, edited by Christian Vandendorpe and Jean-Michel Salaün, Presses de l'Enssib, 2004, p. 61, http://archivesic.ccsd.cnrs.fr/docs/00/06/21/21/PDF/sic_00000291.pdf

Gillespie, Tarleton. "The Politics of 'Platforms'." *New Media & Society*, vol. 12, no. 3, May 2010, pp. 347–64, https://doi.org/10.1177/1461444809342738.

Goldsmith, Kenneth. *Uncreative Writing: Managing Language in the Digital Age.* Columbia University Press, 2011.

Guilet, Anaïs. *Pour Une Littérature Cyborg: L'hybridation Médiatique Du Texte Littéraire.* 2013. Université du Québec à Montréal, Thèse ou essai doctoral accepté, http://www.archipel.uqam.ca/6010/.

Kessler, Franck. *Notes on Dispositif.* 2004. http://frankkessler.nl/wp-content/uploads/2010/05/Dispositif-Notes.pdf

Larrue, Jean-Marc, and Marcello Vitali-Rosati. *Media Do Not Exist: Performativity and Mediating Conjunctures.* Institute of Network Cultures, 2019, https://papyrus.bib.umontreal.ca/xmlui/handle/1866/22937.

Marino, Mark C. *Critical Code Studies.* The MIT Press, 2020.

Mauro, Aaron. *Hacking in the Humanities Cybersecurity, Speculative Fiction, and Navigating a Digital Future.* Bloomsbury Academic, 2022.

Méchoulan, Éric. *D'où Nous Viennent Nos Idées?* VLB, 2010, http://www.edvlb.com/viennent-nos-idees-/eric-mechoulan/livre/9782896491476.

Monjour, Servanne. "La Littérature Numérique n'existe Pas. La Littérarité Au Prisme de l'imaginaire Médiatique Contemporain." *Communication Langages*, vol. N° 205, no. 3, 2020, pp. 5–27, http://www.cairn.info/revue-communication-et-langages-2020-3-page-5.htm.

Monjour, Servanne. "Le Profil Numérique: Au-Delà de l'opposition Homme-Machine?" *Subjectivités Numériques Et Posthumain*, edited by Machinal et al., PUR, 2020.

Monjour, Servanne, and Nicolas Sauret. "Pour Une Gittérature: L'autorité à l'épreuve Du Hack." *Revue*, vol. XXI–XX, no. 2, 2021.

Mougin, Pascal. *Moderne/Contemporain*. Les Presses du réel, 2019, https://www.lespressesdureel.com/ouvrage.php?id=7310.

Müller, Jürgen E. "Intermediality and Media Historiography in the Digital Era." *Acta Universitatis Sapientiae, Film and Media Studies*, vol. 2, 2010, pp. 15–38.

Nachtergael, Magali. *Poet Against The Machine. Une Histoire Technopolitique de La Littérature*. Le mot et le reste, 2020, https://lemotetlereste.com/artsvisuels/poetagainstthemachine/.

Petit, Victor, and Serge Bouchardon. "L'écriture Numérique Ou l'écriture Selon Les Machines. Enjeux Philosophiques Et Pédagogiques." *Communication & Langages*, no. 191, Dec. 2017, pp. 129–48, https://doi.org/10.4074/S0336150017011097

Poell, Thomas, et al. "Platformisation." *Internet Policy Review*, vol. 8, no. 4, Nov. 2019, https://policyreview.info/concepts/platformisation

Rajewsky, Irina O. "Intermediality, Intertextuality, and Remediation: A Literary Perspective on Intermediality." *Intermédialités: Histoire Et Théorie Des Arts, Des Lettres Et Des Techniques*, no. 6, 2005, p. 43, https://doi.org/10.7202/1005505ar

Ruffel, Lionel. *Brouhaha. Les Mondes Du Contemporain*. Verdier, 2016.

Souchier, Emmanuël. « L'image du texte pour une théorie de l'énonciation éditoriale », *Les cahiers de médiologie*, vol. 6, no. 2, 1998, pp. 137–145.

Vissac, Guillaume. *Accident de Personne*. Publie.net, 2011.

Vitali-Rosati, Marcello. "La Littérature Numérique, Existe-t-Elle?" *Digital Studies/ Le Champ Numérique*, Feb. 2015, https://papyrus.bib.umontreal.ca/xmlui/bitstream/handle/1866/13159/La-litterature-numerique_Vitali-Rosati.pdf?sequence=1.

Vitali-Rosati, Marcello. "La littérature numérique francophone : enjeux théoriques et pratiques pour l'identification d'un corpus" *Lire et donner à lire les littératures francophones : Outils critiques et stratégies éditoriales*, edited by Véronique Corinus and Mireille Hilsum, Presses universitaires de Rennes, ISBN 978-2-7535-8316-0, p 209–220, 2022.

3 Reimagining Translation Anthologies

A Journey into Non-Linear Computational Assemblages

Raluca Tanasescu

"Can't date a datum,
simply get lost in the data,
the endless fun of not being one."

—MARGENTO, *"US" Poets Foreign Poets*

Introduction

This chapter introduces a novel approach to curating a literary translation anthology of poetry that diverges from the traditional conception of literary anthologies as historical collections with significant influence on canon formation. It presents *"US" Poets Foreign Poets. A Computationally Assembled Anthology* (MARGENTO), a "radical" literary translation undertaking that offers a reproducible model of selection and demonstrates a holistic understanding of translation. This unconventional approach shifts the primary focus away from concerns related to literary systems, traditions, and canon establishment and, instead, places a greater emphasis on the artistic and formal aspects of poetry, such as meter and rhyme, among others. In addition, and perhaps, most importantly, the emphasis on formal and language aspects related to poetic form are not only concerns regarding interlingual translation but also the main way in which the 53 poems in the anthology were selected from a much larger corpus of poetry, thus offering a scalable model for anthology curation. The fusion between various media (the page, the digital, and the code), the interplay between page poetry and electronic poetry in each of these media separately and in all of them at once and the representation of poems as text, as tf-idf vectors, and as nodes in various graph visualizations warrant an intermedial approach that offers readers a multifaceted, immersive experience with strong creative and analytical undertones. In this way, the anthology becomes a platform embedded both in the print industry and in the digitality of the code, a multimodal type of literary infrastructure that, as we will see, both controls the text and encourages serendipitous emergence.

DOI: 10.4324/9781003320838-5

"US" Poets, as I will refer to it here for brevity, is described by its editing collective as a bridge between the realms of digital and traditional page-based poetry, aiming to unearth connections among a wide array of poems. To visually represent these connections, the anthology employs graph theory: in essence, it uses this approach to analyze and generate poetry, conceptualizing clusters of poems as interconnected networks or graphs. Each poem represents a node in the network, and the relationships between them are established based on shared characteristics derived from various genre-related features, including diction, meter, rhyme, metaphor, themes, syntax, and more, on the grounds of a term frequency-inverse document frequency (tf-idf) vectorization approach. Tf-idf is a popular statistical method based on a numerical representation used in natural language processing to evaluate the importance of a word within a document relative to a collection of documents, with higher values indicating greater significance. The evolving network of digital and page-based poems emerges as a distinctive form of literature, a "graph poem," and as a generative anthology model, while also allowing for the computational expansion and analysis of the poetry corpus. Besides being a poetry anthology, it is also a bilingual one, featuring Romanian translations of the English-language poems. Thus, the proposed model of anthologizing and the nature of the poems included bear implications over the nature of translation, which, as the editors themselves explain, is done on three levels: literal (as in literary translation in the traditional sense), processual (involving the replication of the algorithms that had generated the digital originals, or developing new algorithms to generate the Romanian poems featured as translations of the English ones), and semiotic (the translation of the corpus of poems into network graphs).

As the reader may have already noticed, this type of undertaking differs considerably from the linear model on which most literary anthologies are built (Essmann and Frank; Korte *et al.*, Ferry, Baubeta, Seruya, etc.). At a minimum, it begs the question of reconsidering the codex as the only medium of the category—since it uses algorithms to dig out the most suitable pieces out of a pool of candidate-poems—as well as the understanding of the category as a monolithic construct rooted in established literary traditions (Seruya *et al.*, Frank and Essmann). At a more complex level, it questions the relevance of the many categorizations and distinctions that have been attempted in anthology theory, from anthology vs. collection vs. miscellany to the notion of authorship which, in the case of translation anthologies, is extremely problematic (Pym, "Translation and Non-Translational Regimes") and so much the more so in the case of *"US" Poets* since there is not only one editor but also an editing and translation collective called MARGENTO. The highlighted case study also raises the question of anthologies as scalable platforms serving as infrastructure for corpus analyses as well as the issue of the emerging editor and translator, which Johanna Drucker also approaches in her chapter in the present volume. While MARGENTO indeed uses a machinic model of curation, the output of the model is still dependent on the editor's selection of candidate-poems as well as on the way literary and algorithmic translations are approached; in other words, the model relies on both human input and machine capabilities, just as generally platforms—be they social or technological—condition and are conditioned by their users.

Although the complexity of this anthology is unlikely to be fully addressed in one single contribution, I will discuss its most relevant *translation-related* features with the aim of contributing to the broader conversation about the significant impact of the digital on the literary tradosphere. Just like digital literature, which is "often found, piecemeal, at the fringes of better-established disciplines, such as book history (whose very choice of name signals its unease with contemporary developments), nationalist literary studies (despite the Internet's structural undermining of national boundaries), cultural sociology (though traditionally restive with specifically literary judgements and cultural studies (long more attuned to screen media than to the codex)" (Murray 313), digital literary translation has been approached only in relation to creativity and machine translation. Second, although not of lesser importance, the chapter aims to emphasize the importance of code as a creative medium for literary translation as well as the promise of computational analysis of formal and stylistic issues as scaffolding for the generation of an anthology model that functions as a platform for generating and analyzing poetry. To these ends, we will seek to answer the following questions: What does *"US" Poets* bring new in terms of anthology curation? Does the digital have an impact on the editorial practices surrounding the editing of a poetry anthology? Can such a mode of curating poetry anthologies be separated from the influence of the body politic? And finally, what would a definition of translation anthologies look like in light of the novel practices put forth by the anthology at hand?

The chapter is structured across four further sections and a conclusion. The "Literary (Translation) Anthologies" section provides an overview of existing research on anthologies in literary studies and in literary translation, highlighting features that will be later on placed into a dialog with *"US" Poets*. The "Dynamics and Relationality in Translation Anthologies" section is dedicated to introducing the concepts of dynamics and relationality and their renewed relevance to anthology curation. The "Anthological Relatedness and Multimediality as Translation" section elaborates on the links between relationality and the materiality of anthologies, bringing to the fore the issue of the digital medium. The *"'US' Poets Foreign Poets*. A Case Study of Data Commoning" section describes further characteristics of the highlighted anthology and expands on the ways in which it challenges existing anthology scholarship. Finally, the "Anthologies as Platforms: A Non-Linear, Scalable Model" section answers the questions asked in this introduction and reflects on the elements of novelty that *"US" Poets* brings to the scholarly fields of literature and translation and on its further implications on the theoretical frameworks that inform our thinking about literary translation.

Literary (Translation) Anthologies

In one of the most comprehensive pieces of research on poetry anthologies to date, Anne Ferry argues that anthologies are taken for granted, but they are "peculiar, both distinctive and odd, for the corollary reason that the choices about the book's contents, except for those that went into the making of the poems, are the decisions of someone whose aim is *to make something of a very different kind*: a selection of several or many poets' work, decided and arranged on principles and using materials different from what would be found in a book of poems by only one author" (2, emphasis mine). Although poetry anthologies are a familiar kind of books, there is remarkably little research in cultural studies about the very diverse practices of anthologizing compared to the overall number of such titles published globally, with just under 82,000 entries currently listed by WorldCat. Most studies on literary anthologies flourished over the last two decades of the 20th century, when cultural and literary studies were concerned with the processes underlying canon formation, and translation scholars followed in these footsteps.

In literary studies, various distinctions are taken into account in the classification of anthologies. Certain scholars make a distinction among thematic functions, literary or historical-literary functions, cultural or cultural-historical functions, and ideological, political, or commercial functions, as outlined by Naaijkens. Other classifications start from the quadruple survey anthology, focus (Mujica) or programmatic (Korte *et al.*), textbook anthologies (such as readers), and comprehensive anthologies (Lauter), all sharing the tenet of canon formation (Vale de Gato). Irrespective of the element that drives such classifications, most scholars agree that they are not exclusive and often overlap. Indeed, Patricia Baubeta remarks that anthologies are "a catch all genre, and can be organized in an almost infinite number of ways" (213). Referring to poetry anthologies in the Lusophone context, she rightfully notes that "poems [...] can be grouped together according to a multiplicity of criteria, but all of them are *intensely subjective* and depend quite simply on the anthologist's own reading experience and personal taste" (213, emphasis mine).

Simply described as "a collection of connected or interrelated writings" (di Leo 6)—a definition which has not changed much across literary history—anthologies are overwhelmingly seen as essential for understanding the histories and structure of literary systems (Korte *et al.*). Besides this pervasive historical dimension, one of the main features of such collections is the anthologists' self-consciousness, that is, their subjective awareness of the principles underlying selection and arrangement (Ferry), as well as their ideological identity that turns them into powerful tools for canon formation and revision (Kittler). No matter how they are framed and irrespective of the aspects a certain definition dwells on, all understandings point to anthologists' interests, tastes, and to their own reading experience of the corpora that served as departure points in the selection, to the point that even "readers" (a form of anthology) contain traces of the editor's reading experience (Price, *The Anthology and The Rise of the Novel*).

In line with the post-modern condition's "concern with fragmentation and wholeness, and its alleged crisis of value and evaluation" (Korte 3), many anthologies in Western Europe and North America have focused on multiculturalism. In Portuguese and Spanish contexts, literary anthologies have recently played a consequential role in the formation of new literary histories, with an impact on acknowledging the contributions of women and minorities to canon formation (Baubeta, Guillén). The crisis of value and evaluation mentioned by Korte and her co-editors was marked by the issue of the politics underlying the process of editing anthologies—a highly contentious one in relation to feminist literature (Robinson) as well as to the use of anthologies as teaching tools for literary survey courses in North-American Universities (Damrosch). As Cary Nelson notes, the kind of rearrangements and displacements anthologies create in literary practice and criticism are "figurations of the body politic" (47). Poets appropriate the power of anthologies to serve their own interests and to use them as instruments of criticism: "Nothing is innocent in an anthology, since any presence entails an absence" (Palenque cited in Baubeta 14). The contentious air that surrounds anthologies has an effect on the description of the kind of editor that would take on the task of putting together an anthology: portraits vary from "irresponsible enthusiasts" and "'minor poets' [...] who wish to bully the public into accepting them as major poets through the leverage of their anthologies" (Riding and Graves 39–40) to "a reader who takes upon himself the power to direct the readings of others, intervening in the reception of multiple poets, modifying the horizon of expectations of his contemporaries. A writer of second degree, the anthologist is a super-reader of the first rank" (Guillén 2, translation mine). Irrespective of the angle from which anthologies have historically been examined, it becomes evident that the primary focus is consistently directed toward the subjective role of the human curator. This underscores the fundamental idea that the choices and selections made by the editor are influenced by their personal viewpoints, preferences, and interpretations, and as such, they play a central and subjective role in shaping the content and thematic direction of each particular anthology.

At this point, we can agree that most of the existing scholarly contributions on poetry anthologies have three significant things in common; first, the fact that they rely on the subjective selection of the anthologist; second, the fact that they have a presentation and evaluation function foregrounded in the same subjectivity of the editor; and third, the fact that most anthologies have a historical dimension grounded in the assumption of canon formation: "Composing an anthology creates a miniature canon, no matter how resistant the editor is to the vexed notions of goodness and importance [...] Traditionally, anthologies are compiled on three bases: excellence, representativeness (and/or comprehensiveness), and interest, often working in some combination [...] All three criteria frustrate precise definition" (Kilcup 37).

To these common features, I would like to add a fourth one, which seems to be approached by anthology theorists only as a matter of fact: its printed, book-bound format. In anthology theory, the materiality of such collections has so far been approached almost exclusively in relation to the economics of publishing such volumes. The advent of the printing press in the 15th century significantly influenced the formation of literary canons. The standardization enabled by print allowed for the mass production of books, creating authoritative versions of literary works that became the foundation of these literary canons. Moreover, print technology facilitated cultural homogenization by spreading texts and ideas across regions and languages, thereby impacting the global perspective on specific works and their canonical status. The ability to critically engage with printed texts led to greater attention and critical acclaim for certain works, influencing their inclusion in literary canons. Literary anthologies are among the categories that played an extremely important role in canon formation, alongside books for pedagogical use.

However, authors like textual scholar Jerome McGann refer to "the analytic limits of hardcopy" (McGann 15) as the restrictions or limitations imposed by traditional printed texts or hardcopy literature on the way we analyze and engage with literary works. In this context, McGann notes how printed books or physical copies of texts manifest constraints that can hinder a deeper or more dynamic exploration of literary content. These limitations might include the fixed, linear nature of the printed text, the inability to easily hyperlink or cross-reference to other texts, and the inability to incorporate multimedia elements, among other things. McGann advocates for digital and electronic forms of literature as a means to overcome these constraints and enable more flexible and interactive modes of engagement with literary works. Similarly, N. Katherine Hayles discusses the flatness of the print against the depth of the code in the same context of the differences between traditional print literature and digital or electronic literature: while print is fixed and does not allow for immediate alterations or responses, "the depth of the code" refers to the underlying code that powers digital or electronic literature, that is, the programming and algorithms that govern how electronic literature functions, which enable interactivity, non-linear narratives, multimedia integration, and dynamic responses to user input. Nevertheless, what is more intriguing in relation to the project discussed here is the fact that *"US" Poets* contains twice as many page poets than digital ones and was published in printed book form, making the anthology only an instantiation of a superseding model, which is actually the stake of the whole project. The main objective of this entire endeavor is to leverage the non-linear nature of code in order to highlight previously uncharted connections between vastly diverse poetic works. This approach stands in stark contrast to traditional anthologies, which often establish artificial associations between poems and poets based on the principles of canon formation or revision.

In translation studies, anthologies have been an object of inquiry as a subspecies of more fundamental issues, such as translation proper or the ethnography of translation processes. Translation anthologies became an object of systematic research only in the second decade of the new millennium (Seruya *et al.*), with scholars previously noting that translations had usually been the kind of text that was either left out of literary histories (Lambert) or overlooked by cultural history altogether (Basnett). Unlike literary history, which perceives anthologists as wielding a special kind of authority through the gesture of selection and implicit exclusion, translation scholars regarded anthologizing as a difficult endeavor since "the anthologist has to assume the burden of selection" (Lefevere 141), rather focusing on the challenging task of assessing what makes an anthology piece in translation. Translation scholars have thus approached anthologies in much the same way as most of literary studies and comparative literature: as a textual model on printed support. The reasons for this are translation scholars' focus on a 19th-century notion of text as a verbal and written expression and on the history of translation studies having been dominated by canonic literary texts. In the 1990s, scholars equated anthologies to museum exhibitions featuring literary pieces of cultural importance and providing an interpretation and evaluation of the selected literary corpus, with translation serving as a legitimation of its value.

At the same time, the practice used to be seen in a homogenous way, with similar purposes irrespective of the specifics of the culture in which they were produced:

> Anthologies (i.e., collections of texts and other printed matter) are a special type of widely distributed books. Like museum curators, anthologists select for exhibition items that are considered of cultural importance and/or sales value; by arranging the exhibits, they project an interpretation and evaluation of a given field and invite readers to make use of the cultural store. Translation anthologies serve essentially the same purposes internationally.
>
> (Essmann and Frank 65)

In the 2000s, this homogenous understanding of anthologies becomes more nuanced, and they start to be related to selection and preservation rather than to evaluation, as well as to gestures of contesting the canon and introducing the readers to less circulated pieces of literature. Authors like Judy Wakabayashi see anthologies as pieces of micro-history related to cultural development, a special kind of books that allow, by reducing the scale of the investigation, for a more detailed analysis of the social and political processes surrounding their publication. Most translation scholarship, however, links anthologies with the contestation of existing canons: "All anthologies have inherent (re)canonizing intentions and effects, whether the texts they contain count as canonical already or as unknown, forgotten, marginalized" (Seruya *et al.* 2). They are transplantation acts of domestic literary polemics, acts of deliberate selection and deliberate restructuring and recontextualization of a specific corpus, in which outside narratives collide with inside stories (D'hulst).

With the advent of the sociological turn in translation research in the new millennium, the agency of translators starts to be more and more manifest and their involvement in editorial practices all over the world becomes a recognized reality. Literary translators, especially poetry translators, make their involvement in the local literary scenes known and anthologies become instances of literary poetics and reflections of various politically informed attitudes toward language and culture. Speaking about contemporary mainland Chinese poetry in translation, Maghiel van Crevel notes that generally "[t]ranslation anthologists make very different books and say very different things about them. [...] what anthologists do, and what they say they do, also reflects their individual agency and hence their positionality and their inclination" (318–319). In other contexts, such as India, existing anthology scholarship notes their purpose of counter-narratives of translation practices, "a form of resistance to the celebration of national boundaries" (Israel 398; also, Pym, *Negotiating the Frontier*), that is, translation projects that contests the classification of literary history in strictly nationalistic terms. It becomes thus apparent that, whenever anthology theory scholars are not concerned with a structuralist approach to anthology curation, they are instead concerned with poststructuralist preoccupation for textuality as a site of struggle, for the implications of cultural and historical context as well as for the poststructuralist focus on readers' interpretations of included texts.

Dynamics and Relationality in Translation Anthologies

Translation in Anthologies and Collections (19th and 20th centuries), edited by Teresa Seruya, Lieven D'hulst, Alexandra Assis Rosa, and Maria Lin Moniz in 2013, the most recent systematic translation studies contribution which tackled the category under scrutiny in this chapter, exudes a similarly structuralist stance. I would like to single out two distinct aspects that the authors emphasize in their introduction as definitory for the category. First, as the title suggests, the editors approach two different types: the anthology—a selection and rearrangement of small literary texts—and the collection—a neighboring notion that implies rearrangement, but not as much selection. The editors define both as clusters of elements that the authors, readers, and publishers regard as salient in the making of the category, or a "linguistic, geo-cultural, generic, historical, thematic" set of criteria (D'hulst 20). As we can see, their understanding perfectly mirrors that of literary studies, which does not include materiality and the medium among the salient features of anthologies, with the exception of scholar-practitioners working in electronic literature and in the so-called digital humanities. In the introduction, they note that two of the most important historical principles underlining the editorial process behind anthologies are *dynamics* and *relationality*, which are two central poststructuralist concepts. However, their understanding is far from being poststructuralist. By dynamics they understand "the interplay between the constituent elements of the communication process in which literary anthologies come into being [applied] to the variable combinations of elements such as authorship, genre, themes, language, editorship and readership, some combinations being more foundational or prominent than others at given moments in time" (9). This is different from the understanding of literary dynamics as fluid, complex, and often rooted in the instability of language, the interplay of power, and the intertextual connections between texts, which questions the idea of a fixed, singular meaning and emphasizes the role of the reader and the broader social context in shaping interpretations of literary works. In a similar vein, by relationality, they understand "the variable relation between anthologies and other so-called synthetic forms" (9), and in defining synthetic forms, they use the definition provided by

Popovic and Macri in 1977, according to which such forms are concerned with literary syntheses such as "collection, anthology, author (as sum of all texts), literary group, trend, generation, minority literature, national multilingual literature, 'metropolitan literature', supranational literature, 'European' literature, and world literature" (Popovic and Macri cited in Seruya *et al.* 8). These are all monolithic terms that reflect the consolidation of various traditions under one convenient moniker.

However, synthetic forms in contemporary literature also refer to creative or artistic approaches that involve the construction, combination, or synthesis of elements to create new and often experimental forms of literary expression with innovative and non-traditional structures. Some of these forms are collages—the piecing together of fragments of text from different sources to create new multi-layered poems; ergodic literature— where readers engage in a non-linear reading process to access the text, which might involve navigating footnotes, interactive elements, or various types of non-standard formatting; hypertext fiction—in which the authors use digital technology to create non-linear narratives; and many others. Allowing for a more fragmentary type of literature curation enlarges our understanding of anthologies to include, for instance, periodicals, which in some cultures have a similar synthetic role (Hung).

Another example, now with an established tradition, is that of the poetry assemblages curated and translated by Jerome Rothenberg, the world-famous American poet, and Pierre Joris, the Luxemburg-born American poet, essayist, translator, and anthologist. These assemblages would be difficult to place under Seruya *et al.*'s conservative understanding of anthologies. Rothenberg used for the first time the word "assemblage" to refer to his five-volume anthology project *Poems for the Millenium* (vol. 1, 1995—vol. 5, 2015), whose aim was to offer "a radical and globally decentered revision of American and world poetry" (Rothenberg, "A first anthology/assemblage of the poetry and poetics of the Americas" n.p.) and to push back against "the canonical anthologies we all know as the great conservatizing force in our literature(s), against which—as artists of an avant-garde—many of [them] have had to struggle" (Rothenberg, "The Anthology as A Manifesto" 16). To him, the notion of assemblage meant the act of bringing together "this eclectic range of complex poetics and performances" (Wrighton), in search of all the ways of poetry he could discover, especially native American. Rothenberg's anthologies are perhaps the closest example to MARGENTO's, although the first is more associated with the ethics of the place than with a concern for form or poetic diction. Rothenberg's assemblages bring together poems pertaining to very diverse and understudied traditions and are part of a wider concern for mapping literary geographies (Anderson), but it is not the grounds of a reproducible model because its logic resides in the editors' interests and tastes. In spite of there probably being an internal logic in structuring the assemblages the way he did, Rothenberg did not make the model manifest, instead focusing on the logic of assembling poetries as gathering "or pulling together of poems & people & ideas about poetry (& much else) in the words of others and in their own words" (Rothenberg, "The Anthology as A Manifesto" 19). Nevertheless, his work in the area of ethnopoetics is very similar to the approach proposed by *"US" Poets*: it reflects a multifaceted, interdisciplinary approach to poetry, one which combines oral tradition with translation, performance, sound, and textual experimentation, thus the concern for anthologizing diverse poetries with an awareness of their materiality.

In the case of *"US" Poets*, the appellation "a computationally-assembled anthology" aligns with the selection-driven category but puts a focus on the medium and the process used to curate it, highlighting the affordances put forth by computation as well as the dynamics of the assemblage. Assemblage in the sense of Deleuze and Guattari might be the best way to conceptually describe such a computational approach, as it deals with the play of contingency and structure, organization, and change. "Agencement," the French term used by Deleuze, is a dynamic term: it is not the arrangement or organization but the *process* of arranging, organizing, and fitting together. Thus, an assemblage is not a set of predetermined parts (such as the poems presented in a poetry anthology in the traditional sense) that are then put together in order or into a preconceived structure. Nor is it a random collection of things, but a becoming that brings elements together. The allusion to Deleuze is explicit in relation to the links of the expanding graph as "lines of flight" (MARGENTO 259) and the process of computationally selecting candidate-poems for the anthology is described in the Editor's Note as highly dynamic: "[...] surf the surroundings, dig for a twig, root for a bot, dive in for more of unlike before" (6). The stakes of the anthology are in the process that generates the model: "for flow's sake gotta go with the flow..." (6) because the more the graph grows, the more inclusive it becomes: "Our migration is the integration of the poetries we got in the making into ever vaster and more detailed versions of themselves, of ourselves as poem drivers, 4(D)-rivers, data rivers" (6).

Nevertheless, MARGENTO's assemblage differs in an important respect from Deleuze and Guattari's notion: while the latter emphasizes constant mutation that can lead either to expansion or collapse, the former emphasizes constant growth. Although specifically called an "assemblage" in the subtitle, the anthology collection according to MARGENTO's model appears as a *constantly evolving* collection of poems selected according to the most relevant features of the genre. The key to escaping collapse seems to reside in the anthologist's grip on the code. The tighter the collection of poems is (that is, the higher the weight of the links between vectors), the closer to an anthology design the editors are. The assemblage feeds itself from multiple poem databases but grows according to a well-defined logic apparent in the algorithms used. The values of the tf-idf scores mutate with every poem added to the corpus. Thus, the mutation appears only at the level of the tf-idf vectors, but the result is always expansion, which prompted C. T. Funkhouser to rightfully note in the blurb on the anthology's fourth cover that the volume manifests "an unprecedented propulsiveness" (2018).

One may argue that such an assemblage is closer to the neighboring notions of "collage" and the associated "aesthetics of the fragment" (Joris 38). Literary collages involve the deliberate use of disparate, often fragmented elements such as text and images, juxtaposed and their intention is, indeed, to create a new, complex, and often experimental work that challenges traditional narrative structures, encouraging readers to engage with the text in a non-linear and more participatory manner. In the process, collages often emphasize the beauty and significance of individual fragments and encourage readers to interpret and connect them in unique ways, leading to a deeper exploration of the text's multiple layers of meaning. By contrast, *"US" Poets* is not necessarily (or, rather, not primarily) concerned with the literary value of each anthologized poem, but with the ways in which the features of each poem contribute to the wholeness and expansion of the assemblage.

At this point, we can agree that this example significantly departs from contemporary conceptions of dynamics and relationality in anthology scholarship. Paradoxically, these notions are delineated in conjunction with rather rigid and singular concepts, even though a plethora of more nuanced, fluid, and interrelated ideas are readily accessible in the current intellectual landscape. The treatment of dynamics and relationality in current anthology theory appears out of step with contemporary scholarship. It juxtaposes these concepts with more rigid and monolithic ideas, failing to embrace the wealth of dynamic and interconnected theoretical frameworks that are presently available. In an era marked by the proliferation of flexible, multifaceted, and interdependent conceptualizations, traditional approaches to anthology curation appear somewhat anachronistic.

Anthological Relatedness and Multimediality as Translation

As noted before, of interest for the topic of anthology curation is the fact that poststructuralism emphasizes the interconnectedness of texts and their dependence on cultural and historical contexts, challenging the isolation of individual printed works by highlighting the influence of relationships with other texts and the broader cultural milieu. Relatively recent contributions on anthologies in translation studies have noted the heuristic value of relationality with regard to academic training in literary translation. More specifically, Vale de Gato speaks about the role played by collaborative translation anthologies in literary translation classes, that is "[...] arranging corpora for literary translation teaching purposes according to an anthological design, so as to help achieve its twofold goal: to have a hands-on approach to translating literary texts, and to increase students' competence in literature, from literary and textual criticism to the reading of literature and the understanding of correlations between literary systems, traditions and repertoires" (Vale de Gato 50). Although the historical approach is still overarching, since literary traditions and evolutions form the foundation of any comprehensive literature course, the Portuguese scholar considers it insufficient for the transmission of literary competencies. In order to be suitable to teach and learn collaboratively the practice of literary translation, the proposed anthological design needs to comply with a set of further requirements, such as diversity of text genres, diversity of trends and styles, time-range and historical-textual changes, explicitation of text formatting conventions, etc. The model advanced by Vale de Gato leverages intertextual and translation relatedness as one of the two guiding principles of putting together a literary translation anthology for teaching purposes (the second one being the diasporic literature and translation approach). On the one hand, such use has merit because it takes the issues of relationality and dynamics at least one step forward in comparison with a strictly historical, canon-formation approach. On the other hand, her project factors in the medium in the process of designing the anthology: before becoming a trade edition in printed form, the anthology takes advantage of the relatedness of the digital medium. *PEnPAL in Trans— Portuguese-English Platform for Anthologies of Literature in Translation* started from her anthology model-based syllabus and became an inter-institutional literary translation project and a collaborative environment for teaching and research, consisting of a website, a blog, and a database (Valdez and Oliveira Martins 196). The first output was *Nem cá nem lá: Portugal e América do Norte entre escritas* (*Neither Here nor There: Writings Across Portugal and North America*), an anthology of 29 authors and 56 texts divided into fiction, poetry, memoirs, and historical discourse, children's literature and drama, with authors' biographical notes as well as "some considerations on the translation process and main translation strategies used, such as selective nontranslation as compensation for heterolingualism, explicitation, italicization of passages marked as foreign in the source text, replacement of disruptive language with non-standard target varieties, reliance on mixed literary repertoires, and the systematized replication of orality markers in the target language, among others" (199).

At this point, we can definitely see that such a use, although novel, still focuses on selection criteria (evaluation), recontextualization, authorship (translator's agency), and, perhaps more than anything, on purpose.

The two devised models mentioned above—the intertextual and diasporic models—serve the pedagogical purpose of the enterprise. While they can also serve without a doubt as approaches in building any type of literary (translation) anthologies, especially due to the fact that the historical and canonical dimensions are not set aside but only made more nuanced, we argue that the type of relatedness and dynamics such an anthology promotes is still limited and the models are not necessarily suited for replication in each and every cultural context and with any type of literary translation. Indeed, if by literary translation, we understand the translation of printed canonical literary texts, then the two proposed models may be entirely suitable and easy to replicate.

Nevertheless, if we enlarge the understanding of literary text as a product at the intersection of language and technology, traditional approaches will fall short. It is especially true in the case of contemporary poetry: "Today it is hardly radical to observe that poetry is —or at least is inseparable from— the means by which it is produced and distributed or transmitted" (100), notes Martin Spinelli about this literary form for which technology functions more and more as a writing and a reading medium (Kac). In digital humanities, anthologies and translation have been approached, even if sparingly and indirectly, in the synthetic contexts of electronic scholarly editing (Price) and of digital archiving for gendering purposes (Mandell), exploring the category in relation to the reticulated structure of digital space and facilitating a platform-like understanding of literary collections. The interplay between text and technology is especially manifest in electronic literature (e-lit). E-lit practitioners in general and digital poets in particular avail themselves of the affordances of technology and digital space. In one of his foundational texts, Loss Pequeño Glazier notes that the field of poetry needs to be reconstituted to include new forms of writing:

> The text now revels in radical forms of adjacency; a metonymy that comes from overlaying, collage, juxtaposition of visual elements, and forms of mapping. These are forms, I might add, that innovative print poetry has investigated extensively and from which many lessons can be drawn. Digital innovative practice can add to this the action programs realize and the concept of programming as writing.
>
> (Glazier, *Epilogue*, n.p.)

To go back to relatedness and dynamics, the two key notions on which this chapter has been slowly building, they are of utmost importance in the contemporary understanding of textuality: "writing is a whole and [...] as individuals we are just a part of that whole. How much more interesting the 'text' of a literary conference, for example, becomes when we consider the whole conference a text, rather than looking to an individual presentation for that sort of breadth!" (Glazier, *Epilogue*, n.p.). We can easily see a parallel between Glazier's example of a literary conference and our topic of literary anthologies. To echo his words, how much more interesting a (translation) poetry anthology becomes when we consider a poem in relation to other poems of its type, rather than looking at individual poems taken out of their context or co-text?

An anthology that reflects this sort of contemporary understanding of the literary text is the one edited by the Electronic Literature Organization. Every five years, they publish their *Electronic Literature Collection*, both on the web and as a physical version (CD ROM or USB flash drive)—a tradition started in 2006, with the latest installment published in 2022. The first two volumes do not provide any explicit rationale underlying the selection and publication of the included works although it transpires from the publisher's mission statement: "to assist writers and publishers in bringing their literary works to a wider, global readership and to provide them with the infrastructure necessary to reach one another" (web). Although the curation and archiving intentions are made clear via the explicit moniker "collection" in the very title and the anthological relatedness that implies selection is missing, there is a sense of interrelatedness that comes from a webpage dedicated to keywords. For instance, the page lists two electronic literature pieces under the keyword "translation," defined by the editors as "works in which the process of translation between languages, or between natural languages and code, is referenced, enacted, or otherwise important" (ELO web). One of them is John Cayley's foundational text "Translation," which also appears under the keywords "ambient" ("a dynamic linguistic wall-hanging" cf. Cayley), "appropriated text," "audio," "authors from outside North-America," "collaboration," "constraint-based/procedural," "generative," "multilingual or non-English," "music," "QuickPlayer" (the video-player), and "textual instrument." The latter keyword, especially, reflects an understanding of the text that is multifariously medial:

A work written and coded in such a way that it is capable, by analogy with a musical instrument, of playing numerous compositions. The reader is invited to become an expert player of the piece, for skill at manipulating it, above and beyond familiarity with how with its interface works, yields reading and viewing rewards. A closely related idea is that of the instrumental text, where an interface allows manipulations of a particular piece of writing in an interesting way.

(ELO web)

The second volume does not feature any electronic work related to translation but continues the hyperlink indexing of keywords. Their third volume contains an editor's statement that emphasizes the salience of the digital medium for electronic literature: "If we define literature as an artistic engagement of language, then electronic literature is the artistic engagement of digital media and language" (ELO web). Their mission statement also acknowledges the rise of social media, transnational communication, and new platforms that foster "experimental forms of human interaction" (id.), which reflects a broadening of the perspective, from an understanding of e-literature as occurring at the intersection of textuality and technology and from objectives related mainly to the preservation, to producing "a genealogy that interleaves differing historical traditions, technical platforms, and aesthetic practices" (id.), bringing to the fore underrepresented authors and traditions. "This collection parallels the works collected, operating in symbiotic relation with programs and processes, images and texts, readers and writers—and you" (id.). The relationship between the anthology and its context of publication that Seruya *et al.* referred to as salient for the category thus gains in dynamism, since one can very little control the way in which readers experience their encounter with a piece of electronic literature. This third installment consisted of 114 entries from 26 countries, published in 13 languages. In spite of the language diversity, it does not contain any work with the metadata "translation," which had to do with the community's rejection of English as the dominant language of e-lit.

There are two interesting observations to be made at this point in support of the relevance of a computational approach to translation anthology curation in the new millennium. On the one hand, the first two volumes are perceived by the community of digital practitioners as collections of canonical digital texts, such as Cayley's, thus countering the notion that anthologies traditionally deal with established texts and collections with eclectic selection, while the next two, although much more diverse, are explicitly perceived as anthologies (Marecki and Montfort). On the other, established digital authors such as Cayley and Stephanie Strickland specifically deal with the act of translation, understood in relation to e-lit not only as a linguistic transfer but also as a semiotic process of transfer between codes and media. For instance, Stephanie Strickland's contribution to the *Handbook of Electronic Literature* manifests "the importance of the practice of translation, understood as encompassing acts of transduction, transposition, transliteration, transcription, transclusion, and the transformation we call morphing" (Strickland 25). She sees translation as essential in digital space, especially in relation to conversion media: just as translators of print hieroglyphs do not have much control over the way 21st-century readers of English experience translations, electronic poets have little say over the way in which readers' personal computers and their personal settings mediate their reading experience. Strickland quotes John Felstiner, who famously stated that a poem in the original language seems dormant, while in translation, the same poem goes through a process of "alienating stress" (Searls 5) that resuscitates it and brings it back to life.

The process of alienating stress via translation is so much more acute in the case of digital poetry. Speaking about "Renderings," a project "researching global, non-English [digital] literatures and translating chosen works into English (thus, working against dominating tendencies)" (i85), Marecki and Montfort explain how translation was carried out in this context. They note that the translation of digital creations realized as computer programs introduces novel complexities beyond those encountered by translators of conventional literature, a process which is reminiscent of translating experimental, conceptual, or restricted works, often necessitating the reimagining of the piece in a different linguistic and cultural milieu, and occasionally even the adaptation of the original program into a new programming language. Indeed, the depth of the code involved in digital writing, the multimodality of such works, and their dynamic non-linearity as well as the complexity of other contextual elements all add to the complications of linguistic translation and draw on other dimensions of translation, particularly the inter-semiotic one.

"US" Poets Foreign Poets. A Case Study of Data Commoning.

Anne Ferry notes that answering the question of what makes an anthology piece involves dealing concomitantly with two further questions: one having to do with the nature of the cultural situation that led to a particular poem being featured in an anthology, and one related to the inherent qualities of the poems that made them an obvious choice for a certain anthology.

First off, let us approach briefly the nature of the cultural situation surrounding the publication of this computationally assembled anthology. *"US" Poets* was published in 2018, one year after the third volume of the *ELO Collection* became available online. As I have mentioned, the respective installment seemed to place a great emphasis on the use of code for generating poetry, which was an illustration of already almost decades of interest in this practice of author-driven digital writing. The "computationally assembled" in the subtitle of the *"US" Poets* anthology would immediately make us think that the editors were necessarily indebted to this new mode of making literature, especially since it contains not only traditional page-based poetry but also electronic poetry. However, while this indebtedness is not far-fetched, e-poetry is not the only form of writing that shares commonalities with the anthology under scrutiny. The field of poetry writing experienced a much broader redefinition during the first decades of the new millennium, of which electronic poetry was only one strand. Other poststructuralist forms of writing were much indebted to a Deleuzian mode of conceiving of the text, such as the one described by Pierre Joris, according to whom poetry needed to become "[a] truly open field, visualizable as a rhizomatic space with lines of flight shooting off in all directions, with no up/down, front/back or left/right spatial hierarchization, able to incorporate quasi-instant links to any other text or objects in cyberspace" (Joris 91). Joris also argued at the time that the days of rigidity in form, content, and state had passed and that all revolutions, whether addressing the state or the state of poetry, have transcended any fixed boundaries.

Indeed, in one of the paratexts, the editors explicitly refer to the expansion of the poetry corpus that forms this particular anthology as "lines of flight," while a previous anthology-like bilingual volume signed MARGENTO directly referenced the notion of "nomadism" in the title: *Nomadosofia/Nomadosophy* (2016). *Nomadosophy* was indebted, as one of the blurbs on the fourth cover suggests, to place poetry: "rich with political aptitude and buzzing with lyrical pizzazz - as it seeks to remember our many origins, roaming on toboggans, fishing boats, and taxicabs alike, and searching for a place for the night" (Baker). In *Placing Poetry*, Ian Davidson notes that a poem is not only positioned within its context but also actively shapes the environment it resides in. Poetry is simultaneously contained within its designated space while continually questioning its boundaries and who belongs within it. It traverses various locations through the act of *translation* and seamlessly transitions between different surroundings. The stationary connotations of place give way to the dynamic purpose of action, which, although hinting at a place of rest, remains in perpetual motion. The main editor, Chris Tanasescu, had articulated his views on place poetry in an article published almost at the same time as *Nomadosophy*, in which he noted that the notion of place still needs further exploration, "particularly with a further emphasis on 'placing' read as an action expressed by an intransitive verb, place-in-progress, place-as-process, and specifically, place-as-performance, especially if corroborated with studying the dynamism and processuality instilled and explored by poetry in (and as) place/ing" ("Community as Commoning" 23). Furthermore, Tanasescu argues that the mission of (post/trans)digital poetry is not about extracting data but rather immersing itself within the database and continually expanding it, which is crucial for crafting poetic projects that embody the fundamental characteristics of digital space itself, which include self-generation, self-organization, and self-sustaining (cf. Stephen Kennedy's *Chaos Media: A Sonic Economy of Digital Space*). He also argues that, in addition to considering the diasporic nature of digital poetry, one needs also incorporate the nomadic element to ensure that there are no constraints, fixations, or limitations hindering the free flow of sound and its unending trajectories, noting that the term "nomadic" embodies both the concept of unrestricted mobility and communal utilization. Etymologically, it originates from "[roaming to find] pasture, pasturage, grazing," stemming from the Indo-European root *nem-, meaning "to divide, distribute, allot." This implies sharing resources, goods, and lands, thus promoting a sense of common ownership (Tanasescu "Community as Commoning," 36). Tanasescu's stance aligns with the suggestion made by Jean-Gabriel Ganascia in "The Logic of a Big Data Turn in Digital Literary Studies," according to whom

> [...] computer-aided methods can be seen as a continuation of traditional humanistic approaches. As such, they can afford many opportunities *to renew humanistic methods* and *to make them more accurate*, by helping to empirically confront working hypotheses with datasets that now approach the entirety of our printed record, taking into consideration not only literary works themselves but also *the intellectual landscapes surrounding the authors of these works*.
> (Ganascia 5, emphases mine)

This is exactly one of the purposes the third section of the anthology ("Graph-Poem-Based Corpus Explorations and Expansions") serves: on the one hand, to empirically confront the positioning of certain traditionally central authors against more marginal ones and, on the other, to follow the model's emergence with every datum added. In other words, to use the anthology algorithm's incursions through the corpus to generate alternative views of every poem-node while the corpus expands.

With regards to the second question asked at the beginning of this section—What are the distinctive characteristics of the poems that clearly justified their inclusion in a particular anthology?—Anne Ferry is decidedly not wrong to ask this. However, a certain poem being an obvious choice for an anthology, no matter what the latter's function and purpose are, warrants the questioning of a qualifier like "obvious." While it can be understood as a relational qualifier—as in an obvious choice for the rationale behind the respective anthology as a whole—it totally disregards the poem's relation with the other parts of the whole. This linear view is very common in anthology theory, which posits that although poems are taken out of their "natural" context, they are "juxtaposed with works who's only connection with them may exist in the anthologist's mind" (Baubeta 42). Such understandings of how the parts make the anthology whole reflect a structuralist stance according to which an anthology is the sum of its parts, whereas Tanasescu's model is graph theory-based and projects a completely different understanding of what makes an anthology piece. Furthermore, a structuralist understanding of the category leads to cases in which a certain piece of writing becomes part of an anthology because "it is much easier to compile one's own from previous selections than to sift and resift the book market" (Frank and Essmann 26), emphasizing once again one of the mechanisms by which print contributed to canon formation.

In a seminal article, "International Literature Transfer via Translation Anthologies," Rainer Schulte rightfully argued that anthologists are not much different from those translators who are satisfied with a perfect semantic rendition, although there is more to a text than semantics—and here he enumerates the examples of sound, rhythm, image, and metaphor. Similarly, he suggests, translations anthologies "must transcend the level of that 'literal' existence" (142) and "use the forum [to] create the richness of a particular literature, so that the atmosphere—and not some mechanical arrangement—of that richness be communicated to the reader" (142). He likens anthologies to huge metaphors, shrewdly noting that easy metaphors sell well, and suggests the abandonment of some of the structuring principles of the past "to address the richness of perspectives that emerge in other cultures and languages" (141). Reading today, Schulte's thoughts sound very much ahead of his time, especially considering the fact that not much has changed in the way most anthologies are structured. Finally, he expresses his hope that translators would take up more often the role of anthology editors and structure such collections in a way that reflects their translational experience.

"US" Poets is definitely not in the business of easy sells, although the initial print run did sell out very fast. It is an anthology by a poet very much aware of the opening of the field of poetry (Tarlo) and a translator cognizant of the fact that translation is not only a transfer between languages but also an epistemic and semiotic process. A little background about the main editor and translator, Chris Tanasescu, and the project that fueled this anthology seems in order at this point. *"US" Poets* is one of the lines of flight shooting out of The Graph Poem Project (#GraphPoem), which emerged from Tanasescu's urge to enrich poetic practice by tapping into the synergy between poetic text, translation, and computational tools. Started in 2010, this project has used graph theory and the concept of networks for both analyzing and writing or generating poetry. Essentially, the underlying concept involves representing collections of poems as networks, with each individual poem as a node, and multiple connections (links) between them. These connections are determined by quantifying shared characteristics based on genre, including aspects like vocabulary, rhythm, rhyme, figurative language (such as metaphors), themes, sentence structure (including enjambments), and more. Poems can be integrated

into these networks, and this approach combines computational analysis with the expansion of poetry corpora and creative output. This effectively transforms any growing network of poems into a poem in itself, often referred to as a graph poem or a networked poem.

The postface by Romanian critic Ion Bogdan Lefter attempts to offer "three (of the many more possible) reading keys" (329). One of them is a new stage in the evolution of a certain author whose "writing has meanwhile diversified and became river-like and expansive. He imagines ever-proliferating and pantagruelian discourses, able to swallow the all-encompassing reality together with the language and languages that reflect it, in never-ending combinations, in his and others' phrasings, in a gigantic utopia of a kind of universal intertext" (329, translation mine). Indeed, he openly states in the Editor's Word that he "[c]an't get enough of that" (6). This insatiability signifies the poet-editor's intricate perspective on poetry as communion and on the significance of a poem not in its self-sustaining literary worth—"Can't date a datum[...]" (6)—but in its capacity to emerge from the connections it forms with other poems: "[...] simply get lost in the data, the endless fun of not being one." The encroachments of network algorithms into the data corpus are likened to a search for gold—"the ore in here, the aurum around" (6)—however, while every poem conceals an unnamed latent treasure (the ore), this treasure only reveals itself (the aurum) when surrounded by similar poems. The pursuit of companions (other akin poem-nodes) is all-encompassing: "We don't leave anything or anybody behind" (6).

Another distinctive aspect of the anthology lies in the juxtaposition of digital and page-based poets—part of Tanasescu's "discursive expressionism" (Lefter 330)—and in the printed materiality of the volume, a feature the postface author seems notably enthusiastic about, given his overt partiality toward the value of digital poetry. There are three potential facets to consider within this context: first, it is reasonable to think that one of the reasons behind choosing the printed format over a digital one was to align with the expectations of the Romanian book market, which, at the time, remained largely unacquainted with digital poetry. Moreover, if we consider the widespread availability of digital poetry on the internet, it would have been less logical to release the anthology online. Second, a primary objective of the anthology was to foster a dialog between digital poets and their counterparts in the realm of traditional poetry, arguably a groundbreaking endeavor in world literature. While this dialog indeed transpires within the digital domain at the algorithmic level, it also needs to be made manifest in the medium of page-based poets. In the spirit of Bruno Latour's concept of becoming a "digital trace," the latter must undergo a transformation to become data amenable to processing while the selected digital poets undergo a sort of digital-to-analog conversion. Finally, while the algorithm serves as the model for generating any anthology, *"US" Poets* represents a specific instantiation of this intermedial model, implying that numerous similar anthologies featuring poetry culled from various data sources are within the realm of possibility.

Another novel facet of the anthology pertains to its reshaping of the concepts of selection and authorship. Let us first refer to selection. The editor departs from an initial corpus of 40 poems, but there are not many details on how the selection was made, except for occasional references to "poems and poets we loved" (262). The process of selection is not a manifesto or a "smacking" of traditional anthologies in Rothenberg's terms but an act of care toward the emerging whole rather than toward each anthology piece: "The band of 'and' and 'and' never yielding a sum" (8). While the origins of the selected texts are duly acknowledged, the resultant assemblage incorporates these components, transforming individual journeys into a collective endeavor. In traditional anthologies, content is typically presented in a linear fashion, often organized chronologically, by country of origin, or by language. MARGENTO, on the other hand, initially follows an apparent linear trajectory, commencing with the title's direct reference to American poetry, but ultimately evolves into a non-linear and communal narrative, wherein "US" is reinterpreted as "us," a word encompassing foreign poets as well: "Make it go with a single word. We" (6). The process of going beyond simple equivalence between languages was praised by reputed critic and digital poet Christopher Funkhouser as especially compelling: "I have never, in three decades of study, seen a literary anthology so determined to generate something out of itself, something beyond a 1:1 conversion, and then successfully do so. What an interesting idea, to both transcreate and more literally translate the contents of a collection of writing" (Funkhouser n.p.). Furthermore, the title *"US" Poets Foreign Poets* does away with the distinction between originals and translations whole also reflecting the involvement of the poet-editor, as well as the coming-together of poets via translation irrespective of their national or geographic divides.

In the expansion driven by the algorithm controlled by the editor, the latter assumes the inexplicit role of an author. All the choices made in the processual design of the anthology bear the mark of Tanasescu's persona, equated by David Baker when he spoke about *Nomadosophy* with that of a puppet master. The fact that he equates algorithms with poems—"there is nothing more poetic than our algorithms and there's nothing more algorithmic than our poems" (8)—is reflected in his further academic work (e.g., Tanasescu & Tanasescu) as well as in one of his poetics statements (Tanasescu, "Poetry Thy Name is Translation"). However, he does not see himself as the only author-editor and instead co-opts a band of fellow translators, each of them with a precise task in the design of the model: Vaibhav Kesarwani and Diana Inkpen operating at the level of classifier training, and Raluca Tanasescu and Marius Surleac as fellow literary translators, all five forming a translation and editing collective. Regarding the editor's role, it is worth emphasizing that the authority over the selection process is vested primarily in the training of the poetry classifiers. This implies that the editor's authorial control can potentially diminish as the process unfolds, given that the vectors will act in accordance with their initial training, which will also lessen the potential control the editor may try to exert over the algorithm used in expanding the selection. The editor can thus be likened to someone compressing a spring, without having precise knowledge of the spring's subsequent trajectory once it's released. This understanding is not limited to the human agent involved in the process but grants agentive power both to the human and to the algorithms that operate the platform.

Last but definitely not least, *"US" Poets* has a deep impact on the way we understand and practice literary translation and literary translation scholarship. In the "Note from Translators and Coders," translation features prominently not as a simple linguistic transfer concerned with perfect semantic equivalence but as a semiotic and epistemic one. In these latter two acceptances, translation needs to be understood as a process of transfer between the semiotic code of the codex and the semiotic code of digital space as well as a transaction between translation in the humanistic sense and translation in the computational sense. The "Note from Translators and Coders" identifies three types of translation: literal, literary, and processual. Digital or programming poets use machinic procedures that repurpose, recode, and remediate pieces of traditional text in digital space. In translating such digitally generated poems, the anthology applies the same processual logic, employing the same tools or algorithms to generate the translation whenever that was possible. For instance, the translation of mIEKAL aND's "Stacy Doris Poem" used the same Botnik app that generated the digital original. First, Tanasescu rendered the digital poem into Romanian, then fed this "literary" translation to the Botnik app, which generated the final translation. Another example is Christopher Funkhouser's poem, which was reiterated using the same PyProse app used in producing the original, and then this second iteration was translated into' Romanian. Another interesting example that mirrors the implications of translation as a process is the translation of Romanian poet Serban Foarta's multilingual poem "Papillonage." In order to include the Romanian original in the final corpus featured in the third part of the anthology— "Graph-Poem-Based Corpus Explorations and Expansion"—Tanasescu translated it first into English ("Butterflyçcion") and then included it as if it were an original.

To these considerations that the editors expand on in the paratexts of the anthology, I would like to add a fourth type of translation, which is related to the visual process of translation from the digital to the codex. Irrespective of how many codes a digital poem combines, the digital-to-analog conversion will suffer a simplification, from the depth of the code to the flatness of the print. One of the most interesting examples in the anthology is the translation of Maria Mencia's "The Winnipeg: The Poem that Crossed the Atlantic" (Figure 3.1) In the web version, the lines of the poem are depicted as flowing between South America and Europe, mirroring Mencia's grandfather's trip on the ship The Winnipeg following the Spanish Civil War. In order to transpose this movement of the text between two geographic locations as well as the importance of the two continents for Mencia's family, Tanasescu re-generated the already existing French version of the poem as a double mesostic (Figure 3.2) that read, on the left, MENCIA, and, on the right side, NERUDA (the Chilean poet involved in the rescue operations surrounding her grandfather), a perfectly valid translation into Romanian as well, one which depicts the two words as two spines that "the personal narrative revolves around" (Mencia n.p.).

Anthologies as Intermedial Platforms: A Non-Linear, Scalable Model

Just as *"US" Poets* does not bet on the print vs. digital distinction but on their intermedial fusion, it does not do away completely with subjective selection and does not relinquish control. In the Postface, Lefter notes that "[o]ne should not look for unifying features. This deep-dive into contemporary American poetry does not have the properties of an overview. The idea is to signal variety" (337, translation mine). The observation is blind to the reticulated structure of the assemblage, built on poetic diction commonalities that function as links between the poem-nodes. A common poetic language is what brings together the assemblage without limiting the lines of flight that each of the poems achieves, as one poem that joins the pool of poems can be very similar to the poems in the pool or less so. The tf-idf vectors and the diction classifiers are the building blocks of "the modeling of," the instruments with which the editor assembles the anthology. What the critic refers to then, I surmise (and here he is not wrong), is the fact this particular anthology is not grounded in the tenet of a canon or in a historical dimension; its objective is not to present an overview of canonical contemporary American poetry. Its main ambition is twofold: on the one hand, to bring forth a model of selection that goes beyond a poem's canonical status while also preserving the anthologist's control over the selection, a scalable model which can be easily replicated; and, on the other, to offer a novel type of literary platform, a dynamic and interactive intermedial space

Figure 3.1 Mencía's *The Winnipeg*

MARIA MENCIA
poèMe qui a trAveRsé l'atlantIquE

j 'ai coMmencé   en Argentine je veNais tout juste
sur le WinnipEg personne   d'identité chEz ma mère, dans
civile d'EspagNe, beaucoup   natal de la pRovince de Guada
enfuis en FranCe et avaient fi   presq ue tout troUver sur l'intern
a été un vérItable choc pourdonc   décidé De faire une rec
Pablo NerudA amoureux de   Franciso MencíA Roy, accompagn

travaillait comMe consul chargé   igner ce souveNir bien précis
avec le soutiEn du premier mi   la crítica borrE toda mi poesía
qui devait meNer les 2200 Esp   recuerdo no podRá borrarlo nadi
Valparaiso, au Chili, le 4 août   tique efface toUte ma poésie si
uvez lire «MisIón de amor» [M   e j'écris aujourD'hui personne n
cueil de NerudA Memorial de la   c®oire que mon grAand-père avait

interprété comMe un travail de   ires pour préseNter le prototyp
il appelait ces rEfugiés par leur   surprise m'attEndait au Museo
leurs professioNs. Il les compare   'hôtel des immigRants en raison
semées dans l'oCéan et qui fais   jour de l'inaugUration j'ai apps
'atmosphère étaIt remplie d'émo   des passagers Débarqués au port
Pablo NerudA en a été si tou   rivée de ma grAnd-mère le 12 f

visite à sa faMille accompagné   des questioN je lui dois
ils auront passE sept ans là-bas   ont-ribué à forgEr mes centres d'intérêt
oir une dette eNvers le poète a   soin d'exploreR et d'être curi
d'amour et une Chanson désespérée   de venir d'ailleUrs et d'être di
à mes étudIants en espagnol   évérance et de Détermination un
me Pablo NerudA qui a écrit   ir sauvé mon grAnd-père et son f

et quiconque aiMerait contribue   en avec cet évèNement un poème
isualisation poEtique du voyag   and-père que jE n'ai jamais co

67

Figure 3.2 Translation of Mencia's poem

where readers can engage with diverse poetic forms, exploring the intersections between traditional and digitally engaged expressions as well as between textual and visual elements. To circle back to the first question asked in the introduction that would be the main element of novelty brought about by this anthology, which also emphasizes the impact of the digital on the editorial practices surrounding the curation of a poetry anthology.

To answer the question of whether such a mode of curating an anthology could be separated from the body politic, the answer is both yes and no. On the one hand, it is definitely possible to take distance from the politics of the canon by including as many underrepresented candidate-poems in the selection corpus and by pursuing anthology objectives that are concerned with poetic form rather than with the politics surrounding poetry. But on the other hand, the algorithms used may not be completely neutral tools, in that they may contain algorithmic biases or they can be easily manipulated by the editor, things that readers may not be aware of.

Finally, what would a reassessment of (poetry) translation anthologies look like in light of the novel practices put forth by the anthology at hand? Referring back to Patricia Baubeta's definition according to which anthologies are "a catch all genre [that] can be organized in an almost infinite number of ways" (213) following a logic known only to the editor, it appears that MARGENTO's anthology is a partly self-generated, self-organized, and self-sustained model that can be easily likened to a digital platform. Poetry anthologies would thus beg redefinition as visible intermediaries that move away from an aesthetics of linearity and offer access to various tools for assessing the model they were built on. The category of anthologies would also acquire a scalable dimension that allows editors and readers to employ the model to generate smaller or larger scale projects. Nevertheless, in order to turn this holistic approach to anthology making into a sustainable endeavor, literary translation needs to reconsider its theoretical paradigms to include Actor Network Theory, which would allow the placing of the human and the technological on the same footing, and also complexity thinking, which comes with an emphasis on mixed-method approaches and on non-linear interconnectedness and emergence. In this way, our understanding of the category of anthology will expand just like MARGENTO's poetry corpus: "no ode unless in the communal flow across multiple channels, an n-ode of n-dimensional song throngs" (6).

Bibliography

Anderson, Jon. "Towards an Assemblage Approach to Literary Geography." *Literary Geographies*, volume 1, issue 2, 2015, pp. 120–137.

Bassnett, Susan. *Comparative Literature: A Critical Introduction.* Blackwell, 1993.

Damrosch, David. *Teaching World Literature.* Modern Language Association of America, 2009.

Davidson, Ian and Skoulding, Zoë (eds.) *Placing Poetry*. Rodopi, 2013.

Deleuze, Gilles and Guattari, Felix. *A Thousand Plateaus: Capitalism and Schizophrenia*, translated by Brian Massumi. University of Minnesota Press, 1987.

D'hulst, Lieven. "Forms and Functions of Anthologies of Translation into French in the Nineteenth Century." *Translations in Anthologies and Collections (19th and 20th Century)*, edited by Teresa Seruya, Lieven D'hulst, Alexandra Assis Rosa, and Maria Lin Moniz, pp. 17–34. John Benjamins, 2013.

di Leo, Jeffrey R. "Analyzing Anthologies." *On Anthologies. Politics and Pedagogy*, edited by Jeffrey R. di Leo. University of Nebraska Press, 2004.

Essmann, Helga and Frank, Armin Paul. "Translation Anthologies: An Invitation to the Curious and a Case Study." *Target. International Journal of Translation Studies*, volume 3, issue 1, 1991, pp. 65–90, https://doi.org/10.1075/target.3.1.05ess

Ferry, Anne. *Tradition and the Individual Poem. An Inquiry into Anthologies.* Stanford University Press, 2001.

Frank, Armin Paul and Essmann, Helga. "Translation Anthologies: A Paradigmatic Medium of International Literary Transfer." *Amerikastudien/American Studies*, volume 35, issue 1, 1990, pp. 21–34.

Funkhouser, Christopher. "'US' Poets Foreign Poets: A Computationally Assembled Anthology." *Asymptote*, Jan 24, 2019, https://bit.ly/45RuhpR

Ganascia, Jean Gabriel. "The Logic of Big Data in Digital Literary Studies." *Frontiers in Digital Humanities*, volume 2, pp. 1–5, 2015, https://doi.org/10.3389/fdigh.2015.00007

Glazier, Loss Pequeño. "Epilogue. Between the Academy and a Hard Drive: An E-cology of Innovative Practice." *OL3: Open Letter on Lines Online*, edited by Darren Wershler-Henry. UbuWeb Papers online, 2000, http://www.ubu.com/papers/ol/glazier.html

Guillén, Claudio. "Sobre las antologías." *Ínsula: revista de letras y ciencias humanas*, volumes 721–722 (Antologías poéticas españolas siglos XX–XXI), 2007, pp. 2–3.

Hayles, Nicole K. "Print is Flat: Code is Deep: The Importance of Media-Specific Analysis." *Poetics Today*, volume 25, issue 1, 2004, pp. 67–90.

Hung, Eva. "Periodicals as Anthologies: A Study of Three English-Language Journals of Chinese Literature." *International Anthologies of Literature in Translation*, edited by Harald Kittel, pp. 239–250. Eric Schmidt, 1995.

Israel, Hephzibah. "History, Language and Translation. Claiming the Indian Nation." *The Routledge Handbook of Translation and Politics*, edited by Jonathan Evans and Fruela Fernandez, pp. 386–400. Routledge, 2018.

Joris, Pierre. *A Nomad Poetics: Essays*. Wesleyan University Press, 2003.

Kac, Eduardo (ed.). *Media Poetry. An International Anthology*. Intellect Books, 2007.

Kennedy, Stephen. *Chaos Media: A Sonic Economy of the Digital Space*. Bloomsbury, 2015.

Kesarwani, Vaibhav, Inkpen, Diana, and Tanasescu, Chris. "#GraphPoem: Automatic Classification of Rhyme and Diction in Poetry." *Interférences littéraires/Literaire interferenties*, volume 25, 2021, pp. 218–235.

Kittel, Harald. "International Anthologies of Literature in Translation: An Introduction to Incipient Research." *International Anthologies of Literature in Translation*, edited by Harald Kittel, pp. ix–xxvii. Erich Schmidt, 1995.

Kittler, Friederich. *Discourse Networks 1800/1900.* Stanford University Press, 1990.

Kilcup, Karen L. "Anthologizing Matters: The Poetry and Prose of Recovery Work." *symploke*, volume 8, issues 1–2, 2000, pp. 36–56.

Korte, Barbara, Schneider, Ralph, and Lethbridge, Stephanie (eds.). *Anthologies of British Poetry. Critical Perspectives from Literary and Cultural Studies.* Rodopi, 2000.

Korte, Barbara. "Flowers for the Picking: Anthologies of Poetry in (British) Literary and Cultural Studies." *Anthologies of British Poetry. Critical Perspectives from Literary and Cultural Studies*, edited by Barbara Korte, Ralph Schneider, and Stephanie Lethbridge, pp. 1–32. Rodopi, 2000.

Lauter, Paul. "Taking Anthologies Seriously." *MELUS* [Pedagogy, Canon, Context: Toward a Redefinition of Ethnic American Literary Studies], volume 29, issue ¾, 2004, pp. 19–39, https://doi.org/10.2307/4141840

Lefevere, André. "Translation and Canon Formation: Nine Decades of Drama in the United States." *Translation, Power and Subversion*, edited by Román Álvarez and M. Carmen-África Vidal. Multilingual Matters, 1996.

Marecki, Piotr and Montfort, Nick. "Renderings: Translating Literary Works in the Digital Age." *Digital Scholarship in the Humanities*, volume 32, issue suppl_1, 2017, pp. i84–i91.

McGann, Jerome. "The Rationale of Hyper Text." *Text*, volume 9, 1996, pp. 11–32.

Murray, Simone. "Charting the Digital Literary Sphere." *Contemporary Literature*, volume 56, issue 2, 2015, pp. 311–339.

Naaijkens, Ton. "The world of World Poetry: Anthologies of Translated Poetry as a Subject of Study." *Neophilologus*, volume 90, issue 3, 2006, pp. 509–520.

Nelson, Cary. "Multiculturalism without Guarantees: From Anthologies to the Social Text." *The Journal of the Midwest Modern Language Association*, volume 26, issue 1 (Cultural Diversity), 1993, pp. 47–57.

Price, Kenneth M. "Electronic Scholarly Editions." *A Companion to Digital Literary Studies*, edited by Ray Siemens and Susan Schreibman, pp. 434–450. Blackwell, 2007.

Price, Leah. *The Anthology and the Rise of the Novel.* Cambridge University Press, 2000.

Pym, Anthony. "Translational and Non-Translational Regimes Informing Poetry Anthologies. Lessons on Authorship from Fernando Maristany and Enrique Diez-Canedo." *International Anthologies of Literature in Translation*, edited by Harald Kittel, pp. 251–270. Erich Schmidt, 1995.

Pym, Anthony. *Negotiating the Frontier. Translation and Interculturalities in Hispanic History.* St Jerome Press, 2000.

Robinson, Lillian S. "Treason Our Text: Feminist Challenges to the Literary Canon." *Tulsa Studies in Women's Literature*, volume 2, issue 1, 1983, pp. 83–98.

Rothenberg, Jerome. "The Anthology as a Manifesto & as an Epic Including Poetry, or the Gradual Making of *Poems for the Millenium*." *Revista canaria de estudios ingleses*, volume 52, 2006, pp. 15–18.

Rothenberg, Jerome. "A First Anthology/Assemblage of the Poetry and Poetics of the Americas, from Origins to Present. An Announcement and an Appeal." *Poems and Poetics*, 25 May 2018, https://jacket2.org/commentary/first-anthologyassemblage-poetry-and-poetics-americas-origins-present

Searls, Damion. "Bringing the Poem to Life: An Interview with John Felstiner." *Poetry Flash*, issue 275, Jan.-Feb. 1998, p. 5.

Seruya, Teresa. "Anthologies and Translation." *Handbook of Translation Studies*: Volume 4, edited by Luc van Doorslaer and Yves Gambier, pp. 1–6. John Benjamins, 2013.

Seruya, Teresa, D'hulst, Lieven, Rosa, Alexandra Assis, and Moniz, Maria Lin (eds.). *Translation in Anthologies and Collections (19th and 20th Centuries)*. John Benjamins, 2013.

Spinelli, Martin. "Electric Line: The Poetics of Audio Digital Editing." *New Media Poetics: Contexts, Technotexts, and Theories*, edited by Adalaide Morris, Thomas Swiss, Sean Cubitt, and Roger F. Malina, pp. 99–121. MIT Press, 2006.

Strickland, Stephanie. "Quantum Poetics: Six Thoughts." *Media Poetry. An International Anthology*, edited by Eduardo Kac, pp. 25–44. Intellect Books, 2007.

Susana, Valdez and Martins, Isabel Oliveira. "A Digital Platform for Literary Translation: collaborative translation and teaching." *Humanidades Digitais o Mundo Lusofóno*, edited by Rocardo M. Pimenta and Daniel Alves, pp. 195–214. FGV Editora, 2021.

Tanasescu, Chris. "Poetry, Thy Name is Infinity by Translation." *Poetry International Online*, March 2010, https://bit.ly/3Qc5cA0

Tanasescu, Chris. "Community as Commoning, (Dis)Placing, and Trans(Versing): From Participatory and 'Strike Art' to the Postdigital." *Dacoromania Litteraria*, volume 3, 2016, pp. 10–44.

Tanasescu, Chris and Tanasescu, Raluca. "Complexity and Analytical-Creative Approaches at Scale. Iconicity, Monstrosity, and #GraphPoem." *Zoomland. Exploring Scale in Digital History and Humanities*, edited by Florentina Armaselu and Andreas Fickers, pp. 237–260. De Gruyter, 2023.

Tarlo, Harriet. "Open Field: Reading Field as Place and Poetics." *Placing Poetry*, edited by Ian Davidson and Zoe Skoulding, pp. 113–148. Brill, 2013.

Vale de Gato, Margarida. "The Collaborative Anthology in the Literary Translation Course." *The Interpreter and Translator Trainer*, volume 9, issue 1, 2015, pp. 50–62.

Van Crevel, Maghiel "A Noble Art, and a Tricky Business. Translation Anthologies of Chinese Poetry." *Chinese Poetry and Translation: Rights and Wrongs*, edited by Maghiel Van Crevel and Lucas Klein, pp. 331–350. Amsterdam University Press, 2019.

Wrighton, John. "Ethnopoetics and the Performativity of Place: Jerome Rothenberg and 'That Dada Strain'." *Placing Poetry*, edited by Ian Davidson and Zoe Skoulding, pp. 257–280. Brill, 2013.

Part II

Hermeneutic Modeling

4 Hermeneutic Modeling of Detail in Textual Zoom and Literary Texts

Florentina Armaselu

Introduction

What are the roles of detail in literary texts? How can we interpret these roles? What type of computational modeling can we imagine for this interpretative task? What forms of text making or analysis may be derived from such models? The aim of this chapter is to address these questions, starting from the hypothesis that interpretation in the digital medium always encompasses a certain degree of modeling, understood here in its double sense of building representations of objects and shaping figures in a plastic material. The plasticity of the electronic text is one of the key characteristics of computational text analysis and writing, since it allows for multiple ways of reshaping, restructuring, transforming text, and deriving meaning from the results of these operations. On the other hand, the representational facet of modeling implies both a conceptual and a performative perspective; the former involves pre-interpretation and feature and relation selection from the object or phenomenon to be modeled; the latter is underpinned by the code and its performative capabilities in the digital realm. My approach will combine theoretical and empirical standpoints on detail as an esthetic category and its dynamics interpreted through examples of literary texts and experiments based on the concept of textual zoom.

Detail and its roles in esthetics do not generally seem to be examined through the lens of a unified field of definitions or points of view. Various angles and ways of understanding detail in art and literature have been proposed, and this variety of perspectives demonstrates the complexity, richness, and elusive nature of detail as an esthetic means. Considering that the form of a work of art is determined by the arrangement and interrelation of details, Munro distinguishes four modes of composition in art: *utilitarian, representative, expository,* and *decorative* or *thematic* (15). Therefore, the organization of details in a literary work can serve an instrumental/functional purpose, as in advertising and propaganda; it can

DOI: 10.4324/9781003320838-7

suggest, arouse imagination, and depict objects through narration and description; it can support causal or logical connections; and it can stimulate sensory perception or thematic associations through word-sound patterns, such as rhythm and rhyme, or repetition, variation, and contrast (Munro 15–18). In his study of the maximalist tradition in American literary history, Burns (134) draws attention to the continuum between "facts and gaps" in narrative fictional worlds, which is shaped by the volume of details and the "relative completeness and incompleteness of a world's total construction." From the perspective of knowledge building in human sciences, Ginzburg points out the filiation between the literary clues in Conan Doyle's detective fiction, Freud's theory of psychoanalysis, and Morelli's method of classification and author attribution through the observation of "minor details" (Ginzburg 7), such as the drawing of fingers and ears, in Italian painting. Starting from Morelli's detail-oriented method and the study of four Victorian writers—Ruskin, Browning, Eliot, and Wilde, Pradhan (2) explores the "proliferation of details in Victorian literature and aesthetics" to reflect on the connection between "subjectivity and form in the nineteenth century."

While details were often considered unesthetic or superfluous as forms of artistic expression in earlier times, Schor describes the modern era as an age in which detail has achieved prominence. Her analysis, which traverses different domains—philosophy, literature, painting, photography, cinema, gender studies, and socio-political criticism—retraces the history of detail as connected to the decline of classicism and the ascent of realism, and to events like the invention of the quotidian or the development of consumerism, mechanical reproduction means, and democratization (Schor xlii). While paying attention to the *feminine* connotations of detail in a historical-cultural context and to the shifting nature of esthetic paradigms, she also raises the hypothesis, pointing back to Hegel and Barthes, that every type of artistic medium could involve a specific use or status of detail (Schor 110). Thus, in his *Camera Lucida*, dedicated to the medium of photography, Barthes argues that the expansion energy of certain details may elicit the spectator's subjectivity and a more individualized response, going beyond the mere understanding of the intentional (cultural) framework set by the photographer. Opposed to the *studium*, which posits a set of conventions (historical, socio-cultural, political, ethnographical, esthetic) coded in the photographer's intent, the *punctum* is often an unintended detail which disturbs the unity of the whole and "pricks" the viewer like an arrow unexpectedly raised from the picture (Barthes 26). This incident, which activates the spectator's subjectivity and affective consciousness, has a "power of expansion," firstly, because it tends to fill the whole scene, and secondly, since it represents an "addition" to the photograph, an addition of "*what is nonetheless already there*" (Barthes 45, 55).

Although detail and minutiae are implicit traits of the coding and encoding paradigms as embodied in programming and markup languages, there are not many references to detail as an artistic form in the emerging esthetics of the electronic medium. Specifically, these references seem to be most often implicit and incorporated into broader thematic arguments rather than inquiries targeting detail as an object of study in itself. Theorists of the digital medium from the late 1990s and early 2000s, such as Aarseth, Bolter and Grusin, Ryan, Cramer, and Landow, have therefore paved the way for a form of esthetics that places concepts like cybertext, remediation, immersion and interactivity, computation, hyperfiction, and hyperpoetry within a wider background with roots in modernism, postmodernism, and the history of cultural practices. More recent studies, with a particular focus on historicizing electronic literature, have emphasized its "writing-centered" character as an art that engages the "expressive potential" of digital media and identified three generations of e-lit ranging from the 1950s to the present day (Flores 1, 3). These three waves include pre-Web, Web-, and social media network/API[1]/mobile-based artworks that align with previous formulations pointing to a print-inspired literary experience for the first two and a born-digital popular culture for the third, branded under labels such as digital modernism and digital postmodernism, respectively (Flores 6, 8). Although the second and third e-lit generations currently coexist, there are still distinctive features that characterize them, and implicitly different forms of detail correspond to these categories. Flores discerns a tendency of the second wave to align with literary tradition and the art world, driven by a "poetics of innovation and aesthetic difficulty" and by models such as zines, anthologies, blogs, Web pages, gallery exhibitions, and installations (Flores 8, 10); the third wave is identified by publication formats and models that originate in digital media, inspired by video games and interactive works, and that explore existing platforms, interfaces, and artworks by experimenting with various modes of remixing, derivation, copying, customization, adaptation, and appropriation (Flores 7, 10). New writing and reading practices are also emerging, from linguistic games of "data realism" mixing and mimicking human and machine learning interactions (Pold and Erslev 2) to AI-generated streams of text and a so-called glitch poetics or poetics of error emulating the disruptive and surprising energy of digital breakdowns (Carter 2).

Although detail has yet to acquire a prominent place as a main subject of investigation in digital esthetics, studies on literature in the digital medium and humanities computing have highlighted the particularity of modeling within this area of research as an experimental, epistemological practice directed at the creation of new knowledge or at what Samuels and McGann call "imagining what we don't know" (qtd. in McCarty, sec. 4).

Another type of practice, with applications in literature and computing, stems from the domain of digital hermeneutics, which brings together the rich tradition of text interpretation and methods of meaning-making through digital means, such as data processing and visualization, or "hermeneutic visualization," an emerging field of inquiry in digital literary studies according to Kleymann and Stange.

Going back to the initial questions formulated at the beginning of this chapter, my aim is to focus on a particularity of detail as an esthetic form, i.e., its *dynamic* nature, which can be explored against a background of experimental interplay and hermeneutic modeling in the digital medium. The second and third sections will explain the methodology applied for this purpose and discuss the results of the experiments, while the fourth section will summarize the findings and suggest possible paths for future exploration.

Method

Continuum Logic

To illustrate the methodology, I will first refer to three types of attribute associated with detail which shed light on its dynamic character. In her *Theory of the Portrait*, Schor (53–54) evokes a daguerreotype anecdote published in 1855 by a French man of letters, Francis Wey. After his return to Paris from Athens, a French diplomat used a magnifying glass to examine a daguerreotype taken at the Acropolis a few years earlier and discovered an image of a lion devouring a serpent carved into the stone. Schor's comment on the account highlights the expansion power of the photographic technique which dilates both *space*—by opening the territory of "luxuriant, inexhaustible detail"—and *time*—since the details recorded by the daguerreotype and discovered by magnification are "by definition *delayed details*" (Schor 54, emphasis in original). This power of expansion of photographic detail is better understood if considered in contrast with the pictorial overviews of what Schor calls "earlier modes of recording travel impressions—paintings, sketches, engravings" (53), and Baudelaire's mnemonic art, which was intended to filter out unnecessary detail and retain only the essential characteristics of the represented object (54). Both detail and outline are therefore instances of the same continuum of expressive modes, ranging from precision and profusion to synthesis and abridgment.

Another aspect pointed out by Schor (72, 73) is the projection on a vertical axis of the *individual, special,* and *universal* in Georg Lukács' esthetics. These categories delineate a gradual scale to showcase literary production, from novel to epic, via drama. According to Schor, Lukács' cancellation of the individual in the special represents his "most promising contribution to a theory of the detail" (72). The model allows us to identify the presence of detail even if it appears absent, to find its trace in the totality into which it has been absorbed, and to become aware of its capacity "to persist and to inform in absence" (72). While the first example defines the extremities of the range in terms of modes of expression, from minute accuracy to selectivity and generalization, the second hints at a gradual dynamic linking the presence and absence of detail—pertaining to levels of individuality, particularity, and universality—through scalable configurations underpinned by mechanisms of absorption and traceability. These types of mechanisms allow us to imagine the transition from one level to the other through vertical movements that involve the addition or cancellation of detail and the reformulation of content, evoking the immersion and abstraction techniques characteristic of the exploratory paradigm and metaphor of zooming.

The third attribute of detail considered for discussion is the capability of Barthes' punctum to expand the content of an artwork by sparking the spectator's subjectivity and creativity. While the studium may stand for a common basis of interpretation shared by most observers, the punctum calls for a status of uniqueness, since its very nature and resulting reactions can differ considerably from viewer to viewer. The most interesting part of the punctum therefore consists in its promise (materialized or not after the first shock which punctures the viewer's affectivity) to be eventually articulated in a story that adds new facets to the *already present*. If we change the register from visual to textual, does this promise not represent the very gist of the writing process itself?

The particularities of detail emphasized in this section can be summarized by two main features: power of expansion and capacity to be integrated into a continuum or a variety of scales corresponding to different degrees of artistic expressivity and involvement. While detail can be interpreted as a dynamic entity associated with various forms of action—expansion, delay, absorption, cancellation, absence-presence, traceability—these two properties play a significant role in the process of detail modeling through a digital lens, referring both to reading and writing, as proposed in the next sections.

Textual Zoom

One of the questions often evoked when talking about digital vs. traditional narrative forms relates to the opposition between immersion and interactivity, the former considered emblematic of print and the latter of the electronic medium. Ryan dedicates an interlude chapter, *Dream of an Interactive Immersive Book*, to the description of a science-fiction novel which seems to offer a pathway toward a possible "reconciliation of immersivity and interactivity" (335). The novel is Neal Stephenson's *The Diamond Age: Or, a Young Lady's Illustrated Primer*, which depicts a fictional construct, the primer of a little girl called Nell, whose content expands itself in its interaction with the reader. In printed novels, immersion is generally considered to rely on the capacity of the textual content to induce in the mind of the reader a sort of relocation or "transportation" into the fictional world (Ryan 93). In Nell's primer, immersion appears frequently linked to episode expansion. The reader becomes caught up in the story by asking more details about events and characters that gradually reveal themselves in a question-answering scenario. The salient feature of this type of narrative machine resides in its duality, implying both an interactive mechanism, which generates new branches of the story, and an immersive factor, driven by the curiosity of the reader.

The model of textual zoom or z-text was inspired by this fictional setting of a self-expanding story that grows by answering readers' questions (Vasilescu, *Le livre sous la loupe*; Armaselu and Heuvel). Unlike this setting, in the model questions are not explicitly formulated by the reader but enclosed in the text itself, seen as a collection of potentially extensible entities called z-lexias, which can initiate more detailed representations and be explored by zooming in and zooming out. A z-lexia (inspired by Barthes' *lexia*[2] in *S/Z*, 13, a unit of reading and analysis) can vary from a few words or phrases to one or several paragraphs, including texts and possibly images. A z-textual layout therefore presumes an arrangement of z-lexias on levels of detail, along with the Z-axis. The processes of reading and writing, called z-reading and z-writing, are based on parent-descendant relations. Parent z-lexias are fragments that engender descendants through expansion, by addition or reformulation, to produce more detailed representations on the subsequent levels. Figure 4.1 illustrates the modeling of this type of relation via XML-TEI[3] used by the z-editor, a Java-based interface that I designed for z-text creation and exploration.[4]

Z-editor allows the user to select content (including text and/or images) and expand the selection by additions or paraphrases that contain further information or elaborate on what has previously been said. The selected fragment is marked as a parent z-lexia on the current level, while the content resulting from the expansion is recorded as a child z-lexia that belongs to the next level of the z-text. Each level corresponds to an XML file. The internal representation is based on XML-TEI and is automatically generated by the interface. The TEI element chosen to delimit z-lexias is <anchor> ("Anchor. P5: Guidelines"), with the attributes @*subtype*, @*type*, @*corresp*, and @*xml:id*.[5] The choice of this element was determined by its flexibility. It can be used to mark points of interest within the text, such as the start and end of a z-lexia, and to assign a unique identifier

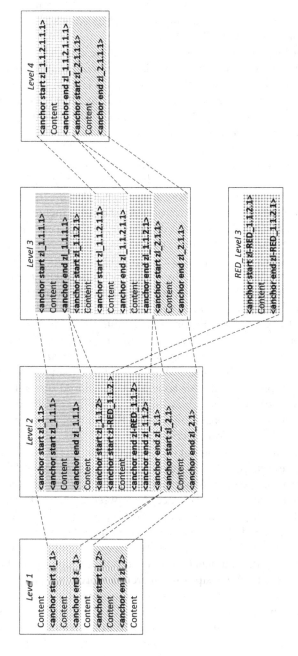

Figure 4.1 Textual zoom, simplified encoding. Modeling of parent-descendant relations between z-lexias marked by hatching patterns (dash, diagonal, vertical, diamond, grid)

to the demarcated segment. Since it is an independent tag (that does not require an opening and closing part), it allows flexible annotations of z-lexias without restrictions regarding the content enclosed by it or the intersections with other XML-TEI elements.[6]

As shown in Figure 4.1, the content can include unmarked (childless) and marked fragments (z-lexias). The identifiers comprise sequences of digits separated by dots which get longer with each level and capture relations between parents, descendants, and siblings (same level z-lexias issued from the same parent, e.g., zl-1.1.1 and zl_1.1.2). The hatching patterns indicate the kinship between the various fragments from different levels. Parallel annotations of the same segment are also possible, to emulate the expansion of the same piece of content through forking interpretations. For instance, z-lexia zl_1 (dash) has a child on level 2, zl_1.1. This descendant contains fragments that are further expanded on the next level, i.e., zl_1.1.1 (vertical) and zl_1.1.2 (diamond), the latter including a parallel expansion, zl-RED_1.1.2 (diamond). The remaining content on level 2 (dash) is not expanded. The TEI encoding, identifier system, and organization of the files are completely transparent to the user and created internally by the z-editor based on the user's interaction with the content. The interface allows for usual word processing functions (insertion of text and image, text formatting, modification, reading) and specific z-writing (expansion) and z-reading operations that enable the textual space to be traversed by zooming in and zooming out, much like the navigation of a map at variable scales. Switching between *read, edit, expand,* and *zoom (in/out)* modes is possible by using different types of cursors. Z-lexias created by parallel expansion can subsequently be explored through magnifying glass cursors of different colors used to zoom in and zoom out and reveal different facets of the same object (see RED_Level3 example above and in the "Parallel Expansion" section).

When referring to the dynamics of detail discussed in the previous section, one can also notice certain affinities with the cartographic zoom model, which allows the user to change the representation scale from a view of the terrestrial globe to the image of a specific place. As Lawrence (4–5), Orford (200–201), and MacEachren (10) observe, the selection of cartographic details is not purely a technical and objective process but includes factors related to the intended degree of generality, the subjectivity of the cartographer, power relations, and the socio-cultural milieu that influenced the production of the map. According to MacEachren, a map is not merely a representation of a region of the Earth, but it can also possess some of the attributes of a "rhetorical discourse." From this perspective, the methods of cartographic analysis are more akin to the methods of literary criticism than those of exact sciences.

The choice of the details to be represented on every layer of a *z-text* is the result of an intentional procedure, too. The z-writing process should assume a certain strategy of stratification and selection of textual material. Whether we are talking about narrative or descriptive techniques, the way of accessing characters' psychology, or the deployment of causal and logical arguments (also recalling Munro's representative and expository functions of detail arrangement), the author of a *z-text* makes choices when creating z-lexias for a particular level. The "surface" levels may correspond to a larger scale of representation, characterized by a higher degree of "generality," while the deeper levels, by including additional details, can move closer, like the variable scale approximation of a coastline, to the entity they portray. In this respect, textual zoom is more similar to cartographic zoom than to a technical zoom on an image, which does not involve the deliberate selection and prior assemblage of details. It also assumes a "scalable" structure, a label that Ryan (213) borrows from Sheldon Renan when speaking of those interactive forms, like Stephenson's primer, offering the choice between "scene" and "summary" or the rapid shift "from the epic perspective to infinite detail."

Conceptual Stratification

The assumption underlying the textual zoom model is that, apart from its visible structure (sections, subsections, paragraphs, stanzas, lines of verse), the text presented on a reading display (printed page or electronic device) also contains a hidden conceptual structure determined by the arrangement of content on different levels of detail. Fragments possessing a certain thematic affinity, or the same degree of generality or specificity, may belong to the same level, even though they are not always adjacent in the visible, surface representation. From this perspective, the whole text can be interpreted as a stratified assemblage of content fragments involving various degrees of conceptual granularity. While the term *structure* may recall debates such as the "structuralism criticisms in computational literary studies" and the "reductionist concept of meaning" considering only "linguistic features" (Gius and Jacke), my aim is to target not only the linguistic manifestations of the scalable structure but also its interpretative and argumentative potential considered within contexts that operate both inside and outside the text.

The question that arises is therefore whether these degrees of detail inherent to a text are detectable through automatic procedures, and what their role is from an interpretative point of view. Do they portray a particular artistic or methodological intention of the author, a cultural tendency or form of reality characteristic to a certain historical period, or are they an expression of the logic of the text itself? In *Text, Fractal Dust and Informational Granularity* (Armaselu), I propose a combination of topic modeling and fractal geometry to detect the levels of generality and specificity in a corpus of texts and create informational granularity maps that show how the segments composing the texts are dispersed at these levels, when different scales of representation are involved. Figure 4.2 illustrates the workflow used to produce such a model.

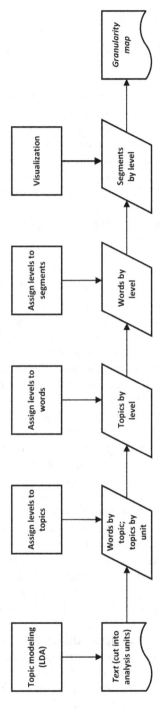

Figure 4.2 Workflow for detecting and representing segment distribution at levels of generality and specificity in texts

An overview of the method is presented below. First, the text is cut into units of analysis (e.g., chapters, parts). It is then analyzed via the latent Dirichlet allocation (LDA) topic modeling method and tool (Blei, McCallum). The topics are assigned to levels of generality and specificity based on an algorithm that takes into account the document entropy measure. Hence, topics that are evenly spread (high entropy) over the different units of the text are considered generic; those centered on only a few parts or just one part (low entropy) are deemed specific. The procedure that I devised for this purpose can differentiate topics and group them by levels of generality/specificity. Once these levels are detected, they are propagated to words, according to the topics to which these words belong. Each word is thus assigned to a level. An additional algorithm was designed to cut the text into segments of various sizes. For instance, I applied several iterations and divided the text by a certain value at each iteration, as inspired by the generation of a fractal structure such as the Koch curve (Mandelbrot, 42–45). The algorithm assigns each segment to the level with the highest score based on the segment size, the number of words belonging to a level, their average word-topic probability, and the inverse of the average distance between them. With the segments assigned to levels, it is possible to build informational granularity maps that show how the different segments contained in the text are scattered across the different levels, ranging from the most generic to the most specific, rather than placed on a single line (see also the "Informational Granularity" section). This type of visualization offers a view of text as modeled through the lens of a detail-based interpretation, which may be applied to literary and non-literary texts (Armaselu). In his study of the macro and micro dimensions in historical writings, Kracauer observes that "the big must be looked at from different distances to be understood; its analysis and interpretation involve a constant movement between the levels of generality" (122). As previously pointed out in Schor's discussion of Lukács' esthetics or Ryan's account of scalable interactive forms, these perspectives, ranging from high-level overviews to minute detail, can also function in literary contexts. The following section will present various types of such detail modeling.

Results and Discussion

Going back to the properties of plasticity and performativity of an electronic text evoked at the beginning of this chapter, in this section I will explore the idea of interpretation through *deformance* by means of a series of examples derived from experiments with the z-text model and z-editor interface and the topic stratification procedure mentioned above. In their essay *Deformance and Interpretation*, following Dickinson's proposal of reading a poem backward, McGann and Samuels dwell on the distinction between *intelligible* and *possible* in the process of interpretation, which in the case of a poem relies on revealing not what it means but the *possibilities* of the poem's meaning (108). The question that I will try to address is, therefore, what can possibly be learned from the deformative and detail-informed perspective on the processes of interpretation and creation of a text?

Analytic Fusion

While McGann and Samuels fed their "experimental analysis" (129) on experiments with poetry, perhaps one of the most persuasive examples of such practice applied to novels is Barthes' analysis of Balzac's *Sarrasine* in *S/Z*. Two things sparked my interest in playing the deformative-interpretative game with this text: firstly, the theoretical constructs that resonated with detailed-driven modeling, such as *lexia* and the broken text cut into contiguous "blocks of signification" where a plurality of meanings can be observed (Barthes 13–15), and the *step-by-step* method of slow, gradual analysis allowing us to study the text "down to the last detail" and to work back along its "threads of meaning" (12); and secondly, the "writerly" nature of the text that prompted an interpretation of the interpretation of *Sarrasine* by *S/Z*. Figure 4.3 (top down) depicts a z-textual layout of *S/Z* excerpts and the results of successive zoom-ins on the selected fragments.

Figure 4.3 Barthes' *S/Z* z-text visualization (z-editor). Successive zoom-ins, levels 1–5

The succession starts with the Balzac text marked with numbers for lexias, as it appears in the Appendix of the consulted edition of *S/Z*. The text is then gradually enriched and transformed by adding details from Barthes' argumentation on each level:

- annotations with interpretation codes: *hermeneutic, symbolic, seme* (HER, SYM, SEM) (level 2);
- descriptions and justifications of the step-by-step analysis and interpretation method and its codes, as a way to understand the plurality of text defined as a "galaxy of signifiers" (level 3);
- insights into the "readerly" vs. "writerly" dichotomy, by paying attention to text as a process rather than product, and to the reversibility of the writerly text proven by the transformation of Balzac's *Sarrasine* into Barthes' *S/Z* (levels 4, 5); the inverse trajectory is also possible by zooming out.

This type of fusion between the text to be analyzed and the gradual deployment of the analytical arguments provides another perspective on Barthes' text. Although on the printed page the content appears as deployed on a flat surface, a closer examination of the details and their role in the argumentation suggests a multi-plane structure with several conceptual levels that can gradually be revealed under a magnifying glass. The subtraction and addition of details as a deformative-interpretative procedure may therefore function as a device for experimenting with the hidden mechanisms of text composition determined by the arrangement and interrelation of details, as suggested by Munro. The reason why different levels of detail can coexist in a text would need further examination. Possible answers could be related to the discursive logic and expressivity of language that allow for variable distance from or description granularity of the observed and represented object through words. Other explanations may be rooted in the genesis of the text itself and its potential development from generic or schematic representations that become more and more precise or rich in detail with the progress and refinement involved in the creative process.

Similar experiments were imagined for other analytical texts that are based on an initial fusion with or close examination of the analyzed text, and which move away from the object of investigation through gradual expansions of the interpretative framework ranging from minute observation to broad-coverage syntheses. Examples of this type are texts such as Auerbach's *Mimesis* and Greenblatt's *Will in the World*, or those associated with the technique of "thick description" popularized by Geertz in his *Interpretation of Cultures*.

In the *Epilogue*, Auerbach synthesizes the articulation points of his analytical method in *Mimesis*, i.e., "the interpretation of reality through literary representation or 'imitation.'" The goal of his approach is not a comprehensive history of realism in general but an inquiry about the gradual incorporation of "realistic subjects" (like daily life) into literary representations that treat them "seriously, problematically, or tragically." According to Auerbach, the classical doctrine of the separation of styles places this kind of everyday reality within the literary frame of a low or intermediate style, going from "grotesquely comic" to "elegant entertainment." It is with the story of Christ and its mixture of "everyday reality" and "sublime tragedy" that the classical rule of levels of styles begins to fade (554–556). Since this process spans a long period of time, Auerbach studies a selection of texts corresponding to different epochs and literary movements, from Antiquity to Modernism, and analyzes various factors that influenced their production (cultural, social, economic, etc.). Each chapter implies a methodological schema, including elements like citation, close reading, and comparative analysis, as well as cultural, socioeconomic, and historical considerations about the context that determined the production of a specific work or the development of a specific trend.

We can therefore assume that the book is organized according to a layered structure where the first level is that of direct citations and the argumentative space is structured in depth along the analysis axis. Taking as an example *Odysseus' Scar*, although the two fragments that are closely analyzed later are not directly reproduced in the text, unlike the opening texts in the other chapters of *Mimesis,* we can imagine adding them on the first level of the z-textual representation. The second level of the structure can contain the two accounts in Auerbach's words: the foot-washing scene when Euryclea recognizes her master by his scar and the episode of God testing Abraham's faith by asking him to sacrifice his only son, Isaac. While the second level of representation implies a survey of what is narrated, the third level may add more elements from the stylistic perspective (how it is narrated), such as the "foreground" strategy in the scar episode completely filling the stage and the reader's mind in the Homeric text or the laconic, mysterious way of leaving unexpressed things that call for interpretation in the Genesis fragment. Zooming further, on the fourth level the reader can discover new components linking the two analyzed chunks and directly comparing the two texts belonging to different forms: the perfectly illuminated, externalized phenomena in the Homeric poems and the undefined, unexpressed details left in obscurity in the biblical accounts. The analysis can continue on a deeper level by adding more general reflections on the "great and sublime" in Homeric poetry, which always supposes events and characters related to the "ruling class," while in the Old Testament stories the "sublime, tragic and problematic" can occur in the "domestic and commonplace," to conclude with the influence of the two styles upon the "representation of reality in European literature" (Auerbach 22, 23).

The experiment involved a number of assumptions and approximations in order to illustrate this kind of interpretative study "under a magnifying glass" and the gradual movement from particular literary texts to the general context that shaped them or was influenced by them. As the example shows, in terms of content, there is no strict rule that the traversal of a z-textual structure from surface to deeper levels should always imply a movement from *general* to *particular.* Other alternatives are also possible (particular to general, simple to complex, concrete to abstract, abstract to concrete, etc.) depending on the author's intentions and strategy to derive new z-lexias. For this case, it was assumed that the layers of the argumentative space can be built by extracting and then adding back details, so that after traversing all five levels (from the citations to the general assertions on European literature), the whole Auerbachian text is retrieved. The z-text layout was intended to capture a form of interpretative-deformative perspective in movement, taking shape gradually, as it emerged from my reading of *Mimesis,* like the double-sense progressive transformation of *Sarrasine* and *S/Z.* These hypotheses were based upon the observation that certain elements may stir up folding and unfolding of arguments (narrative, stylistic, comparative, and historical), an argumentation which for me took the shape of a stratified, dynamic, and elastic structure.

Similar z-text layouts[7] can be created for Greenblatt's new-historicist reconstructions of the historical and socio-cultural context that inspired the Shakespearean work, or Geertz's multilayered, stratified interpretations of ethnographic miniatures, or thick descriptions, such as Cohen's story of the stolen sheep in Morocco in 1912 (Geertz 7–10).

Gradual Reveal

While the examples presented above can be associated with Munro's *expository* function of details intended to convey certain types of information, relation, or argumentation, this and the following two sections[8] will bring to the fore the *representation* function related to the gradual uncovering of detail in description and narration. Table 4.1 shows the results of subtracting and adding back details in three literary texts. The highlighted fragments are objects of interpretation through this "zoomification" process (left to right). The aim of the exercise was to determine what happens, from an interpretative point of view, if certain details are *canceled* (to borrow Schor's expression) and then put back into their original context.

The first excerpt, from *The Fellowship of the Ring,* unrolls over two levels. On the first level, some seemingly insignificant details are removed, then they are restored on the second level. A comparison of the two versions sheds some light on their role in the narrative and descriptive processes. In my interpretation, three groups of details act together to create an atmosphere that is otherwise less effective within the story world on level one. These are the words *west* and *late,* in "looking out *west* on to the garden" and the "*late* afternoon," and the whole sentence that starts

Table 4.1 Gradual unfolding of narrative and descriptive details (Tolkien, Tolstoy, Shakespeare)

Inside Bag End, Bilbo and Gandalf were sitting at the open window of a [...] room looking out [...] on to the garden. The [...] afternoon was bright and peaceful. [...] "How bright your garden looks!" said Gandalf. "Yes," said Bilbo. "I am very fond indeed of it, and of all the dear old Shire; but I think I need a holiday." Kitty danced in the first couple [...]. Vronsky and Anna sat almost opposite her. [...] [...] When Vronsky saw her, coming across her in the mazurka, he did not at once recognize her, she was so changed. "Delightful ball!" he said to her [...]. "Yes," she answered. Love keeps his revels where they are but twain; Be bold to play, our sport is not in sight: These blue [...] violets whereon we lean Never can blab, nor know not what we mean.	Inside Bag End, Bilbo and Gandalf were sitting at the open window of a small room looking out west on to the garden. The late afternoon was bright and peaceful. The flowers glowed red and golden: snap-dragons and sunflowers, and nasturtians trailing all over the turf walls and peeping in at the round windows. "How bright your garden looks!" said Gandalf. "Yes," said Bilbo. "I am very fond indeed of it, and of all the dear old Shire; but I think I need a holiday." **(Tolkien, 33)** Kitty danced in the first couple, and luckily for her she had not to talk [...]. Vronsky and Anna sat almost opposite her. She saw them with her long-sighted eyes, and saw them, too, close by, [...] and the more she saw of them the more convinced was she that her unhappiness was complete [...] [...] When Vronsky saw her, coming across her in the mazurka, he did not at once recognize her, she was so changed. "Delightful ball!" he said to her, for the sake of saying something. "Yes," she answered. Love keeps his revels where they are but twain; Be bold to play, our sport is not in sight: These blue [...] violets whereon we lean Never can blab, nor know not what we mean.	Inside Bag End, Bilbo and Gandalf were sitting at the open window of a small room looking out west on to the garden. The late afternoon was bright and peaceful. The flowers glowed red and golden: snap-dragons and sunflowers, and nasturtians trailing all over the turf walls and peeping in at the round windows. "How bright your garden looks!" said Gandalf. "Yes," said Bilbo. "I am very fond indeed of it, and of all the dear old Shire; but I think I need a holiday." **(Tolkien, 33)** Kitty danced in the first couple, and luckily for her she had not to talk [...]. Vronsky and Anna sat almost opposite her. She saw them with her long-sighted eyes, and saw them, too, close by, when they met in the figures, and the more she saw of them the more convinced was she that her unhappiness was complete. She saw that they felt themselves alone in that crowded room. And on Vronsky's face, always so firm and independent, she saw that look that had struck her, of bewilderment and humble submissiveness [...]. Anna smiled, and her smile was reflected by him. She grew thoughtful, and he became serious. Some supernatural force drew Kitty's eyes to Anna's face. [...] Kitty admired her more than ever, and more and more acute was her suffering. Kitty felt overwhelmed, and her face showed it. When Vronsky saw her, coming across her in the mazurka, he did not at once recognize her, she was so changed. "Delightful ball!" he said to her, for the sake of saying something. "Yes," she answered. **(Tolstoy, 98)** Love keeps his revels where they are but twain; Be bold to play, our sport is not in sight: These blue-vein'd violets whereon we lean Never can blab, nor know not what we mean. **(Shakespeare, lines 123–126)**

with "flowers glowed red and golden." If we consider that the scene happened shortly before Bilbo's big birthday party on September 22nd, we can infer that it was a late, sunny September afternoon. The two characters are looking west onto the garden, which at that hour, given the position of the sun to the west, should have been bathed in sunlight.

The perception is therefore one of warmth and brightness, as confirmed by Gandalf's remark. The description of the flowers, red and golden and "trailing all over the turf walls," enforces the idea of warmth (warm colors), beauty, and peacefulness. This warm, sunny, serene ambience is contrasted with an ingredient that prefigures Bilbo's spectacular disappearance from the birthday party, the evil power of the ring, and all the dramatic events that follow. This is the surprising "holiday" plan that contrasts with Bilbo's fondness for his house and garden and "all the dear old Shire." The antithesis is skillfully built upon a background that brings color, light, warmth, comfort, and tranquility to the scene and, at the same time, adds a component of enigmatic and imminent tension that enlivens the narrative and arouses the reader's curiosity.

On the other hand, the fragment describing the red and golden flowers, trailing and "peeping in at the round windows," represents a stylistic device that offers additional fields of vision. While the first sentence places the spectator inside the room with the two protagonists, the "flowers" detail seems to be observable from a perspective that situates the viewer outside, either at a certain distance, to embrace the whole picture of the house adorned with flowers, or close enough to peep in at the round windows like the nasturtians trailing on the walls. The function of the last detail, the adjective *small* from the "small room," is less clear. It can probably be interpreted as related to the peculiarity of the Hobbits as being little people, living in small houses, but also in connection with or anticipating another scene between the two characters, within the same setting, when the matter of size takes another turn as an expression of power imbalance. It is soon after the birthday party, when Gandalf, angry with Bilbo's refusal to give the ring away, grows "tall and menacing," his shadow filling the "little room," then, once the dispute is resolved, shrinks again to an "old grey man, bent and troubled" (Tolkien 44, 45).

The second experiment includes a fragment from the ball scene in *Anna Karenina* and three levels of detail. The first level contains an abridged version of the scene that is closer to what Palmer calls, in line with Gerald Prince, a "behaviorist narrative," conveying the characters' behavior through words, actions, and appearance, but not thoughts and feelings (Palmer 328). In this type of narrative, it is the reader's task to "join up the dots" and construct the fictional minds when less information is available (325). On the second level, the reader is given more access to Kitty's field of vision (*long-sighted* and *close by*) and feelings (*unhappiness*). The narrator's comment on Vronsky's phrase addressed to Kitty, "for the sake of saying something," is less direct and hints at an attitude that arises more out of convenience than from any real feeling. In Palmer's terms, as applied to a study of Evelyn Waugh's *Vile Bodies*, this would correspond to an intermediate status in the "thought-action continuum," when the state of mind of a character is indirectly indicated (Palmer 336). The third level spotlights a whole spectrum of emotional values reflected through the characters' interactions and mainly filtered through Kitty's perspective. It also shows how a scene can gradually incorporate into the narrative both acuity of behavioral observation and psychological finesse.

The third example elaborates on the three-level description of the bed of flowers on which the two protagonists of *Venus and Adonis* lean. The progression of *violets—blue violets—blue-vein'd violets* seems not only to suggest what, in Greenblatt's words, denotes a "sustained close-up" that intensifies the impression of "physical and emotional proximity" (Greenblatt 243); it also evokes a gradual and astonishing shift of attention from the floral freshness and color of spring to the tiny world of vessels carrying the sap of life but ignoring the meaning of love.

Parallel Expansion

Another type of experiment focused on the capacity of some details to engender different descendants on the deeper levels of the z-textual representation and to multiply the interpretation or the diegetic axes through parallel expansion and by forking the narrative or the descriptive flow. The two examples presented in Table 4.2 (left to right) try to capture this form of detail modeling.

The first example contains excerpts from Hart's analysis of García Márquez's *Chronicle of a Death Foretold*. As explained in the "Textual Zoom" section, the textual zoom model allows for different expansions of the same fragment, such as the short account of Bayardo and Angela's marriage (level one). The second level of the representation provides two different perspectives on Bayardo's character, the former portraying him as a rich man who always gets what he wants, the latter as a symbol of the "invasion" of Latin America by the "ebullient capitalism" of North America. While the first interpretation can be regarded as a depiction of the character through the lens of his own actions, the second suggests a view nuanced by broader considerations on the historical, social, and economic conditions that shaped the context of the drama.

Similarly, the different narratives derived from Princess Ateh's entry in Pavić's *Dictionary of the Khazars* are modeled through separate extension paths that unravel the mystery of the Khazar polemic through multiple and contradictory tales of the same entity, following the red, green, and yellow books and the three facets of an ungraspable truth built out of conflicting sources.

Table 4.2 Interpretative and diegetic forking through parallel expansion of details (Hart, Pavić)

A rich man, Bayardo San Roman, arrives in a small town which remains unnamed, and impresses and marries a beautiful young woman, Angela Vicaro, of humble origins. The marriage takes place in great splendour. **(Hart, 23)**	A rich man, Bayardo San Roman, arrives in a small town which remains unnamed, and impresses and marries a beautiful young woman, Angela Vicario, of humble origins. (23) [...] The first impression we have of him is his legendary wealth [...] He is also presented early on as a man who will stop at nothing to get what he wants; he decides to marry Angela after seeing her quite by chance in the street (p.47; II; 28) and he drives the widower Xius out of his house simply because his future bride casually mentioned that she liked his house. (36) The marriage takes place in great splendour. (23) A rich man, Bayardo San Roman, arrives in a small town which remains unnamed, and impresses and marries a beautiful young woman, Angela Vicario, of humble origins. (23) [...] Another critic has suggested that his ebullient capitalism can be read as a symbol of the North-American invasion of Latin America, specifically in relation to the impoverished Vicario family (91 and 92). (36) Angela is portrayed as [...] being a potential non-conformist [...] However, because of her family's traditionalism, she has no choice when Bayardo proposes to her. (40) The marriage takes place in great splendour. (23)
ATEH **(Pavić)**	(9th century)—the Khazar princess whose role in the polemic concerning the Khazars conversion was decisive. (21) [...] something like a cult of Princess Ateh once existed among Greek and Slavic monastic circles. This cult originated in the belief that Ateh had defeated the Hebrew theologian in the Khazar polemic and had adopted Christianity along with the kaghan, about whom it is uncertain whether he was her father, her husband, or her brother. (22) **(The Red Book)** (beginning of 9th century)—According to Islamic legend, the Khazar kaghan had a relative living at his court who was renowned for her beauty. (130) [...] Ateh took fervid part in the [Khazar] polemic, successfully out-arguing both the Jewish and Christian participants, and in the end helping the Islamic representative, Farabi Ibn Kora. Together with the Khazar kaghan, her lord and master, she converted to Islam. (131) **(The Green Book)** (8th century)—Name of the Khazar princess who lived at the time of the Judaization of the Khazars. (205) [...] Princess Ateh helped Isaac Sangari, the Hebrew participant in the Khazar polemic, by out-arguing the Arab participant, and so the Khazar kaghan opted for the Jewish faith (206) **(The Yellow Book)**

While the exercise can be understood as another form of playing the interpretative-deformative game through the simulation of detail discovery and construction under different types of magnifying glass, it also draws attention to the multiple ramifications that the process of reading and analyzing a text can encompass. This feature recalls Barthes' reading and analysis method in *S/Z*, which takes account of the plurality of the text and its potentiality as an exploratory space, and McGann's observation that books and literary works "organize themselves along multiple dimensions" (*Marking Texts*).

Creative Prompting

While the previous sections have dealt with the reinterpretation of existing texts through detail-driven reconfigurations, the current section will elaborate on another characteristic of detail as an expressive form, namely its function as a creative prompt. Figure 4.4 shows two phases in the writing of a z-text that I created for demonstrative purposes.[9]

The incentive for an extended account of the initial setting was Vallotton's painting and its synchronicity within the two events involving the narrator, the simultaneous TV watching and browsing of the postcard collection. Further developments of the storyline can be imagined by expansions of the fragments of text or the image (e.g., zooming in on it will display an interpretation of the painting, which may be further expanded), following the omen-coincidence path together with a concomitant recording of the writing process itself. This writing-recording by gradual expansion, which enables subsequent exploration of the layers of conception and the history of the text's creation by zooming in and zooming out, allows for a form of detail modeling that keeps track not only of the result but also of the process of becoming of the text.

Analogies may be drawn with approaches in genetic criticism intended to reveal the dynamics of the writing process and the secrets of the laboratory (Grésillon). Experiments of this type can include the published version of a text on the first level, and stratified fragments of manuscripts or *avant-texte*,[11] interconnected through a parent-descendant arrangement in an anti-chronological order, on the deeper levels. Such a layout would enable the examination under a magnifying glass of the backward chains of additions, erasures, replacements, and dislocations that led, for instance, to the descent of the *Antonia tower*, a symbol of Roman pride, from its predecessor, the *Jerusalem temple*, in Flaubert's *Hérodias*, by combining the published text with its folios from Bonaccorso's *Corpus flaubertianum*.[12] In this case, the zoomable model of detail as a creative prompt can be used to trace back the threads of gradual transformation underlying the genesis of the text and Flaubert's laborious quest for the right word.

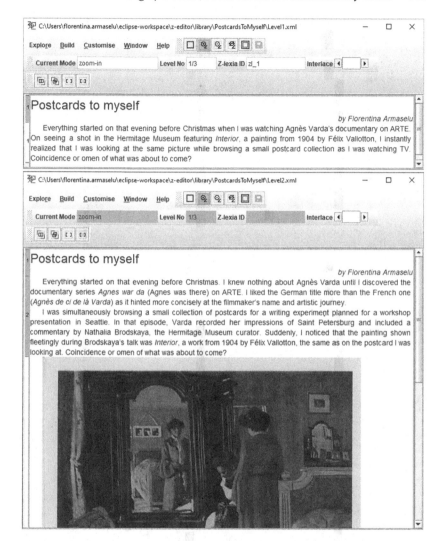

Figure 4.4 Postcards to myself visualization (z-editor).[10] Zoom-in, levels 1–2

Informational Granularity

As explained in the "Conceptual Stratification" section, it was assumed that the levels of generality and specificity of a text, or its conceptual stratification from a detail-driven perspective, can be detected by means of automatic processing and represented through informational granularity maps. Figure 4.5 displays such a visualization obtained by applying this method to Swift's novel *Gulliver's Travels*.

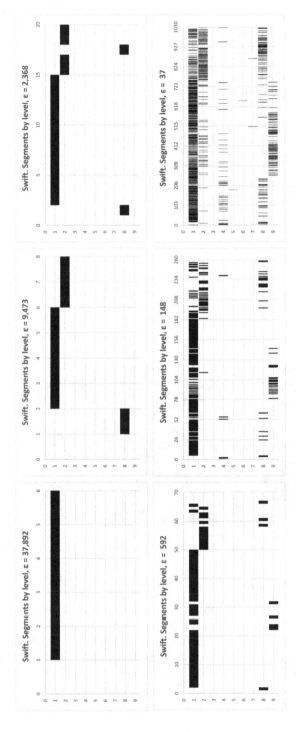

Figure 4.5 Gulliver's Travels (Swift). Segment distribution (horizontal axis) by level of generality and specificity (vertical axis) and ε, the segment size in number of words

Applied to Swift's text, the procedure produced nine levels of generality/specificity. The book contained 37,892 words (after stop word removal)[13] and was cut into five units of analysis corresponding to five parts of the book,[14] which were stored in separate documents. The segmentation included six iterations, with the segment size ε obtained by repeated division by 4 at each iteration (except for the first one corresponding to the whole book). As shown in the figure (read left to right and top down), the algorithm generated a distribution of segments mainly concentrated on the most generic levels, 1 and 2 (top row), and a gradual dispersion of segments toward the more specific levels, 8 and 9 (bottom row), with some items occupying the intermediate levels, 4–7. Granularity here may be interpreted in two ways: firstly, as a measure of the scale of observation, represented through the segment size; and secondly, as an expression of the generality and specificity of the content itself. Therefore, when considered at larger scales, the algorithm indicates a dominance of high-level, generic topics, whereas at smaller scales, the segments exhibit fluctuations between generic and specific themes.

The alternation of fragments with different degrees of generality and specificity is more discernible for smaller sizes (148 and 37 words). While higher level segments offer general descriptions of the settings of each voyage (dates, goal, weather, ship, money) or matters that are familiar to the reader (people, countries, customs), the deeper level segments encompass the oddities of the countries visited (edicts commanding the subjects to break eggs at the "smaller end;" inhabitants "tall as an ordinary spire steeple;" praises expressed by "rhombs, circles, parallelograms, ellipses, and other geometrical terms;" virtues of quadrupeds "placed in opposite view to human corruptions") (Swift, part I, ch. 4; part II, ch. 1; part III, ch. 2; part IV, ch. 7). These different levels of granularity and strata of detail that connect and contrast the odd with the familiar and the general with the particular seem to represent the main artistic means used by Swift to satirize the society of his time.

Concluding Remarks

The chapter proposes a type of modeling based on the interpretation of detail as a piece of content (one or more words, sentences, or paragraphs, including text and possibly images–as shown in the "**Creative Prompting**" section) that can be expanded, absorbed, delayed, tracked, and placed within a continuum as a form of artistic or argumentative expression. The selected examples provided an overview of the possible applications of such a model to the analysis and production of literary texts, with a selection of works that mainly originated in the print medium. Future work may include the study of electronic literature and new AI-inspired or generated productions, and the combination of the z-text model with the automatic analysis of informational granularity.

Although centered on the domain of computing, literature, and literary analysis, these examples draw attention to more general scale- and detail-related mechanisms that seem to be part of our cognitive system and information coding apparatus involved in the production and interpretation of knowledge and artistic artifacts. For instance, Dretske defines the difference between perceptual, informationally rich, and cognitive, detail-selective processes, as a matter of analog-to-digital conversion. This transformation is understood as involving a loss of information that results from higher order processing such as classification, generalization, and recognition (Dretske 139–142). DiCaglio also notes that a change in resolution, understood as the amount of detail discerned within a certain observation range or scale, involves a revision of the observed field into a new set of objects and relations applying within it. This form of conceptual shift also pertains to knowledge production, where operations such as accumulation, aggregation, and categorization can expand the scope of inquiry beyond immediate experience or the study of single entities and isolated phenomena (DiCaglio 23, 38–41).

To these views, we can add that this type of conceptual mechanisms appear to underlie different degrees of information granularity or detail profusion or various scales of observation and representation, which can operate in both learning or reasoning and creative settings. The question of how the change of scale and degree of detail may influence the processes of text creation, understanding, and esthetic reflection requires further attention. While associative thinking has been extensively considered by hypertext theorists and creators and digital media analysts, the interplay between detail modeling, scale, cognition, and creativity needs to be more systematically explored. With its dynamic nature, its ability to bring into focus the text as a mental process rather than a product, and its potential to enable scrutiny and immersion as gradual discovery, detail represents a category that may open new avenues of investigation at the intersection of digital esthetics, literary and analytical computing, hermeneutic modeling, and cognitive studies.

Acknowledgments

The author would like to thank the editors and reviewers for their suggestions and Sarah Cooper, from the Language Centre at the University of Luxembourg, for English proofreading.

Notes

1 Application Programming Interface (API).
2 The term *lexia* is also used by hypertext theorists and electronic literature creators, for instance, to define—along the lines of Barthes—the "blocks of text" joined by "electronic links" that form a hypertext (Landow 3), or the "sections" of a piece of

electronic fiction such as Memmott's *Lexia to Perplexia*, that allows users to "[c]lick and mouse over elements of the lexia to expand the content and introduce new elements" (https://collection.eliterature.org/1/works/memmott_lexia_to_perplexia.html, accessed August 4, 2023).

3 Extensible Markup Language (XML). Text Encoding Initiative (TEI).

4 http://zoomimagine.com, accessed March 4, 2023. https://github.com/florentina-a/z-editor, accessed August 22, 2023.

5 For instance, the content corresponding to the first z-lexia is delimited by the tags *<anchor subtype="start" type="z-lexia" xml:id="zl_1"/>* and *<anchor corresp="#zl_1" subtype="end" type="z-lexia"/>*. The identifier may also comprise the number corresponding to the level of representation, which for reasons of simplicity was not included.

6 The current implementation of z-editor imposes the restriction of *no overlap* between z-lexias, except for parallel expansion, for simplicity of the model.

7 For examples of z-text layouts with excerpts from the cited works by Auerbach, Greenblatt, and Geertz, see Vasilescu (*Le livre sous la loupe* and *Du texte électronique*).

8 Experiments with earlier versions of z-editor and z-texts with extracts from the cited authors (Bonaccorso, Flaubert, Greenblatt, Hart, Pavić, Shakespeare, Tolkien, Tolstoy) are presented in Vasilescu (*Le livre sous la loupe*). See also Armaselu (*The Book under the Magnifying Glass* and *The Text as a Scalable Structure*, in *The International Journal of the Book*, edited by Howard Dare and Mary Kalantzis, vols. 3, 4, nos. 1, 4, Common Ground, Melbourne, Australia, 2006, 2007; http://zoomimagine.com/MyPage.html#jarts; accessed March 4, 2023).

9 Armaselu, Florentina. *Postcards to myself*. http://zoomimagine.com/ZEditor.html, accessed March 5, 2023. https://github.com/florentina-a/z-editor, accessed August 22, 2023.

10 See https://github.com/florentina-a/z-editor, accessed August 22, 2023.

11 *Avant-texte*, term proposed by Bellemin-Noël (13).

12 For more details on the experiment, see Vasilescu (*Le livre sous la loupe*, 191–200).

13 All word counts are expressed in number of words after stop word removal.

14 *A letter from Captain Gulliver to his cousin Simpson*; PART I. *A Voyage to Lilliput*; PART II. *A Voyage to Brobdingnag*; PART III. *A Voyage to Laputa, Balnibarbi, Luggnagg, Glubbdubdrib, and Japan*; PART IV. *A Voyage to the Country of the Houyhnhnms*.

References

Aarseth, Espen J. *Cybertext: Perspectives on Ergodic Literature*. The Johns Hopkins University Press, Baltimore and London, 1997.

"Anchor. P5: Guidelines for Electronic Text Encoding and Interchange." TEI Consortium, version 4.5.0. Last updated on October 25, 2022, revision 3e98e619e https://www.tei-c.org/release/doc/tei-p5-doc/en/html/ref-anchor.html Accessed March 1, 2023.

Armaselu, Florentina. "Text, Fractal Dust and Informational Granularity: A Study of Scale." In *Zoomland. Exploring Scale in Digital History and Humanities*, edited by Florentina Armaselu and Andreas Fickers. Studies in Digital History and Hermeneutics series. De Gruyter Oldenbourg, Berlin, Boston, 2024, pp. 287–334. https://doi.org/10.1515/9783111317779-012.

Armaselu, Florentina, and Charles van den Heuvel. "Metaphors in Digital Herme-neutics: Zooming through Literary, Didactic and Historical Representations of Imaginary and Existing Cities." *Digital Humanities Quarterly* (DHQ), vol. 11, no. 3, 2017. http://www.digitalhumanities.org/dhq/vol/11/3/000337/000337. html. Accessed March 1, 2023.

Auerbach, Erich. *Mimesis. The Representation of Reality in Western Literature.* Princeton University Press, Princeton and Oxford, 1953, 2003.

Barthes, Roland. *S/Z*, translated by Richard Miller. Hill and Wang, New York, 1974.

Barthes, Roland. *Camera Lucida. Reflections on Photography*, translated by Richard Howard. Hill and Wang, New York, 1981.

Bellemin-Noël, Jean. *Le texte et l'avant-texte. Les brouillons d'un poème de Milosz.* Librairie Larousse, Paris, 1972.

Blei, David M. "Introduction to Probabilistic Topic Models." *Communications of the ACM*, vol. 55, 2011. https://www.researchgate.net/publication/248701790_ Introduction_to_Probabilistic_Topic_Models. Accessed March 2, 2023.

Bolter, Jay David, and Richard Grusin. *Remediation: Understanding New Media.* The MIT Press, Cambridge, MA, London, 2000.

Bonaccorso, Giovanni, et al. *Corpus Flaubertianum II. Hérodias. Edition diplo-matique et génétique des manuscrits*, vol. I. Librairie Nizet, Paris, 1991.

Bonaccorso, Giovanni, et al. *Corpus Flaubertianum II. Hérodias, Edition diplo-matique et génétique des manuscrits*, vol. II. Sicania, Messina, 1995.

Burns, Daniel Warren. "Exceptional Scale: Metafiction and The Maximalist Tradi-tion in Contemporary American Literary History." PhD dissertation, University of North Carolina, 2015. https://libres.uncg.edu/ir/uncg/f/Burns_uncg_0154D_ 11801.pdf. Accessed February 19, 2023.

Carter, Richard A. "Generative Unknowing: Nathan Allen Jones' Glitch Poetics." *Electronic Book Review*, December 4, 2022. https://doi.org/10.7273/F72Z-AC69.

Cramer, Florian. *Words Made Flesh: Code, Culture, Imagination.* Piet Zwart Insti-tute, Rotterdam, 2005. https://www.netzliteratur.net/cramer/wordsmadefleshpdf. pdf. Accessed February 23, 2023.

DiCaglio, Joshua. *Scale Theory: A Nondisciplinary Inquiry.* University of Minnesota Press, Minneapolis, London, 2021.

Dretske, Fred I. *Knowledge and the Flow of Information.* The David Hume Series. Philosophy and Cognitive Science Reissues, CSLI Publications, Stanford, 1999.

Flaubert, Gustave. *Trois Contes. Un Cœur simple. La Légende de saint Julien l'Hospitalier.* Hérodias, Editions Garnier Frères, Paris, 1961.

Flores, Leonardo. "Third Generation Electronic Literature." *Electronic Book Review*, April 6, 2019. https://electronicbookreview.com/essay/third-generation-electronic-literature/.

Geertz, Clifford. *The Interpretation of Cultures.* Basic Books, New York, 1973.

Ginzburg, Carlo. "Morelli, Freud and Sherlock Holmes: Clues and Scientific Method*." *History Workshop Journal*, vol. 9, no. 1 (March 1, 1980), 1980, pp. 5–36. https://doi.org/10.1093/hwj/9.1.5.

Gius, Evelyn, and Janina Jacke. "Are Computational Literary Studies Structuralist?" *Journal of Cultural Analytics*, vol. 7, no. 4, December 2022, https://doi.org/ 10.22148/001c.46662.

Greenblatt, Stephen. *Will in the World: How Shakespeare became Shakespeare.* W.W. Norton & Company, New York, London, 2004.

Grésillon, Almuth. *Eléments de critique génétique. Lire les manuscrits modernes.* Presses Universitaires de France, Paris, 1994.

Hart, Stephen M. *Gabriel García Márquez: Crónica de una muerte anunciada,* second, revised, edition. Critical Guides to Spanish Texts Series, edited by Alan Deyermond and Stephen Hart, 57. Grant & Cutler Ltd, London, 2005. https://bulletinofadvancedspanish.files.wordpress.com/2022/06/3rd-edition-stephen-hart-cronica-de-una-muerte-anunciada_removed.pdf. Accessed March 5, 2023.

Kleymann, Rabea, and Jan-Erik Stange. "Towards Hermeneutic Visualization in Digital Literary Studies." Digital Humanities Quarterly (DHQ), vol. 15, no. 2, 2021. http://www.digitalhumanities.org/dhq/vol/15/2/000547/000547.html. Accessed February 27, 2023.

Kracauer, Siegfried. *History. The Last Things before the Last.* Markus Wiener Publisher, Princeton, 2014.

Landow, George P. *Hypertext 3.0: Critical Theory and New Media in an Era of Globalization.* Parallax: Re-visions of Culture and Society, edited by Stephen G. Nichols, Gerald Prince, and Wendy Steiner, series editors, The Johns Hopkins University Press, Baltimore, 1992, 1997, 2006.

Lawrence, George Richard Peter. *Cartographic Methods.* Methuen & Co Ltd, London, 1971.

MacEachren, Alan M. *How Maps Work. Representation, Visualization, and Design.* The Guildford Press, New York, London, 2004.

Mandelbrot, Benoit B. *The Fractal Geometry of Nature.* W.H. Freeman and Company, New York, 1983.

McCallum, Andrew Kachites. "MALLET: A Machine Learning for Language Toolkit," 2002. http://mallet.cs.umass.edu. Accessed March 2, 2023.

McCarty, Willard. "Knowing …: Modeling in Literary Studies." In *A Companion to Digital Literary Studies,* edited by Ray Siemens and Susan Schreibman, John Wiley & Sons, Ltd, Oxford, 2013, pp. 389–401. https://doi.org/10.1002/9781405177504.ch21. Accessed February 21, 2023.

McGann, Jerome. "Marking Texts of Many Dimensions." In *A Companion to Digital Humanities,* edited by Susan Schreibman, Ray Siemens, and John Unsworth, Blackwell Publishing Ltd, 2004. https://companions.digitalhumanities.org/DH/?chapter=content/9781405103213_chapter_16.html. Accessed March 5, 2023.

McGann, Jerome, and Lisa Samuels. "Deformance and Interpretation (with Lisa Samuels)." In *Radiant Textuality: Literary Studies after the World Wide Web,* by Jerome McGann, Palgrave Macmillan, New York, 2001, pp. 105–135. https://doi.org/10.1007/978-1-137-10738-1_5,

Munro, Thomas. "Form in the Arts: An Outline for Descriptive Analysis." *Journal Of Aesthetics and Art Criticism,* vol. 2, no. 8 (Autumn 1943), 1943, pp. 5–26.

Orford, Scott. "Cartography and Visualization." In *Questioning Geography. Fundamental Debates,* edited by Noel Castree, Alisdair Rogers and Douglas Sherman, Blackwell Publishing, Malden, 2005, pp. 189–205.

Palmer, Alan. "The Mind Beyond the Skin." In *Narrative Theory and the Cognitive Sciences*, edited by David Herman, CSLI Publications, Stanford, CA, 2003, pp. 322–348.

Pavić, Milorad. *Dictionary of the Khazars: A Lexicon Novel in 100,000 Words (Female Edition)*, translated from Serbo-Croatian by Christina Pribićević-Zorić. Vintage Books, New York, 1989.

Pold, Søren, and Malthe Stavning Erslev. "Data-Realism: Reading and Writing Datafied Text." *Electronic Book Review*, 2020. https://doi.org/10.7273/N381-MK15.

Pradhan, Pritika. "'Not Simple Truth but Complex Beauty': Details in Victorian Literature and Aesthetics." PhD dissertation, Rutgers, the State University of New Jersey, 2019. https://rucore.libraries.rutgers.edu/rutgers-lib/61909/PDF/1/play/. Accessed February 19, 2023.

Ryan, Marie-Laure. *Narrative as Virtual Reality: Immersion and Interactivity in Literature and Electronic Media*. Parallax: Re-visions of Culture and Society, edited by Stephen G. Nichols, Gerald Prince, and Wendy Steiner, series editors, The Johns Hopkins University Press, Baltimore and London, 2001.

Schor, Naomi. *Reading in Detail: Aesthetics and the Feminine*, first edition, 1987. Routledge, New York, London, p. 2007.

Shakespeare, William. "Venus and Adonis," published in 1593. *The Bard of Avon: Shakespeare in Stratford-upon-Avon*, 2002–2008. http://www.shakespeare-w.com/english/shakespeare/w_venus.html. Accessed March 3, 2023.

Swift, Jonathan. *Gulliver's Travels into Several Remote Nations of the World*. The Project Gutenberg eBook, release date February 1, 1997 [EBook #829], most recently updated August 17, 2021, first published in 1726. https://www.gutenberg.org/ebooks/829. Accessed March 3, 2023.

Tolkien, J.R.R. *The Fellowship of the Ring: Being the First Part of the Lord of the Rings*. Harper Collins Publishers, London, 1994.

Tolstoy, Leo. *Anna Karenina*, translated by Constance Garnett. The Modern Library, New York, 1950.

Vasilescu, Florentina. "Le livre sous la loupe. Nouvelles formes d'écriture électronique." PhD dissertation, Université de Montréal, 2010. https://papyrus.bib.umontreal.ca/xmlui/handle/1866/3964. Accessed March 4, 2023.

Vasilescu, Florentina. "Du texte électronique au contexte culturel." In *Performances et objets culturels. Nouvelles perspectives*, edited by Louis Hébert and Lucie Guillemette, Presses de l'Université Laval, Québec, 2011, pp. 483–493. https://www.pulaval.com/livres/performances-et-objets-culturels-nouvelles-perspectives. Accessed March 4, 2023.

5 The Novel's Factory of Opinions

Adapting Sentiment Analysis Tools to ELTeC Prefaces

Ioana Galleron, Roxana Patras,
Rosario Arias, Javier Fernández-Cruz,
Frédérique Mélanie-Becquet, Olga Seminck

Introduction

The preface is one of the most prototypical, well-delineated, and homogenous types of paratext. In his seminal work on "thresholds of interpretation," Gérard Genette documents the preface's empirical historicity by cataloging the variations caused by cultural codes, printing routines, and authors' stylistic choices and lays it out that, along time, its repertory of features is quite "stable," hence "a history of the preface would not be very meaningful" (Genette 161). Admitting his own shortage of statistical data, which would have perhaps "clarified for us the distribution... according to period, genre, author, and national tradition" (163), Genette analyzes prefaces by assembling various case studies and quotations. The French theorist provides us with a lengthy inventory of types (original/authorial, delayed, allographic, actorial, fictional) and also remarks on the wealth of "para-synonyms" used to name the liminal texts: "introduction," "prologue," "note," "warning," "preamble," "prelude," "preliminary discourse," "exordium," etc. Prefaces may also overlap with other types of liminal matter as in the case of the dedicatory epistles, whose literary life seems to span especially along the nineteenth century (123–124). There are more fine-grained differences between "prefaces" and "introductions," especially when they occur in the same book, but these variations do not influence consistently, in Genette's view, the functional performances of the liminal text. Thus, even if the introduction's proper and similar essay-kind introductory texts are meant to be more systematic, less bound to (historical) circumstances, and prone to anticipate the main text's foci, a bundle of thematic wires and a couple of "prefatorial functions"—such as to hold the reader's interest and to guide her/him by explaining the why's and the how's of reading—are features that connect prefaces from all ages. This means that the liminal matter might provide us with a quasi-homogenous object of study (Genette 161–292), or, at least, with a unifying practice specific to the entire European cultural environment (Galleron *passim*).

DOI: 10.4324/9781003320838-8

Three decades after the publication of Genette's work, theorists un-veiled the impasse of "paratextual limits," and in the case of prefaces, the problem in proving there is a formal contrast between the liminal matter and the main text (Gallerani et al. 4, Ruokkeinen and Liira *passim*). So, it has been suggested a switch from the macrolevel understanding of para-texts to a micro-level exploration (Peikola and Bös 3–33). This new view on textual fluidity obliterates the thematic concerns—more specifically, the themes of the how and the themes of the why mentioned above—and brings to the fore, in turn, the pragmatic and functional aspects.

Rich and multilingual literary corpora, sampled distribution, and sta-tistical data were lacking when Genette published his *Thresholds* (1987). Fortunately, such resources have been produced in recent years and con-stitute one of the most valuable contributions of digital humanities to the study of literature. Affirmations about prefaces can now be tested on large corpora, with a digitally renewed functional approach, aimed at grasp-ing the attentional signals and at showing how "the factory" of opinion-making works. In line with the volume's idea to bring to the fore examples of hermeneutic modeling in computational literary studies, this chapter seeks to offer a two-layered approach to the extracted material: on the one hand, a critical take on the results yielded by various sentiment analy-sis algorithms after they had been tried on, and tested by means of, a literary corpus that is multilingual and patrimonial at the same time; on the other, an internalization *sur le vif* of sophisticated theoretical concepts (e.g. paratext, preface), which have not been previously operationalized by literary computational research. We expect the data patterns to provide information for us to propose a new functional typology of prefaces, while enabling us to pay careful attention to the prefaces' "double historicity" (Chartier 149), to evaluate the prefaces' potential in holding or drawing away the attention (focus), to analyze the prefaces' capacity to generate affective bias, and, moreover, to question their presupposed "prototypical-ity" (Peikola and Bös 14) or homogeneity.

The new insights sentiment analysis (SA) and emotion analysis have re-cently yielded for literary studies (Kim and Klinger, Klinger et al. 237–268, Schmidt et al. *passim*, Elkins *passim*, Moreno-Ortiz 133–140), on the one hand, and the preface's relative comparability to product reviews and product teasers (Fang and Zhan *passim*), on the other, supply a good ar-gument for trying SA on liminal matters. Indeed, prefaces—and chiefly the authors' original prefaces—may be considered the moment's harvest because, regardless of textual strategies, they are supposed to play up the affective movement of the prefatorial situation of communication, as well as to introduce the dominant affective notes of the main text, and, even-tually, to form opinions. Reactions to criticism, confessions, accomplice addresses, or enthusiastic dispositions toward the author's future success prepare the reader to perceive the main text's stakes. As treatises of rhetoric advise, *exordia*, thus also prefaces, should count on pathos; more specifically, they should catch, hold, or draw away the readers' attention in order to create, if possible, a reader-friendly disposition (Salmi 187–207). Therefore, beside their obvious cognitive goal (explanation of why and how), prefaces are always about giving and receiving emotions and about striking the right opening "note." Such affective bias surfaces not only in "positive prefaces" but also in "negative prefaces" whose orientation is eventually positive too, because they are meant to work as "antidotes" and to make up for the defects of the elements involved in the situation of communication (Arrington and Rose 306–307). All in all, an SA-based modeling of prefaces appears as a viable approach for unveiling the specificities of this genre.

This discussion of the opinion-making process in prefaces is also meant to supplement our former analysis of titling practices in the European novel (Patras et al 163–187), chiefly by exploring further "the seduction/attraction function" and by revealing how the focal accent is retrieved in larger paratextual units. If our study on titling has shown interesting clusters and brought in new suggestions about how to deal with both cross-national influences and unchanging practices, then it would be fascinating to visualize a similar patchwork in prefaces. If the titles' foci might be related with the tendency of entities (person, places, other) to show up unattended or in relatively fixed combinations (e.g. person entities tend to favor pairing with place names rather than with alike entities), it would be interesting to devise an SA-based solution for digging up those "pointer sentences" that indicate "the unspoken assumptions" of the preface or of the main text (Gascoigne 20). Thus, SA may help in better understanding how cognitive and pragmatic goals are intertwined in prefaces.

Notwithstanding the myriad of exceptions that have been lengthily discussed by theorists, our study draws on a rather plain definition of prefaces: they are understood as autonomous units of the work, characterized by a special locutionary regime, and serving as an introduction to the main narrative, either because it clarifies some of its features or because it contextualizes its creation process. Developing on this working definition, the study will dedicate a first section to the presentation of our corpus, a second one to some technical choices, and a third, to our findings. We will adopt a rather descriptive than interpretative stance toward the results generated via our pipeline. We are, however, confident in stating that our digital approach brings new insights about the liminal texts, completing previous takes on what prefaces usually do, as well as on whom (and why) mobilizes this device throughout European literary traditions.

Our Corpus

Our investigation is based on the European Literary Text Collection (ELTeC),[1] built through a collaborative effort within the COST Action "Distant reading" (Schöch et al.). Our aim is to correct Genette's shortcomings of noncanonical illustrations as far as prefaces are concerned. As the number of authors involved in writing the present chapter is much more limited than the group who participated in the above-mentioned title study, we were able to explore only four ELTeC collections, English, French, Romanian, and Spanish. The four sub-corpora are part of the ELTeC "core," which is formed of ten collections having a high degree of compliance with a set of sampling criteria. Thus, they include both canonical and noncanonical novels, as evenly spread over four time slots (T1: 1840–1859, T2: 1860–1879, T3: 1880–1899, T4: 1900–1919) as possible, and balancing author gender. Moreover, often-explored literary traditions, such as the English one, are counterbalanced in our corpus by examples from lesser established literary traditions, such as the Romanian one. However, this also means that the present endeavor remains open to further validations and refinements that might come from the enlargement of case-studies pool. Therefore, what we offer here is mainly an amendable method rather than firm conclusions.

ELTeC texts are freely downloadable files in an XML TEI[2] format, from which extractions of specific sections can be made with an XPath (or XQuery) expression, or with a Python script. We concentrated on the divisions (marked-up with the TEI tag <div>s) that ELTeC contributors labeled "liminal" via an attribute. Not all output txt files contain text or appropriate text: in some cases, liminal <div>s are inexistent or empty, while in others they contain a title page only. Finally, in some rare cases annotation errors—e.g. liminal divisions placed at the end of the work or agglutinated in the <body> with the first chapter—caused some data leakages. Once the errors were corrected and the non-relevant <div>s filtered out, we obtained a total amount of 178 texts out of 400 candidates (44.5%).

Out of these texts, many had to be discarded as not corresponding to our working definition. Thematic or more largely semantic relations can be construed from the coexistence of any kind of liminal section with a narrative within a same book, but they were not what interested us. Consequently, we decided to exclude the epigraphs,[3] such as those opening Colombine's *Los Inadaptados* (SPA4007)[4] where the reader enters the fiction with a quotation from Saint Matthew's gospel, followed by a statement abstracted from or even signed by "LIFE." In others, we found only a short and conventional dedicatory text (e.g. Liviu Rebreanu's *Ion*, ROM076). In some cases, the liminal texts appeared to be penned by someone who was not the author of the novel: for instance, Octave Mirbeau puts a letter by Alphonse Daudet in the opening of his *La Maréchale* (FRA02802), despite a Parthian spire it contains. Finally, we had combinations of any of these various possibilities—epigraph and dedication, but no preface; preface and epigraph; etc.—all of them forming complex paratextual instances.[5]

The general distribution by collection of the different types of liminal matter can be seen in Figure 5.1.

A further difficulty was also related to the fact that texts titled "introduction" or "prologue" were not, according to our definition, prefaces; others, bearing no title, appeared to be dedicatory epistles, which offered quite deep insights into the novels. For instance, the dedicatory text written by Mme Adam to Alexandre Dumas (FRA00102) is informative and details the themes of the main text. On the contrary, the dedicatory text written by Hector Malot to his wife (FRA02601) is highly subjective and personal, shedding little or no light over the following narrative. We have thus decided to retain the first text and to exclude the other. Borderline cases, such as introductory units written in verse (e.g. Al. Pelimon's *Hoţii şi hagiul*, ROM096) or the episode of Saint Theresa's life opening George Eliot's *Middlemarch* (ENG18721), have also been excluded. However, this exclusion did not fall indifferently over all dedicatory texts. For instance, we decided to retain Alphonse Allais' jocular defense of Captain Cap's existence (FRA00401), as well as "Ganconagh's Apology" in the preamble of *John Sherman and Dhoya* (ENG18910) insofar they both contain an explicit reference to the following text, defining it as a work of art. All in all, a total of 92 liminal <div>s have been selected for conducting our

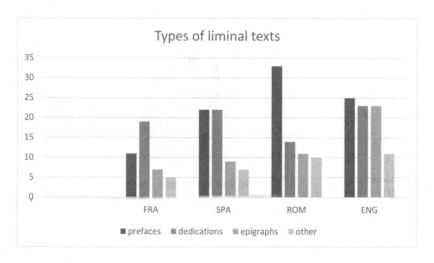

Figure 5.1 Types of liminal texts

analysis. Only nine of them come from the French collection, while the others are spread quite evenly between the English, the Romanian, and the Spanish collections.

Further analysis of these 92 liminal divisions (<div>s) revealed that some novels contain more than one preface. For instance, *Yeast: A Problem* by Charles Kingsley (ENG18510) presents two prefaces, one accompanying the first and another one the fourth edition of the book. The two texts are different and perform the prefatorial functions in quite different ways. This is also the case in Romain Rolland's *Jean-Christophe* (FRA04202), or in Aricescu's *Misterele căsătoriei* (ROM031), with the first having three preceding texts and the second four. We have split manually the successive prefaces of the same novel in different files, completing their identifier.[6] The total number of units submitted to analysis is therefore slightly higher (110) than the number of liminal divisions (<div>s) labeled performing prefatorial functions. As a consequence, the relative weight of the four collections is a bit different from Figure 5.2, with the Romanian corpus becoming the richest (37 prefaces, 34% of the total), followed by the Spanish one (33 prefaces, 30%), the English one (27 prefaces, 25%), and finally the French one, still the poorest (13 prefaces).

Tools and Methods

The aim of performing SA on texts in four languages quickly appeared as a bold endeavor and thus came with a methodological challenge. After reviewing related bibliography, we realized that most of the SA

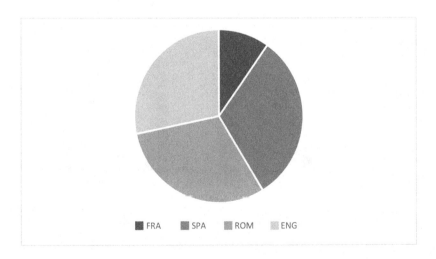

Figure 5.2 Prefatorial divisions in the four collections

tools work only with English. There were, however, a few exceptions such as Lingmotif, TextBlob, and XED. Lingmotif, an analytic text suite created by the Tecnolengua Group at the University of Malaga, supports English and Spanish, but not Romanian or French (Moreno-Ortiz et al. 511–568).[7] In a similar way, TextBlob, a quite popular tool, supports the analysis of English and French, but not that of Spanish and Romanian texts. Trained on the alignment of quotes from movies, XED promises to cover a larger variety of languages (Öhman, et al. 6542–6552), but after fine-tuning it on our corpus, it appeared that many sentences were skipped, while those that got parsed were assigned with a sentiment score that was not concordant with the annotator's reading.[8] All in all, we could either lead separate studies for each language, with different tools, and obtain no comparability, or exclude pairs of languages (Romanian-Spanish, not supported by TextBlob, or Romanian-French pair, not supported by Lingmotif), and obtain a debatable comparability.

In order to keep a ground for comparability and to overcome the difficulties posed by language diversity, the decision has been taken to translate all texts to English and to parse them with two of the tools that have been mentioned above, Lingmotif and TextBlob. In spite of some noticeable divergences,[9] Lingmotif and TextBlob function quite similarly, by giving a score to a portion of text rather than emotion labels (anger, trust, fear, etc.) appended to it.[10] The Spanish, French, and Romanian prefaces were translated into English with DeepL; in order to achieve a better performance with DeepL translation, the Romanian collection was beforehand normalized and slightly modernized. Also, to evaluate the bias introduced by the automatic translation and considering that pairs of languages (Spanish and English, and French and English) were supported by the chosen tools, we decided to set side by side the results of the SA performed on translations and those obtained with original texts. We did not, however, carry out reverse translations from English to French or Spanish, so as to further check the performances of the tools.

In addition to the first round of annotation, described above, which helped us to target, within the liminal divisions, the portions of prefatory text, we have conducted a second one, targeted at a deeper semantic layer, possibly tensed between the preface's competence and performance, between its aspiration toward autonomy and its introductory duty. While, except for a few borderline cases (e.g. verse, lengthy citations of recommendation letters), the first round of annotation did not raise problems, the second round of annotation needed a careful assessment of the categories that might be informative, directly or indirectly, for the polarity, the subjectivity, and the intensity of the prefaces, three aspects computed by the considered tools. Even though the preface expresses "an unbalanced and even shaky situation of communication" (Genette 237), Genette detects in the prefaces a prototypical pentadic structure: form, place, time, sender, and addressee (Genette 161–196). Elaborating on this structural analysis and emending the theorist's take on "the functions of the original preface" (Genette 196–229), we decided to annotate six categories. Two of them ("voice" and "engagement") are pragmatically oriented, thus SA tractable, while the other four ("topicality," "reference to characters," "context," and "aesthetics") represent types of textual and contextual information—also referentiality markers—that might feature, albeit indirectly, some sort of sentiment-related pattern.

a   Voice ("personal" or "fictional")
    We defined as being articulated by a "personal" voice all those prefaces in which the author assumes authorship, speaking on his/her behalf either in the first person (SPA4022: "You are still in time to leave me, my reader and master. Forget that you spent a few pesetas to read me; add them to the many you have misused or have been robbed or demanded, and throw this book away without reading it, if you don't know how to read."), or in the third person (ROM095: "In publishing this book, *the author* has had no other desire than to give his country, now as in the past, as always, the tribute due to it from all talents according to their measure and strength."). We defined as being articulated by a "fictional" voice all prefatory matter that introduces the main text through a fictional device such as a conversation with the intradiegetic storyteller, an allegory of the main character's progress through the narrative or any other device that may be characterized with Thackeray's metaphor "before the curtain." Here is one example: "To finish, I make known that I have always been a weaver of my state, and that I remain in the house where my father stayed, in Saint-Brunelle, near Morlincourt, Oise; moreover, that Fructueux Cellier is my name" (FRA00101).
b   Topicality (yes/no values)
    The question here is to what extent the preface gives an idea about the contents of the novel, containing one or several thematic hints. For instance, in Thackeray's *Vanity Fair*, the topicality has a positive value because the prefatorial matter represents an amplified explanation of the allegory that also gives the title of the novel: "I have no other moral than this to tag to the present story of 'Vanity Fair'. Some people consider Fairs immoral altogether, etc." (ENG18480). On the contrary, in Ioan Pop-Florantin's *Horea*, there is no direct indication of the main text's topics or themes.

c References to characters in the main text (yes/no values)

We decided to annotate as referring to characters both the prefaces that mention individualized characters (by proper names such as "Chantal" in Octave Mirbeau's *La Maréchale* or "Horace" in George Sand's novel), and the collective or characters indicated metonymically like in the sentence "The style is that of *the speakers*" (ROM025). In the example given under point (b), that of Ioan Pop-Floratin's *Horea*, while no direct indication about the themes is available, the reader finds an anticipation about the main character: "Romanian mothers still teach their children today to pray to God for the soul of that savior and martyr. Who was that matchless man? And what did he do on this earth?" (ROM050).

d Engagement (yes/no values)

This aspect yields data about the author's reactiveness against or in favor of someone/something. The refutation of the critics' reviews and the invitations to the public to perform a friendly reading represent two good examples of engagement with the main text's message. For instance, Iuliu Dragomirescu's preface to *Cele şapte candeli. Pe Catafalc* contains more than one bitter arrow toward the critics and scribes: "Come now, you ignorant critics, you scribes... violating art and deflowering the dream, spread, impudent, the hour of your orgy, prepare the feast of your putrefaction" (ROM038). In Silverio Lanza's *La rendición de Santiago*, we have found both refutation of critics and flattery of readers: "I am sorry, influential gentlemen, that I have troubled you, writing books and worshipping women... In the meantime ... I continue to adore women, and to write little books with all my powers and senses. And enough of this portrait! Be content with this one, readers, and pin me to the wall, or hang me wherever you please" (SPA4022).

e Context (yes/no values)

Prefaces detailing the when, where, and/or how of the writing situation were labeled bringing information about the context. For example, Romain Rolland's preface to *Jean-Christophe* explains how the author conceived the main character and the theme of the novel: "I must explain the conditions in which I undertook the whole of my work. I was isolated. I was suffocating like so many others in France in an enemy moral world, etc." (FRA04202).

f Aesthetics (yes/no values)

The annotation of this aspect is triggered by the presence of specifications about various aspects of the novel, such as the style, the genre, the type of language, and the tone. For instance, Catherine Sinclair's reflection, in her preface to *Modern Flirtations* (ENG18410), on "light reading," has been annotated as an aesthetic consideration. The mentions of aesthetic categories such as the ideal of beauty or genres (novel, poetry) were annotated in Ghica's *Don Juanii din Bucureşti*: "The novel can take all forms, tell us everything, and Sdescribe everything. The great facts of history, the strong feelings of the soul, the habits of life, the novel contains everything, expresses everything" (ROM015).

At the end of the process, consisting, on the one hand, in an SA performed twice, once with Lingmotif and once with TextBlob, and, on the other hand, in a manual annotation of the six above-detailed aspects, we obtain, for each collection in English (whether original or translated), several Excel files with the following data:

- global Lingmotif scores for each preface;
- global TextBlob scores for each preface;
- sentence scores with TextBlob for each preface;
- manual annotations of each preface with respect to the voice it displays, its topicality, the anticipation of a character, etc.

In addition, specific sets of data exist for French and Spanish, obtained with TextBlob, respectively, Lingmotif.

In what follows, we discuss the main findings these spreadsheets support and invite the reader to consult them for further insights (Galleron 2022). What we are looking at is a potential correlation between voice, topicality, character anticipation, engagement, contextualization, or aesthetic consideration, with stronger or meeker, more or less frequent sentiment expression. The aim here is not only to capture these aspects via SA but also to see if any of these orientations of a preface translates into specific sentiment profile. Such an identification may help, in return, within a distant reading protocol to the identification of a specific type of preface in a large corpus.

Findings

The first element of interest is the distribution of the prefaces. The prefatory practice seems to be culture dependent, with a large number of such texts existing in the English, Spanish, and Romanian collections, and a noticeable lower presence in the French one. Also, this last collection is the only one displaying less prefaces than dedications (see Figure 5.1). Another cultural specificity seems to be the epigraph, much more frequent in the English novel (in absolute values and by comparison with the other liminal types) than in French, Spanish, or even Romanian texts. In addition, the distribution of the types in this last collection shows that the Romanian novelist is more prone than his/her colleagues from other countries to offer all types of preambles in his or her novel. As shown by Mircea Vasilescu, the rich variety of liminal matter is a prominent feature of the premodern Romanian literature (Vasilescu 63–141). Thus, for nineteenth-century novels, the diversity of the paratextual apparatus might point backward rather than forth, that is, premodern literary practices. Other explanations have been provided for these contrasts: in the Romanian culture of the 19th century, the novel is a brand-new product for the partially literate readership and should be advertised accordingly, by promising a friendly and quality reading (Anghelescu *passim*, Drace Francis *passim*). This is further validated by the statements one finds in the authorial prefaces of the Romanian collection: "Autorul ştie ce grea sarcină şi-a impus, dar el ştie asemenea că publicul nu necunoaşte marginile posibilităţii ce împresoară, la noi, cariera literară. Or cum însă, el se resemnă în aprecierea cea dreaptă a acestui public, şi, încurajat de imparţialitatea sa ca şi de buna voinţă cu care a salutat totdeauna modestele sale scrieri, îi dedică şi acum fructul vegherilor sale. Autorul." (ROM095).

On the contrary, the French public looks well introduced to the genre; prefaces are therefore deemed as less necessary, unless the novelty of the topic asks for some clarifications: for instance, the American way of life, mentioned in the preface to *Les Trappeurs de l'Arkansas* (FRA00301). However, well-established novelistic traditions, such as the English and the Spanish ones, do not translate similarly in very low numbers of prefaces: whether this is justified by a greater urge to underline the novelty of the contents in competitive book markets, or by other factors, such as the publishers' demands or the inertia of publishing practices, remains to be examined.

The hypothesis about a link between less well-established novelistic traditions and a large number of prefaces is supported to a certain extent by the decrease in the proportion of novels with prefaces one can observe when looking at the distribution by timeslots. Overall, 40.54% of the texts in all languages from the T1 (1840–1859) have a preface. This figure drops to 21.98% in the following period (1860–1879), and to 12.5% in the third period (1880–1899), as if, along with the evolution of the genre, the European writers consider the novel more and more self-explanatory, or maybe the prefatory device appears more and more outdated: already in the seventeenth century, the French poet Boileau was mocking the authors for trying to capture the benevolence of their readers through prefaces, instead of counting solely on the merits of the book. This kind of genre fatigue is overcome in the fourth period (1900–1919), where we can see a sharp increase in the number of prefaces. Their proportion gets to a level close to that observed for T2 (22.76%), probably because the authors find new ways of engaging with the liminal text. There is some evidence that national literatures may have changed in more significant ways during the first decades of the 20th century to which T4 corresponds than between T2 and T3[11]: the increase in the number of prefaces may be a result, or a side effect, of this. In this sense, it is necessary to expand the corpus to the previous and following periods to have a clearer view about the trends.

Another argument pleading for a link between the use of a liminal device and the degree of comfort, or familiarity, with the novelistic practice is to be found in the distribution of our corpus by gender. At the scale of the entire corpus, women do not write more or less prefaces than men; in both cases, roughly one in five novels has a preface, whether written by a male (23.53%) or a female author (22.58%).[12] A similar observation has been made in the title study, with women's practices of denomination appearing quite close to those of their male counterparts. However, it is significant that prefaces by women are concentrated in the T1, with 17 out of the 28 items coming from this period. Women writers are not a novelty in 1840, but their involvement in the literary field is not yet banalized at the time. This may have triggered a higher need, from these authors, to release their works with a liminal text, meant to offer a kind of protection through all kinds of *captatio benevolentiae*:

> PREFACE [To all] After this paper will follow, the third and final part of my conception. The delay, of this second volume—was due to the hardships of life. This delay, however, did not harm me. On the contrary. Events—and in the meantime, important works—have come to me, which have made me aware that I have been thinking for myself, when the synthesis directed by experience was so rightly guided by my personal intuition (ROM082).

As the novel develops, and women writers become more accepted, if not more numerous, the urge to contextualize the topics of the novel, to justify their literary choices, and to prepare their public for a good reading decreases, thus leading to considerably lower numbers of prefaces on their side: 14.81%, 6.45%, and 12.82% of the feminine novels from T2, T3, and T4 have prefaces, as opposed to 35.94%, 17.95%, and 34.94% of the masculine novels from the same period.

Anticipating the SA, developed further down, and in addition to these observations about male and female uptake of the liminal practice, let us also note that, at the scale of the whole corpus, feminine prefatorial voices do not appear more sentiment prone or more subjective than the masculine ones: while Lingmotif finds female voices more positive than the masculine ones (57 vs. 49 in terms of sentiment expression), as well as more subjective (74.67 vs. 73.03), TextBlob figures do not concur, indicating little difference between male and female writers in terms of sentiment expression, with a short advantage given rather to the first ones (0.10 vs. 0.09 of polarity). If women write more prefaces, especially at the beginning of their journey in the novelistic land, these prefaces are not necessarily "hotter" than the masculine ones, except when specific topics ask for a stronger worded argument.[13]

In turn, the higher or lower success of a novel on the market does not seem to be correlated to the presence or the absence of a preface. Overall, 24.31% of the success novels have a preface, a figure slightly more important than the one achieved by less reprinted texts (22.37%), but the difference is not that significant, especially considering the quite low numbers we are dealing with. Therefore, neither does the preface appear to be a feature of the "good" novel nor the characteristic of a less successful one, and this ambiguity seems to be a staple of the prefatorial practice.

SA helps refining and, to some point, understanding these distributions, even if the figures are not easy to interpret, insofar as the tools are at odds about certain aspects, in spite of a certain correlation between the results. Generally speaking, when looking with TextBlob (Figure 5.3), prefaces do not show much contrast in terms of sentiment score: most of the texts are rated between 0 and 0.2 (in other terms, "neutral," while, potentially, the score range spans from −1 ["extremely negative"] to 1 ["extremely positive"], as indicated in note 10).

On the contrary, as it can be observed in Figure 5.4, Lingmotif tends to characterize more neatly the prefaces, with only some 19% among them occupying the middle ground of "slightly positive" or "slightly negative." As the following image shows, some prefaces are rated by Lingmotif with 0 ("extremely negative") or 100 ("extremely positive"), which are the minimum and respectively the maximum scores the tool can award.

In addition, extreme values (more specifically, values outside the standard deviation[14]) tend to be rather in the category of "extremely positive" with Lingmotif (eight prefaces with scores over 80) and in the negative category with TextBlob (ten prefaces with scores inferior to 0). Also, with some exceptions, Lingmotif does not place among the extremes the same prefaces as TextBlob, and vice versa.[15] This is not unexpected, since the tools implement very distinct algorithms, but this fact complicates the analysis and invites to constantly return to the texts.

Keeping these differences in mind, it is highly significant when the two tools meet. In three cases (FRA00102, ROM004-1, and SPA2020), Lingmotif and TextBlob both evaluate certain prefaces as highly positive. In fact, the Romanian and Spanish prefaces are dedicatory epistles that have been recategorized during the manual annotation. More generally, extreme positivity achieved with either tool is an indicator of hybridity: both Alarcon's book (SPA3006, 83 points with Lingmotif, but only 0.19

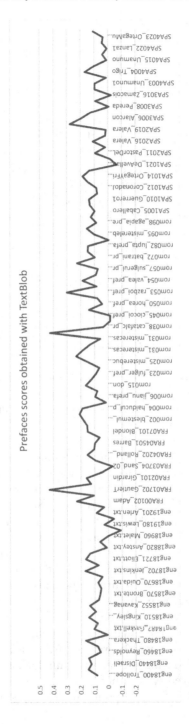

Figure 5.3 Prefaces scores obtained with TextBlob

Figure 5.4 Prefaces scores obtained with Lingmotif

with TextBlob) and Boerescu's novel (ROM034, 0.42 with TextBlob, but no more than 56 with Lingmotif, meaning "fairly positive") deal with the contents of the work while dedicating it to a friend or a member of the family. Less often, highly positive scores pick up other borderline cases, such as the discussions about the Romanian book market one can find in ROM004-2 or ROM053-1. This is an interesting finding from a methodological point of view, which may help us to better document the non-homogeneity of prefaces in future studies based on other ELTeC collections.

Another meeting point concerns the Romanian prefaces. Both tools put them among the most polarized, in terms of sentiment expression. This is visible not only when looking at the extreme values, with more than 40% among them coming from this collection (8 values out of 18 with TextBlob, 12 out of 25 with Lingmotif), but also when considering the mean values per collection, shown by Figure 5.5.

It seems, therefore, safe to argue that, in distinction to their English and French colleagues, and, to some extent, differently from the Spanish writers, Romanian novelists tend to express stronger opinions in the liminal texts, either infusing enthusiasm to their readers, or deploring misconceptions about their books, denouncing injustices, and so far.

In a quite similar way, as it can be observed in Table 5.1, writers from the most remote period (1840–1859) use stronger words than those from more recent eras, judging by the mean scores their prefaces get with both tools. The decrease is neater when looking at the "sentiment score" obtained with Lingmotif and to the "polarity" calculated by TextBlob: both tools indicate thus that sentiment expressions tend to become less frequent over time.

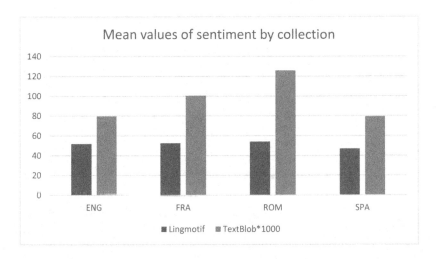

Figure 5.5 Mean values of sentiment by collection[16]

Table 5.1 Scores per period with each tool; see note 10 for the explanation of column heads and calculations

	Lingmotif		TextBlob	
	Sentiment score	Intensity score	Polarity	Subjectivity
T1	53.4	76.36	0.11	0.38
T2	50.14	72.37	0.10	0.40
T3	51.06	66.5	0.09	0.37
T4	51.16	75.19	0.08	0.38

In this respect, too, SA converges with the ideas one could draw from the mere count of prefaces, suggesting that, over time, prefaces get less buoyant. Lingmotif further supports this idea by calculating for T3 a lower score in terms of intensity of the expression, as compared to T2 and T1. Also, intensity of prefaces reaches during T4, a level comparable with T1, which comforts the idea that the turn of the century puts back into the light the liminal devices. However, this argument needs to be taken with some care, as the figures are not corroborated by the subjectivity score obtained with TextBlob, which singles out T2 in terms of involvement of the author with the situation or the ideas the preface conveys. Whatever the tool, T3 remains the period during which prefaces appear to have more undertones. A partial explanation can be found when crossing these figures with what we can see about the evolution of fictional prefaces (Table 5.2). Both tools calculate low sentiment and subjectivity scores for this kind of text, as if the voice of a character was taking the edge of the affirmations made in a liminal text. Since T3 is precisely the period during which the fictional preface is more prevalent (25% of the prefaces use this device vs. 10% in T1 or 8% in T4), its score is bound to be lower on both aspects.

Differently from our initial expectations, the orientation of the prefaces in terms of topicality, character anticipation, engagement, or contextualization does not translate to striking differences in sentiment scores. On all these aspects, the mean values group around 50 with Lingmotif ("slightly positive") or stay between 0.09 and 0.10 with TextBlob. The

Table 5.2 Scores per preface orientation (fictional/personal)

	Lingmotif		TextBlob	
	Sentiment score	Intensity score	Polarity	Subjectivity
Fictional	48.33	63.6	0.0938	0.34
Personal	52.06	75.12	0.101	0.39

Table 5.3 Scores per preface aspect

	Topicality	Character	Engagement	Context	Aesthetics
TB polarity*1000	10.66	9.73	10.48	9.83	10.86
LM polarity	49.72	49.90	48.53	51.45	50.29
TB subjectivity*1000	39.24	37.9	41.36	39.48	40.35
LM subjectivity	76.2	73.22	74.46	73.41	73.94

only concordance Table 5.3 allows to identify refers to prefaces mentioning one or several characters from the following novel: both tools award the lowest intensity/subjectivity scores for such texts, and even the lowest polarity score with TextBlob. In the meantime, it is quite surprising to observe that engaged prefaces are not among the "hottest" and that aesthetic considerations, when they appear, supersede the other prefatory foci in terms of sentiment expression and intensity.

A potential explanation is that the five above-mentioned aspects are always intertwined in prefaces. Thus, a more neutral presentation of a character may dilute the impact of an ideological stance expressed in the text, while topicality and aesthetic considerations may support each other. More generally, working with mean values compromises to a certain extent the identification of some strong prefaces in terms of sentiment expression and personal involvement of the writer: a very negative paragraph gets easily counterbalanced, mathematically speaking, by a more neutral one, but this does not mean that the impression the first one leaves to the reader is less prominent than the one produced by an entirely negative preface. A more fine-grained approach appears therefore necessary to observe how the authors play the sentiments in the liminal texts at the sentence level. This means abandoning Lingmotif for this last part of the chapter, since this tool does not calculate a score at the sentence level. Furthermore, in order to benefit both from the information brought by the polarity and by the indication given by the subjectivity, as calculated by TextBlob, we decide to create a "combined value" as a multiplication of the two.

Thanks to these last choices and calculations, it becomes possible to draw sentiment graphs text by text. Among many insights such an approach allows, this facilitates the identification of the strongest sentence in a preface, i.e. a sentence characterized both by a choice of words that conveys sentiments and by a significant subjective involvement. As an illustration, we can look at the following preface to the French novel *Jean-Christophe*.

The peak observed in Figure 5.6 corresponds to the following sentence: "C'est qu'il n'était pas seulement ma voix mais celle de mes amis" [it wasn't only my voice but also that of my friends too]. Romain Rolland uses it to explain the success of his book, a conveyor of a more general

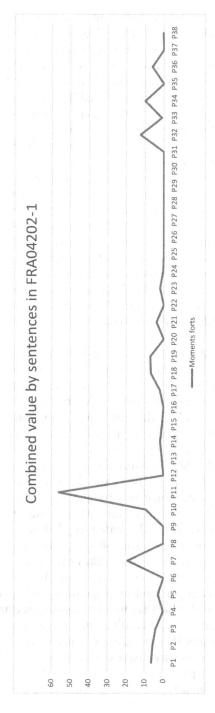

Figure 5.6 Sentiment graph in FRA04202-1

opinion, the expression of the people, and even the output of the best part of the nation. The higher combined value corresponds therefore to the main idea of the preface, offering a lens for interpreting the entire novel. A systematic reading of the sentences obtaining the highest combined value in all our prefaces leads to quite similar conclusions. Except for some short, exclamative sentences (e.g. "But alas!"),[17] the concerned portion of text is in all cases highly relevant for understanding the book, providing a kind of abstract of the following novel, focused either on its topics and main character, on an ethical or aesthetic principle driving the writing, or on the context in which it has been created.

Differently from what we expected, this new approach continues to put the engaged prefaces in a middle ground of sorts, in terms of their sentimental value. Sentences in particular, and prefaces as a whole,[18] discussing about the character and the topic of the work, get superior mean values to all the other potential foci. On the contrary, sentences about context continue to obtain the lowest scores, just as those calculated on the whole prefaces, even if they involve mentions of close relatives and friends, to which the author is very attached. In other words, fictional elements are presented in a more stringent, or appealing way, than ethical or contextual ones, something that has probably to do with the seductive function of the prefaces.

Thus, the identification of the strongest value appears rather as an indicator for defining, among other elements, the prefatorial strategy of writers. Three kinds of prefaces can be described with regard to the situation of the sentiment "peak": those situating the strongest sentence in the first part of the preface (roughly, the first third of the total number of sentences); those leaving the strongest sentence for the last part of the preface, and in some cases, for the very last sentence (e.g. ENG18841, SPA1012, ROM034); and finally, those in which the strongest sentence is to be found somewhere in the middle. In the first case, the preface draws the attention with a strong statement, which is subsequently explained and nuanced in quite a didactic manner. This is, for instance, the strategy adopted by Girardin in FRA02101, where the statement that love is a curse, occurs in the sixth sentence out of 273, the following (and much longer) part of the preface clarifying why the author makes such a sad and surprising affirmation. In the second case, the preface engages in a journey progressing toward a climax, creating a kind of suspense whose fulfillment through the strong affirmation is conducive to a favorable expectation with regard to the novel to come. Thus, *Vlasia*'s writer narrates a tortuous finding of a manuscript, placing the strongest sentence of the liminal text[19] just before concluding "this is why I have entitled this book *Vlasia or the new upstarts*." The third type of preface puts the reader in the situation of a treasure seeker: the main focus of the preface and, subsequently, one of the most interesting hints about the novel to come is somewhat hidden, challenging the analytical skills of the public. This is also corroborated by the fact that middle text strong sentences get a lower mean value (0.36) than similar phrases placed at the beginning (0.43) and at the end of the preface (0.40). A peak in the middle is less visible, and the corresponding prefaces appear a bit more puzzling with regard to their main foci. Data-driven, our finding improves upon Birke and Christ's typology of prefatorial functions: "interpretative," "commercial," and "navigational" (Birke and Christ 65–87).

Interestingly enough, the "didactic" preface (i.e. placing the strongest sentence at the beginning) is never the dominant strategy, whether looking by time slot or by collection. In this respect, T1 prefaces seem to prefer a climax toward the end (ratio 0.92),[20] while the following periods place the highest sentimental sentence in the middle (ratios between 0.5 and 0.66). Collection-wise, the French one and the English one display a preference for the first of these strategies, with ratios of 0.71 and 0.95, while the Spanish and the Romanian prefaces adopt rather the second (ratios of 0.59 and 0.61). These figures hide, however, important differences between the authors from the same country, and sometimes even between prefaces written by the same author for the same book,[21] inviting to project each preface on its historical and cultural background, a too individualized approach, which goes beyond the scope of the current contribution.

Conclusions

Our study about the novel's factory of opinions was designed as a methodological experiment. The small number of collections that we have taken into account and the shortcomings of the tools, neither trained on literary texts nor working on all envisaged languages, demand further work, aimed at enlarging and diversifying the corpus, at perfecting the tools, and at refining the analytical strategy. A specific training for performing sentiment analysis via further fine-tuning of language models offered by fastText[22] and BERT is promising leads. Also, a valuable complementary approach would consist in conducting an unsupervised classification of the liminal texts, so as to see if judgments made by manual annotators coincide with automatically generated labels, and to what extent the clustering proposed by the machine meets the subjective descriptions of prefaces in terms of orientation (topics, characters, context, etc.). So far, as shown above, only the aesthetic considerations formulated in a preface and the prefiguration of a character seem to have a specific effect on its sentiment profile, an observation that needs both to be consolidated by the study of a larger number of collections and to be better explained. In particular, the lack of a firm correlation between the SA profile of the preface, on the one hand, and the voice, topic, engagement, and specifications about the context in which the work has been conceived, on the other, needs to be deepened so as to understand if this is related to a structural inadaptation of the tool to the literary text, to the shortcomings of our methodology, or rather to the characteristics of the genre.

In spite of these limitations, some interesting regularities emerge regarding the liminal devices in the novels. Overall, prefaces appeared more numerous, more female-authored, and more polarized during the first time slot, even if the two last aspects (female authorship and polarization) are not necessarily linked. T2 and T3 are those of a certain lull in the prefatorial practices, translating both in lower numbers, and in little contrast with regard to the sentiment scores of the texts from these periods. At the end of the covered era, the preface becomes again a genre of interest, in which authors get more engaged, as shown both by the manual annotations and by the subjectivity trend calculated with the SA tools.

The limitations of the tools have impaired, to a certain extent, our deployment of sentiment analysis. However, the various scores we have calculated, especially that of the strongest sentence, can help with a distant reading of large collections, as well as with the identification of alternative or more fine-grained periods by the scholars in literary history. They need to be integrated with other stylometric methods, thus progressing toward a more comprehensive digital criticism framework.

Notes

1 https://distantreading.github.io/ELTeC/
2 eXtensible Markup Language (XML) is a standard for creating annotated documents that can be read both by humans and by machines, allowing the storage and the interchange of data. Text Encoding Initiative (TEI) is a specification of XML for text documents.
3 Epigraphs are quotations (or, in some cases, phrases with unclear authorship) placed at the beginning of a novel. To the difference to the dedications, they are not directed to a specific reader.
4 We provide the identifier of the novel in the corresponding ELTeC collection, insofar it allows retrieving easily all metadata related to a specific text, as well as access to the text itself.
5 Our initial analysis and annotation of liminal divisions can be found online at the following address [https://doi.org/10.5281/zenodo.7418386].
6 For example, in Silverio Lanza's *La rendición de Santiago*, we found two liminal texts and named them SPA4022-1 and SPA4022-2.
7 Lingmotif's web app is available at http://lingmotif.com
8 A sentence such as "N-am ce-ți trimite alt, fratele meu, pentru atâtea trude nesuferite, decât această simplă povestire a timpilor trecuți, în care-mi am găsit adesea refugiul, și am căutat să mă consolez de atâtea nevoi! [For such unbearable toils, I have nothing to send you, my dearest brother, except for this story of passed times, in which I found refuge often and I sought to be comforted

from so many needs!]" (ROM034) is annotated as conveying disgust, but the system does not take into consideration the fact that this sentiment is expressed in a subordinate sentence and therefore superseded by the positive sentiment expressed in the main clause.

9 Lingmotif does a segmentation of the text in ten equal parts but offers a global score; it is virtually possible to read from a graph the values attributed to a phrase, but the tool is clearly not meant to function this way. On the contrary, TextBlob works at sentence level only, with no aggregated score calculated for the whole; also, to the difference of Lingmotif, it does not underline the most important tokens justifying its decision to class a text as positive or negative. In the following study, TextBlob scores at the scale of a preface have been calculated as the arithmetic mean of the scores received by each sentence.

10 Lingmotif awards a sentiment score and an intensity score, on a scale from 0 to 100. TextBlob offers a polarity and a subjectivity score, on a scale from -1 to $+1$. In spite of the difference in scale, if a text obtains 10/100 with Lingmotif and -0.9 with TextBlob, it can be deemed very negative: the two tools concord in their analysis. It is important to note that we have met few cases of important discordance between the two tools. This is further supported by the correlation one can observe between the scores obtained with Lingmotif and those calculated with TextBlob. We obtain a correlation score of 0.29 (calculated with Pearson's test), which is low, but the p-value ($1.16*10^{-52}$) shows that this correlation is not coincidental. Also, the Pearson test yields much higher values for certain collections, such as the Spanish one (correlation: 0.61; p-value: $8.31*10^{-21}$).

11 This is at least the case for French literature: *La Recherche du temps perdu* by Proust, a true game changer in terms of novel writing, was first published in 1913 (and included in the ELTeC corpus). From this point of view, the timeslot spanning from 1900 to 1919 does not pertain any more to "the long 19th century," but rather to the 20th century.

12 The figures consider the disproportion between male and female writers as corpus contributors, with the first ones writing 2/3 of our ELTeC collections. We calculate the total number of liminal divisions containing prefatorial matter per gender (28 for the women, 64 for the men), divided by the total number of texts penned by author of each sex (124 vs. 272). In four cases, we do not know the author's gender.

13 This is the case in George Sand's *Horace*, for instance, the preface depicts an attitude that could be defined, with a modern term, as "masculine toxicity." The topic results here in a negative score with TextBlob, and a classification as "fairly negative" with Lingmotif.

14 The standard deviation is a measure of the dispersion of a set of values, by comparison with the mean value, and by taking into account the extreme values.

15 For instance, SPA1021, the most negative text for TextBlob, gets a score of 35 with Lingmotif, which puts it in the category of "fairly negative" (distinct of "very negative" and of "extremely negative"). The tools agree about the negativity of this text but do not situate it in the same region on their respective scales.

16 Since the scale for sentiment analysis is not the same in the two tools, we have multiplied the values obtained with TextBlob by 1000, so as to create comparability within the same graph. The score of 120 obtained by Romanian prefaces with TextBlob means that, in fact, Romanian prefaces obtain a score

of 0.12, as opposed to the French prefaces (0.10) or the Spanish ones (0.08). There are no values under 0, since we are dealing here with mean values.

17 This kind of sentence poses more largely the problem of the punctuation in sentiment analysis applied to literary texts. The quoted sentence has little semantic content in itself, but this is only because the hard punctuation (an exclamation mark) isolates it from the following sentence. With a comma ("But, alas, what a disappointment," ROM045-1), this short sentence would have become longer and more meaningful, fulfilling the task of anticipating on the contents of the novel and that of contextualizing its conception.

18 This distinction points toward the fact that two means have been calculated, both based on the combined value of the strongest sentence. First, we have looked at the correlation between the orientation of the sentence (is it talking about the characters? the topics? the context? etc.) and its combined value, then we looked at the correlation between the orientation of the preface (as annotated with yes/no on five aspects, see the methodological section) and the mean value of the strongest sentence. With the first approach, topic gets a score of 0.5, and character a score of 0.49. With the second one, topics are at 0.46 and characters at 0.44. In both cases, these values are the highest of the five aspects.

19 "To reach or approach this ideal, we all race to climb the ordeal of this world, sprinkling the path with our tears, sweat and blood, the rocks bleeding our feet, the thorns tearing our vestments!"

20 This ratio is calculated as follows. First, the ordinal number of each strong sentence is divided by the total number of sentences in the preface. For instance, the highest combined value for ENG18400 is obtained by the 9th sentence over a total of 18 sentences, which translates in a ratio of 0,5. Second, mean values for each time slot and for each collection are calculated based on these ratios.

21 The first preface of ROM025, *Misterele casatoriei*, places the strongest sentence in the middle (ratio 0.63). The second accentuates the very last sentence of the liminal text (ratio 1). Finally, prefaces to the third and fourth editions become didactic, with ratios of 0.22 and 0.32.

22 https://fasttext.cc/.

Works Cited

Anghelescu, Mircea. *O istorie descriptivă a literaturii române. Epoca premodernă.* Tracus Arte, 2019.

Arrington, Phillip, and Shirley K Rose. "Prologues to what is possible: introductions as metadiscourse." *College Composition and Communication*, vol. 38, no. 3, 1987, pp. 306–318.

Birke, Dorothee, and Birte Christ. "Paratext and Digitized Narrative: Mapping the Field." *Narrative*, vol. 21, no. 1, 2013, pp. 65–87.

Chartier, Roger. *The Author's Hand and the Printer's Mind: Transformations of the Written Word in Early Modern Europe.* Polity, 2014. https://www.deepl. com/translator.

Drace Francis, Alex. *Geneza culturii romane moderne. Instituțiile scrisului si dezvoltarea identității naționale (1700-1900).* Polirom, 2016.

Elkins, Katherine. *The Shapes of Stories. Sentiment Analysis for Narrative.* Cambridge UP, 2022.

Fang, X., and J. Zhan. "Sentiment Analysis Using Product Review Data." *Journal of Big Data*, vol. 2, no. 5, 2015, https://doi.org/10.1186/s40537-015-0015-2. Date of access: December, 15, 2022.

Gallerani, Guido Mattia, et al. "Le paratexte, trente ans après," *Interférences littéraires/Literaire interferenties*, n° 23, "Seuils/Paratexts, trente ans après," edited by Guido Mattia Gallerani, Maria Chiara Gnocchi, Donata Meneghelli, Paolo Tinti, 2019, pp. 1–14. http://www.interferenceslitteraires.be

Galleron, Ioana. Introduction. *L'art de la préface au siècle des Lumières*, edited by Iona Galleron. 2007. Presses universitaires de Rennes, 2016, pp. 1–26. https://books.openedition.org/pur/29081.

———. "Prefaces from 4 ELTEC subcorpora: original and English translations (Deep-L)." [Data set]. *Zenodo*, 2022. https://doi.org/10.5281/zenodo.7418634

Gascoigne, David. "Paratext Rules OK." *Masking Strategies. Unwrapping the French Paratext*, edited by Alistair Rolls and Marie-Laure Vuaille-Barcan. Peter Lang, 2011, pp. 13–27.

Genette, Gérard. *Palimpsests: Literature in the Second Degree*. Trans. by C. Newman and C. U of Nebraska P, 1997.

Kim, Evgeny, and Roman Klinger. "A Survey on Sentiment and Emotion Analysis for Computational Literary Studies." *Computation and Language*, 2018, July 11, 2022, https://arxiv.org/abs/1808.03137. Date of access: December, 15, 2022.

Klinger, Roman, et al. "Emotion Analysis for Literary Studies: Corpus Creation and Computational Modelling." *Reflektierte algorithmische Textanalyse: Interdisziplinäre(s) Arbeiten in der CRETA-Werkstatt*, edited by Nils Reiter. Axel Pichler and Jonas Kuhn, De Gruyter, 2020, pp. 237–268.

Moreno-Ortiz Antonio. "Lingmotif: a user-focused sentiment analysis tool." *Procesamiento del Lenguaje Natural*, vol. 58, 2017, pp. 133–140.

Moreno-Ortiz, Antonio, et al. "Análisis de sentimiento basado en corpus." *Lingüística de corpus/The Routledge Handbook of Spanish Corpus Linguistics*, edited by Giovanni Parodi, Pascual Cantos-Gómez and Chad Howe. Routledge, 2020, pp. 511–528.

Öhman, Emily, et al. "XED: A Multilingual Dataset for Sentiment Analysis and Emotion Detection." *Proceedings of the 28th International Conference on Computational Linguistics*, edited by the Association for Computational Linguistics, Barcelona, 2020, pp. 6542–6552.

Patras, Roxana, et al. "Thresholds to the 'Great Unread': Titling Practices in Eleven ELTeC Collections." *Interférences littéraires/Literaire interferenties*, edited by Chris Tanasescu, n° 25, 2021, pp. 163–187.

Peikola, Matti, and Birte Bös. "Framing Framing: The Multifaceted Phenomena of Paratext, Metadiscourse, and Framing." *The Dynamics of Text and Framing Phenomena. Historical Approaches to Paratext and Metadiscourse in English*, edited by Matti Peikola and Birte Bös, John Benjamins, 2020, pp. 3 33.

Ruokkeinen, Sirkku, and Aino Liira. "Material Approaches to Exploring the Borders of Paratext." *Textual Cultures*, vol. 11, no. 1–2 (2017 [2019]), pp. 106–129. DOI: 10.14434/textual.v11i1-2.23302.

Salmi, Hanna. "The Dynamics of Text and Framing Phenomena: Historical Approaches to Paratext and Metadiscourse in English." *The Dynamics of Text* and Framing Phenomena. *Historical Approaches to Paratext and Metadiscourse in English*, edited by Matti Peikola and Birte Bös. John Benjamins, 2020, pp. 187–207.

Schmidt, Thomas, et al. *Using Deep Learning for Emotion Analysis of 18th and 19th Century German Plays.* Melusina Press, 2021.

Schöch, Christof, et al. "Creating the European Literary Text Collection (ELTeC): Challenges and Perspectives." *Modern Languages Open*, vol. 1, no. 25, 2021. DOI: http://doi.org/10.3828/mlo.v0i0.364.

https://textblob.readthedocs.io/en/dev/

Vasilescu, Mircea. *"Iubite cetitoriule…": Lectură, public și comunicare în cultura română veche*, Paralela 45. Bucharest, 2001.

6 Reflective Modeling (Modeling What Would Be There)

A Critical, Creative, and Constructive Approach to Data Modeling

Jan-Erik Stange

Introduction

There is a long tradition of employing models as devices for generating knowledge both in science and the humanities. But while models in science have become more and more central to the scientific process, their use by humanities scholars has often been implicit or even denied (see Bod 79). This changed with the establishment of the digital humanities (DH), which made formalization and consequently modeling an essential premise for being able to conduct humanistic research with computational methods.

Willard McCarty refers to this circumstance as "computational tractability," which forces "us to confront the radical difference between what we know and what we can specify computationally" ("Modelling" 256). This particular kind of translation of knowledge into computable structures is usually referred to as *data modeling* in DH (see, e.g., Flanders and Jannidis, "Data Modeling"). In recent years a debate developed around the idiosyncrasies and epistemological premises of data modeling in DH, at times comparatively to other disciplines.

Generally, the view on data modeling in DH can be considered pragmatic, which is something DH has in common with the empirical sciences. A pragmatic view on models understands models as being representative *of* something (an object or part of an object under investigation) and being *for* something, so they are created with a certain function in mind (see Stachowiak; Mahr; Flanders and Jannidis, "Data Modelling"; McCarty, "Knowing").

Though there are views in DH describing all modeling as data modeling (see, e.g., Flanders and Jannidis, "Data Modeling"), for the sake of argument, in this chapter distinction will be made between different kinds of models: theoretical models and representational models. Representational models can be further differentiated according to their function as being either informational or pragmatic. Data models can be considered a specific form of pragmatic modeling.

DOI: 10.4324/9781003320838-9

There are differences in the way that representation is understood with regard to modeling. According to the *Stanford Encyclopedia of Philosophy*, models of data are a

> [...] corrected, rectified, regimented, and in many instances idealized version of the data we gain from immediate observation, the so-called raw data.
>
> (Suppes quoted in Frigg and Hartmann)

Such description of data models is characteristic of a practice-based scientific perspective. In that case, data is usually thought of as empirical data somewhat inherent to a situation and independent of the observer's perspective, a view also implied by the term "raw data." Accordingly, modeling is seen as an act of cleaning and optimizing the raw data, rather than a constructive activity. In reality, however, scientists usually implicitly model data from early on in the process, e.g., when selecting what (and how) is to be observed or measured in the first place, as has been discussed at length in recent years in areas such as the philosophy of science and science and technology studies.

While empirical scientists employ representations in order to represent empirical or statistical data describing certain aspects of an object or system (Gelfert), literature on data modeling in DH highlights the role individual scholars and their viewpoints play in the creation of data. Data modeling is described as a subjective, iterative, creative, and constructive process (see, e.g., Flanders and Jannidis, "Data Modelling;" Ciula and Eide; Ciula et al.).

Unlike in the empirical sciences, through the modeling activity itself, existing data is changed or completely new data is created (e.g., digital annotation in the tool CATMA creates a data structure of text segments that are defined by their start and end points in the text and by the tags assigned to them [Gius et al.]).

Nonetheless, if we look at the practice of modeling in DH, I argue that there is a gap between the claims made in the literature, on the one hand, and, on the other, the reality of the tools, their user interfaces, and visual representations whose epistemological foundations are stemming from the empirical sciences (see Drucker, "Visualization and Interpretation").

Therefore, drawing from design studies I suggest taking a look at the so-called reflective practice (Schön, "Reflective Practitioner") of design as an inspiration for data modeling tools. In design practice external visual representations like sketches, prototypes, and mock-ups play a central role in creative and critical thought especially at the beginning of the design process. In contrast to representations in science that claim to represent existing objects, these early stage design representations can be thought of as representing something that could at some point exist but does not have to. Therefore, by comparing numerous representations of possible outcomes, practitioners are able to critically evaluate these and identify the most promising ones. Donald Schön called this process a "reflective conversation with the situation" ("Reflective Practitioner," 90). It is enabled through a number of particular qualities these representations exhibit like indeterminacy or argumentation, for example, that support a circular process of alternation between part and whole that resembles the hermeneutic circle in literary studies (see, e.g., O'Toole).

If we take the above-mentioned two characteristics of models, representation and purposefulness, as a basis, we can call all data representations models, if they are instrumental in achieving certain goals. This is true for data visualizations as well, since they are representations that help make patterns in the data visible that would otherwise go unnoticed. However, current data modeling interfaces in DH and their visual representations do not exhibit most of the qualities necessary for reflective practice. I will get back to this point later in the chapter. On the other hand, data visualizations are often not understood as modeling devices, but rather as means of showing modeled results, similar to their use in the empirical sciences.

In this chapter I will take a look at the critical, creative, and constructive[1] qualities of external representations in design practice and examine their potential for what I call "reflective modeling" in digital user interfaces for data modeling in DH. I will start therefore with a short overview of perspectives on modeling in science and the (digital) humanities, outline the current state of the debate, and identify research desiderata. In the following section I will describe the characteristics of reflective practice in design and identify seven qualities that I deem essential and which, as I argue, could be beneficial to data modeling in DH as well. This will be followed by an elaboration on how these qualities could be implemented in a digital environment for modeling data, accompanied by examples of how current tools fall short in this regard. Finally, the application of these qualities will be demonstrated with an interactive mock-up for modeling corpus data of European plays in the subsequent section, followed by a conclusion.

Modeling in Science and DH

While the deployment of models has a long history especially in science, surprisingly, the terms model and modeling have not been the subject of debate in either science or the humanities for a long time. Gelfert situates the beginning of a systematic inquiry into the potentials and limitations of models in the nineteenth century and the philosophical interest in the epistemology of modeling even as late as the middle of the twentieth century (5).

Generally, theoretical and pragmatic perspectives on modeling can be differentiated. Theoretical views in turn can be separated into syntactical and semantic approaches. Both perspectives determine a dependency between theory and models, in which "models play a subsidiary role to theories" (Frigg and Hartmann).

The syntactic conception understands models as part of a logical system of sentences in a "metamathematical language" (Winther). Proponents of the semantic theoretical approach criticized them for "conflat[ing] scientific theories with their linguistic formulations" (Gelfert 12). With the introduction of semantic views, models slowly gain more traction in the discourse on scientific epistemology because here they play a more significant role as the "building blocks of which scientific theories are made up" (Frigg and Hartmann).

As a side effect of the spread of semantic approaches and their argumentation for a conception of models as representations, representation became a central topic of debate in the discourse on scientific theory (see, e.g., Frigg 3).

Influenced by empiricist epistemology many views in the philosophy of science range from an understanding of representations as depicting reality or the real-world and objective representations of particular systems to the idea of representations being user-dependent (Gelfert 26). What unites these conceptions is the idea that there is a represented entity that is independent from the act of representing it. Knuuttila criticizes the fact that the discourse has been rather ignorant toward other fields: "... [it] seems to me that the present discourse on scientific representation has remained a rather solitary enterprise. It has been first and foremost interested in how (and by virtue of what) models represent reality" (14). She suggests not to lose track of research conducted in other areas like cognitive science, philosophy of mind, and especially science and technology studies, where the use of models and representations has been studied extensively since the 1980s (Knuuttila 14). Laboratory studies and cognitive science in particular put an emphasis on the central role of artifacts in the production of knowledge in scientific work (see, e.g., Latour and Woolgar; Giere; Pickering). Such artifacts have also been referred to as "epistemic things" or "epistemic objects" (Rheinberger; Knorr-Cetina).

With respect to theoretical approaches to modeling, Knuuttila argues that contrary to prevailing claims both syntactic and semantic approaches assign a rather subordinate role to models (39). While syntactic and semantic views understand models primarily as representations of already established theoretical knowledge, there have been attempts to define models in a more pragmatic perspective in mathematics and computer science. Stachowiak, for example, defines models as having three characteristics: 1. They represent an object ("Abbildungsmerkmal"), 2. They represent only selected aspects of the object ("Verkürzungsmerkmal"), and, finally, 3. They always serve a particular purpose ("Pragmatisches Merkmal") (131ff.). Similarly, Mahr speaks of models being *of* and *for* something (11f.).

The way that representation has been commonly understood in science and philosophy for a long time has also been referred to as representationalism: The notion that objects in the real world cannot be perceived directly, but rather through mental images that represent them. In this view what is being represented is an observer-independent objective reality. In her book *Meeting the Universe Halfway*, Karen Barad describes, how the separation between representation and the represented has been criticized in poststructuralist and performative approaches:

> Performative approaches call into question representationalism's claim that there are representations, on the one hand, and ontologically separate entities awaiting representation, on the other, and focus inquiry on the practices or performances of representing, as well as the productive effects of those practices and the conditions for their efficacy. A performative understanding of scientific practices, for example, takes account of the fact that knowing does not come from standing at a distance and representing but rather from a direct material engagement with the world.
>
> (28)

Her own concept of "agential realism" draws on theories of performativity but supplements them with a special attention to the materiality of represented entities, particularly in the way she foregrounds the role of matter in the process of materialization.

With an increasing amount of cultural artifacts available in digital form, data modeling in DH has grown into an important part of the scholarly process. An awareness of the ontological and epistemological premises of modeling and models only recently became a subject of discussion, however. Since DH also incorporates digital tools and methods into its practice that have their origins in science, scholars risk to borrow the latter's ontology and epistemology along with those tools and methods. Data visualization is such an example, as it involves representations of empirical or statistical data that have been adopted for use in DH without questioning the underlying epistemological assumptions. These representations then model data in a way that is similar to epistemic practice in science. For example, typical network diagrams used in science depict relationships between entities as simple lines. These lines inform the viewer about the existence or absence of a relationship; they do not provide further information as to the quality of the relation. In the humanities, however, such information can be fundamental for interpretation.

Johanna Drucker has been referring to such visualizations as a kind of "intellectual Trojan Horse, a vehicle through which assumptions about what constitutes information swarm with potent force" (1).

Though discourse on models and representations within DH recognizes the need for the development of a specific (conceptual) framework for modeling in DH, postmodernist or feminist views expressed by scholars like Johanna Drucker or Karen Barad have not been discussed more widely in the community. In recent years, however, there seems to be a new awareness of such topics (see, for example, Mandell; Bode).

While critical perspectives remain a marginal phenomenon in DH, there seems to be a prevalence of pragmatic attitudes toward modeling in the literature, evidenced by the aforementioned characterization of models as being *of* something and being *for* something (for example, McCarty 255; Ciula and Eide 9; Tversky) with a special focus on the aspects of *modeling for*. This is also mirrored by an increasing interest in the field of laboratory studies and the agency of artifacts on individuals as well as on networks of actors in processes of knowledge production. In the past recent years, there have been several initiatives to conceptualize and situate work in DH as laboratory practice. As a result of these efforts, several labs came into existence (see Pawlicka-Deger for an overview).

Attributes typically used in describing modeling in DH literature are "subjective," "constructive," "creative," "iterative," and "explorative" (see, e.g., Flanders and Jannidis, "Data Modelling"; Ciula et al., McCarty, "Modelling"; Flanders and Jannidis, "Shape of Data") elucidating that the DH community expects more from modeling than representation alone.

As a contribution to a pragmatic understanding of modeling combining the *of* and the *for*, Ciula and Eide have proposed a semiotic perspective drawing on the work of Kralemann and Lattmann, and Elleström. In this view, the authors claim, external representations assume the role of icons in the Peircean sense of the term,[2] and therefore, modeling can be understood "as a strategy to make sense (signification) via practical thinking (creating and manipulating models)" (Ciula and Eide 34). While this take on modeling seems promising indeed, Ciula and Eide remain short on what this "practical thinking" would actually look like. A look at another discipline might be helpful here: modeling in design practice. Thus, in the next section I will describe the kind of subjective, critical, creative, and constructive modeling employed in design processes referred to as "reflective practice" (Schön, "Reflective Practitioner") that proceeds in a circular, explorative fashion.

These explications will then serve as a basis for the user-interface-design principles for modeling in DH advanced in the subsequent section.

Reflective Practice in Design as a Hermeneutic Process Involving External Representations

The Interplay Between the Mind and External Representations in Reflective Modeling

Modeling plays a fundamental role in design practice and is used for communicative and pragmatic purposes, just as in science. However, its function and nature differ from the ones it has in science, as we will see in this section.

Usually, what is referred to as *models* are representations of products or architecture of already advanced or finalized designs. These could be physical scale models or 3D architectural models and objects created in rendering software. The purpose of such models is communication, be it as part of a presentation before the client toward the end of a project or for internal coordination within an organization. Ordinarily, such models are used for approving the results of a long design process, including several iterations and consultations with a client. At this point in the process, it is rather uncommon for clients to question the design concept and designers would in most cases be genuinely surprised if they did (such incidents do happen nevertheless, judging by the popularity of anecdotes among designers addressing this topic). In most cases, the alterations to such models will be minimal.

There are, however, other visual representations employed earlier in the design process that are not called models but would qualify as such in the sense of the above-mentioned definition of being representative *of* something and used *for* something. Such representations distinguish themselves by their indeterminacy, uncertainty, or ambiguity (see, e.g., Schön, "Reflective Practitioner" 156; Fish and Scrivener 120–5; Hasenhütl 345; Cross 92). In the literature it is predominantly the sketch that is described as exhibiting these attributes, and to a lesser degree prototypes and mock-ups. It is through these attributes that they prove themselves valuable to the design process because they facilitate exploration. In that regard they are similar to the "epistemic objects" of scientific practice as described in laboratory studies. Knorr-Cetina speaks, for example, of a "lack in completeness of being" and a "tendency to unfold indefinitely" typical of epistemic objects. She goes on:

> [T]hey continually acquire new properties and change the ones they have. But this also means that objects of knowledge can never be fully attained, that they are, if you wish, never quite themselves.
>
> (Knorr-Cetina 181)

However, sketches and other visual representations involved in the design process exhibiting indeterminacy seem to have another characteristic making them valuable for designers: They promote a conversation with the material. Donald Schön speaks of having a "reflective conversation with the materials of a situation" (Schön, "Reflective Conversation" 5). Schön's concept of design situations is based on John Dewey's more general understanding of situations of practice[3] as "not problems to be solved but problematic situations characterized by uncertainty, disorder, and indeterminacy" (Schön, "Reflective Practitioner" 25), which are "apprehend[ed] through the experience of worry, trouble or doubt" (410). In his work *Logic: the Theory of Inquiry*, John Dewey defines the transformation of an indeterminate situation of practice into a determinate situation as "inquiry":

> Inquiry is the controlled or directed transformation of an indeterminate situation into one that is so determinate in its constituent distinctions and relations as to convert the elements of the original situation into a unified whole.
>
> (Dewey 104)

In order to understand why designers need representations that allow for conversation, it is helpful to take a look at the special kinds of problems designers usually try to solve.

In design studies, there seems to be consensus that designers deal with "Wicked Problems," a term coined by design theoretician Horst Rittel (Rittel and Webber). Such problems are characterized by a lack of a clear definition, complex interdependencies, and contradictory and changing requirements. Such problems cannot be solved by applying a rational, linear problem-solving approach. Problem definition and solution strategy are closely intertwined: "The information needed to *understand* the problem depends upon one's idea for *solving* it" (Rittel and Webber 161).

This has implications for approaching these kinds of problems. Since such problems can only be better understood and defined by trying out different solution strategies, designers iteratively work on finding a proper problem-solution pair that solves the issue in a manner that produces the most benefits (Rittel and Webber 162).

Dorst compares the design process to scientific reasoning and argues that in "productive thinking" (i.e., design practice) the reasoning pattern is "abduction." This is in contrast with the reasoning patterns of deduction and induction, where, in the first case, we know the *what* and *how* of a situation enabling us to predict *results*, and in the second, we know the *what* and the observed *results* of a situation allowing us to infer the *how* (Dorst 523). In design practice, Dorst continues, the initial situation is a little different, insofar as there are no *results* to be observed or obtained but rather *values* to be achieved by creating something new. He then differentiates between two forms of abduction. In the first one the *values* and the *how*, i.e., the working principles, are known, in the second only the *values* aimed for. Designers thus have to define the *what* and the *how* of the situation. According to Dorst, experienced designers make use of so-called frames in order to develop problem-solution pairs. The process of framing is exemplified by the "key thesis": "IF we look at the problem situation from this viewpoint, and adopt the working principle associated with that position, THEN we will create the value we are striving for" (Dorst 525). Like Rittel and Webber, Dorst describes an iterative process, in which the designer comes up "with proposals for the 'what' and 'how,' and test[s] them in conjunction" (Dorst 525).

Schön describes this process of reflective practice by means of an example, in which reflective conversation takes place between a student in architecture and a teacher. The student explains the problems she is confronted with in developing her design concept for an elementary school. As Schön describes it, in a constant oscillation between drawing and talking, the teacher reframes the problem as he deems the student's framing inadequate. Through drawing, the teacher conducts a "web of moves" that together form "experiments" that lead to unintended consequences and shifts in meaning. The result is a new understanding of the situation and the potential for additional reconceptualizations. Schön speaks of a situation that "talks back" ("Reflective Practitioner" 156). Consequences arising from earlier actions are judged based on

> whether they [the practitioners] can solve the problem they have set; whether they value what they get when they solve it [...], whether they achieve in the situation a coherence of artifact and idea, a congruence with their fundamental theories and values; whether they can keep inquiry moving.
>
> ("Reflective Practitioner" 166)

For this conversation to be effective, the designer has to be able to work in a kind of test environment that Schön calls a "virtual world, a constructed representation of the real world of practice." According to him, reflective practice is dependent on this virtuality, which, being "rapid and spontaneous," reduces or eliminates certain "real-life" constraints while focusing on others. Virtuality leads to a situation, where "[n]o move is irreversible" ("Reflective Practitioner" 185f.).

Like Schön, Goldschmidt, Fish, and Scrivener speak of "seeing as" and "doing as" to describe the act of reframing a situation. Designers do this by drawing on their past experience to create frames, which they try to adapt to the situation at hand, i.e., they change the visual representation according to a frame and assess the consequences, as described above. The frame they have chosen determines the problem but also suggests a certain strategy for approaching a solution.

While Schön's description of reframing seems rather abstract, there have been attempts to characterize the interplay between external representations (sketches in particular) and mental images. Fish and Scrivener characterize sketches as "records of a sequence of attentive acts combining information from our eyes with images generated from memory" (118f.). It is exactly the particular qualities of sketches that allow this back-and-forth. According to them, there are three qualities (Fish and Scrivener 118f.):

1 Indeterminacy or ambiguity
2 Use of abbreviated sign systems to represent three-dimensional experience
3 Use of selective and fragmentary information

Goldschmidt uses the term "dialectics" to characterize the alternation of the two modes of "seeing as" and "seeing that," when designers are sketching:

> The designer is 'seeing as' when he or she is using figural, or 'gestalt' argumentation while 'sketch-thinking.' When 'seeing that,' the designer advances nonfigural arguments pertaining to the entity that is being designed. The process of sketching is a systematic dialectics between the 'seeing as' and 'seeing that' reasoning modalities.
>
> (Goldschmidt 131)

This circular process of approaching a good fit between problem definition and solution strategy might remind us of another process commonly described as circular: the hermeneutic circle and interpretation in the humanities more generally. And indeed, there have been attempts of likening the design process to the process of hermeneutic interpretation. Snodgrass and Coyne drawing on Gadamer's ideas on dialogical understanding argue that interpretation in the humanities as well as designing are characterized by a "dialectical process of question and answer" (77). They also highlight the many parallels between terms used in hermeneutics and terms used in design studies contributions such as Donald Schön's "The Reflective Practitioner." Schön, for example, describes a circular process of alternating between whole and part, of projected preunderstandings of a whole whose consequences on the parts (the particulars of a design situation) are then evaluated, which leads to new understandings and new projections and so forth:

> Designers come to the design situation with a pre-understanding of what the designed artefact will be. Even as they begin to examine the 'text' of the design situation—the parameters that 'define' it—they have a pre-understanding, a vague projection of the completed product. As they proceed with their interpretation and as their understanding increases by way of an interpretation of the parts, the projected whole is modified, refined, and clarified. This process is fluid, repetitive and continuous. It furnishes a kaleidoscope of ever-changing reflections, revisions, false starts and back-tracking, leading eventually to a clarification of the projection.
>
> (Snodgrass and Coyne 81)

It is exactly this similarity between designing and interpretation that leads me to believe that an investigation into the conditions that enable reflective conversations might prove valuable for the design of reflective modeling environments.

In our earlier research, Kleymann and I explored the role of, and proposed guidelines for, developing data visualizations based on hermeneutic assumptions and for hermeneutic purposes. These guidelines, which are explicitly based on epistemological premises of hermeneutic theory and thus rooted in a literary studies perspective, can be followed in transforming traditional data visualizations into hermeneutic visualizations.

In this chapter, however, I am approaching the problem from a different angle: Because of the similarity between reflective and hermeneutic practice and the potential of reflective practice to enable a creative, constructive, and critical modeling process, I am looking more closely at the material designers are working with and the techniques they rely on in shaping the material in specific ways.

The goal of this endeavor is to identify characteristics of reflective situations that can serve as principles for designing digital user interfaces enabling DH scholars to model in a reflective manner. These principles could then support the design of individual interface elements as well as their interplay in such a modeling environment. Thus, on the one hand, by drawing on the material-related hermeneutics implicit in design per se, this chapter takes a broader approach to the feasibility and prospects of hermeneutic practice in digital environments. On the other hand, it provides specific principles for designing and combining interface elements conducive to manipulating and structuring the digital material—i.e., the data—of the modeling situation (understood in the above-mentioned definition by Dewey as a "problematic situation").

Characteristics of Reflective Practice

I contend that there are seven main qualities that are characteristic and drive the process of reflective practice in design. In the following I will introduce them and explain why they are beneficial to the design process. These qualities, as described in the literature, are usually referring to design practice in the analog world. This means that the material and the tools used for shaping the material are of physical nature, whereas, in the case of data modeling, we are dealing with bits and bytes. There have been, however, attempts of transferring reflective design practice into the digital. Looking at insights gained from these studies might prove valuable (as further argued below).

Indeterminacy

In all accounts describing reflective practice or, more general, creative interaction with external visual representations, indeterminacy or uncertainty is of central importance. Indeterminacies such as gaps (e.g., lines left out of sketches) generate ambiguities requiring creativity on the part of the designers who need to fill them with their imagination. Fish and Scrivener see the value of indeterminate sketches in their ability to "preserve alternatives": "Because the parts of a composition are visually interdependent, an artist may invent signs to represent global structure without specifying detail prematurely" (120). They further specify that "[...] in sketching it is important to omit denotational marks that may hinder imagery movement and that it is necessary to leave space within the sketch for its imagery components" (Fish and Scrivener 124).

Schön describes it in a more abstract way, as he only refers to the situation in general: "The unique and uncertain situation comes to be understood through the attempt to change it, and changed through the attempt to understand it" ("Reflective Practitioner" 154).

It is the indeterminacy that allows designers to fuse visual representations with their mental representations, so that the phenomenon to be modeled can be reframed iteratively until a coherent framing is achieved that aligns a stated problem with a certain solution strategy. Each iteration leads to new situations of ambiguity, forcing designers to question their preunderstanding and preconceived notions and keeping the conversation going. Maintaining ambiguity through indeterminacy is important in order to not "crystallize ideas too early and freeze design development" (Goel 193).

Selectivity

"Virtuality," as Schön calls it, makes it possible to focus on certain aspects of a design situation without interfering with other parts. In the context of prototypes as visual representations Lim et al. speak of "filtering dimensions" to describe the possibility of focusing on "particular regions within an imagined or possible design space" that gives designers the chance to screen "out unnecessary aspects of the design" (Lim et al. 3).

They further elaborate: "For example, a two-dimensional prototype of a three-dimensional building can help us to determine the spatial relationship of the rooms, without placing any constraints on the materials used for walls and floors" (Lim et al. 7).

By employing external representations, virtuality makes it possible to focus on partial understandings of a problem, for which partial solutions can be developed. These partial solutions in turn allow designers to further understand the problem, which again leads to new rounds of partial solutions and so on (Yamamoto and Nakakoji 516).

Developing the whole and the parts is tightly interconnected: A preunderstanding of the whole at any time is projected and formulated in individual parts. Working on the parts and their interrelations then leads to a new understanding of the whole in turn and new projections and so forth. The design process is determined by a sequence of "constant revisions" that lead to an increasing understanding of the whole situation (Snodgrass and Coyne 81).

Unrestrictedness

External representations like sketches afford quick and effortless changes to the material enabling designers to create situations that would be too complex or expensive to model with the materials intended to be used in the finished object. For example, architects can experiment with certain shapes for buildings on paper or in simple physical and digital models and explore a design space without actually having to build anything. Generally, the threshold to experiment and try out things has to be low, if a conversation with the situation is supposed to unfold. This has been referred to as "viscosity" in the context of programming languages and describes the amount of work users have to invest in order to change something (Green and Petre 35).

Immediacy

The typical design situation is a sequence of iterations of trying things out and observing how the situation responds to it. Therefore, it is often a matter of being able to develop and compare as many alternatives as possible in a given period of time to determine a good fit between problem and solution. By using a pencil on paper, designers can observe the effects of their actions instantly without any delay. In this way, the fast exploration of alternatives is supported by activities like sketching because they allow quick formulations followed by immediate evaluations of design ideas (Resnick et al. 2; Goldschmidt 123).

Reversibility

Since designers deliberately work with external visual representations that can be easily manipulated, they can freely explore different design options without risking to do any irreversible damage. The cost of erasing strokes in a sketch, discarding sketches or prototypes completely and starting over is relatively low compared to remodeling buildings, for example. In that sense, as Schön describes it, "[n]o move is irreversible" (Schön, "Reflective Practitioner" 185f.). Fish and Scrivener point out that it is precisely "the need to foresee the results of the synthesis or manipulation of objects without actually executing such operations" (Fish and Scrivener 117) that make sketches such an important tool for designers and artists.

Argumentation

All accounts of creative design practice describe the process as a communication between designer and the material that occurs when "moving an idea out into the world" (Lim et al. 9). For example, Schön speaks of "conversation" and "back-talk" ("Reflective Practitioner"), Goldschmidt uses the terms "dialectics," "dialogue," and "argument" (Goldschmidt), and Snodgrass and Coyne mention a "dialogical cycle of question and answer" (83) to characterize the process. For Goldschmidt, these arguments are short sequences in the process of design that can either be characterized as "seeing that" or "seeing as" (138). While "seeing that" describes the critical or reflective examination of configurations present in the external representation that often trigger the questioning of preconceived notions, "seeing as" can be understood as a reinterpretation of such configurations that then may lead to new sketching activity and changes in the representation, enabling another round of "seeing that" and "seeing as" and so on. With such visual experiments designers are testing if certain configurations work with respect to the context of the design situation. Therefore, it is of central importance that the medium they are working in allows them to easily try out different approaches, compare them with each other, and decide which of these alternatives provides the most coherent solution to the specific problem.

Preunderstanding

The circular nature of the design process is of fundamental importance and relies heavily on the ability of visual representations to represent indeterminacy and uncertainty and to allow designers to interact with representations without restrictions. Although it is enabled particularly by these qualities, its success is also dependent on the material and information available at the start.

As explained above, at the beginning of a design process, the situation may not be fully understood by the designer. Often it is only the briefing handed to them by the client, maybe some additional material and the designers' own experience from other projects that are available to them. It seems the better the preliminary understanding of the situation is, the better will the starting point of the reflective conversation be and the easier will it be for designers to make progress in their endeavor.

In the next section I will investigate how these qualities can be reproduced in a digital environment for modeling.

Reflective Modeling and Data as Material

In reflective practice designers move the design forward by interacting with and manipulating the materials of a design situation. Since we are interested in applying qualities of reflective practice to data modeling in a digital environment, we have to ask if digital data and software in general can be considered to possess material properties.[4] In line with Hutchby's conception regarding technological materiality as being defined by its "affordances" (Gibson cited in Hutchby), I argue that digital data in a modeling environment can also be understood as material. This is exemplified by the fact that it exhibits affordances relevant to specific goals and contexts of users working in such environments (447f.).

In the following paragraphs I propose strategies for implementing qualities of reflective practice in a digital modeling environment and describe how existing DH visualization tools fall short in this regard. The overarching goal of these strategies is, as explained in the preceding section, to enable scholars to have a reflective conversation with the modeling situation. When conducting such a translation, we have to keep in mind that the process is two-fold: It involves not only the translation from analog to digital, but it is also the translation from one form of representation to another. Sketches are representations that have a pictorial relationship to the represented, while, when representing data, we are mainly interested in the relations between data entities, and therefore, the representation can be called diagrammatic.

Indeterminacy

Indeterminacy in sketches is expressed with respect to the shape of the represented object. Since visual representations of data (or short: data visualizations) represent relations, indeterminacy and uncertainty have to be thought of in terms of the relations between data entities. Relations between entities are represented by so-called visual variables (Bertin) and with the help of the Gestalt laws. Visual variables are, for example, size, position, shape, color hue, color intensity, brightness, orientation, movement. Gestalt laws (or principles) describe how humans perceive patterns in their visual environment. For example, objects that are close together are perceived as belonging to the same group (the law of proximity).[5] All of these can be used to compare qualitative (i.e., nominal or categorical) or quantitative (numerical) values. Indeterminacy and uncertainty can be represented by the visual variable itself, for example, by using fuzziness, blurriness, or animation between different states to express a number or range of values for a certain entity. It can also be represented by displaying possible configurations of the data in parallel, providing different affordances[6] for users to consider and compare, and continue their exploration. Their role is to ensure and make apparent the fact that there is more than one way of representing the data and we have to be careful not to rely too much on one particular result. (For example, different temporal binnings could be suggested and their effect shown visually: How does the visualization change, if I look at 50-year-spans instead of 100-year-spans? What other patterns emerge?)

Existing DH visualization tools like *Palladio*[7] or *NodeGoat*[8] offer a multitude of different visualizations that can be compared, but these visualizations usually only represent the model of the data as it existed in the input data file (e.g., *Palladio* and *NodeGoat*) without providing the means of changing the model by manipulating the visualization. *Voyant Tools*[9] automatically creates data models from text files that are structured according to the formats different data visualizations expect. For example, for a visualization called *collocates graph*, the software analyzes which words occur together in the same context and creates a graph connecting words that frequently occur together. The context is defined by a figure that indicates the number of words before and after a particular word and can be changed by users with a slider resulting in different graph representations. However, the arbitrariness of the context selection is not represented by the data visualization, which could as well, for example, represent a model that looks at the average distances between occurrences of words within other words' contexts (we might call this "degrees of collocation"). These distance measures could then be represented by positioning words that are on average closer together in the text and closer together in the visualization.

Selectivity

Practitioners working with sketches often decide to focus on partial problems of a design situation. For example, the purpose of a sketch in architectural design might be to figure out the spatial relationships between rooms in a building. A prototype's role in the product design process might be to explore the ergonomics of the planned product. These visual representations are stripped-down versions of the planned product that consciously omit details that are not relevant to the targeted problem.

In a digital data modeling environment, such selectivity can be facilitated by giving users the ability to visually represent only some properties of the dataset relevant to a research question, to filter out various dimensions of the represented data, and to hand-pick data subsets that emerge as interesting clusters (for example, by drawing a circle around them). Such subsets can then be further explored with other visual representations toward a better understanding, otherwise harder to achieve when analyzing for instance the dataset as a whole.

Dataset filtering is a common function in existing tools (e.g., *Palladio* and *Gephi*[10]) and the information that is shown by the visualization can be adjusted to show only particular properties, a really helpful aspect in exploring the data. However, (inter)actions (or interactive actions) such as filtering out data dimension(s) usually model the data directly, which will show in the visualization per se as well. In that case, the visualization is not conducive to modeling the data in and of itself. Interacting with the visualization directly, and having the possibility to select subsets of it that way, would have the benefit of making possible focusing on sections of the data that cannot be filtered out since subsets are not defined by dimensionality but rather by content.

Unrestrictedness

Accompanying the increasing performance of personal computers and the development of ever more sophisticated graphical user interfaces from the 1990s on, there have been attempts at reproducing analog situations of reflective practice in digital environments, some of which have already been quoted in other contexts (see Schön, "Reflective Conversation"; Fish and Scrivener; Resnick et al.; Yamamoto and Nakakoji). An important requirement for such environments has been the fact that they should be as simple as possible (Resnick et al. 7) and that practitioners should feel as if they were interacting with representations directly, not with a computer, which should "stay invisible to the user" (Yamamoto and Nakakoji 523). Since digital visualizations can only represent data visualizations (e.g., a straight line needs at least the x and y coordinates of its start and end points in order to be digitally visualized), it is not hard to imagine that the represented data is indeed the data a scholar is using for her or his modeling activities. The points of the line could, for example, represent actors in a network diagram, while the line signifies a certain relationship between these actors. Dragging the points closer to or further away from each other, and, consequently, changing the length of the line in order to qualify the closeness of the relationship, would then have a direct effect on the data behind it. While the visual representation ensures an overview of the whole dataset, this local manipulation of the data can then be critically evaluated with respect to its impact on the dataset as a whole.

Recent web applications with modern GUIs have evolved into tools that are much easier to use than early DH desktop applications, Python scripts, or even command-line tools. However, in most cases, the interaction is conducted by taking a detour through interface elements controlling the visualization (see, e.g., *Gephi*). In the case of reflective modeling though, the possibility to interact directly with the visual representation is a must.

Immediacy

As specified in the "Reflective Practice in Design as a Hermeneutic Process Involving External Representations" section, for reflective conversations to be possible, actions undertaken should have an immediate impact. This is an established principle of graphical user interfaces, called "direct manipulation" (Shneiderman), and has been introduced by Ben Shneiderman in the field of human-computer interaction (HCI). An environment for reflective modeling should support this principle by immediately and constructively representing a modeling operation's impact on the visualization as well as the data, thus providing visual and textual feedback for critically assessing whether the operation is in line with a scholar's research question or not.

While most GUI-based visualization tools in DH offer "direct manipulation" and show changes made to the visualization immediately (like visually representing the changes made to a filter in *Palladio*, for example), there usually is no back-channel that connects the visualization to the data that would allow modeling data via the visualization and evaluate the results of such operations right away.

Reversibility

When it comes to reversing actions, it seems a digital environment is particularly well-suited to enable this functionality. In software applications being able to "undo" actions has become a standard feature and there are expert applications making it possible to view a history of recent actions and returning to previous versions of the files at hand. Software versioning has been an established practice especially in the area of software development since the 1970s.

Since we want the interaction with the user interface to be as effortless as possible; we need to make sure that spontaneous modeling experiments can be conducted without breaking the flow of the reflective conversation. For this reason, trying out things and returning to earlier states should be a natural part of the interaction with the user interface and work as fluidly as erasing strokes from a sketch with an eraser.

Many DH visualization tools offer a way of undoing actions, although this is not always as easy as clicking an "undo"-button (see, e.g., *Gephi*). They do not, however, offer a history of actions undertaken in the interface (something we are familiar with in the case of tools like *Open Refine*,[11] for example) that can be individually revisited to return to earlier states.

Argumentation

The most important part for enabling a reflective conversation is the indeterminacy and uncertainty of the representation that allows to interpret and explore the material in different ways.

Since indeterminacy and uncertainty lead to ambiguity in the representation, it is usually possible to argue for different approaches to modeling. Ideally, a digital modeling interface allows scholars to easily create, compare, and discard various modeled configurations. This is first and foremost a feature crucial to the scholars themselves, but it is also important for communicating with others, like presenting the modeling process to an academic audience, for example.

To explore a design space creatively means trying out as many approaches as possible. In design, sometimes practitioners have to start from scratch, other times they build on something already in place and create variations of it. The digital modeling environment should therefore allow to represent the history of the actions undertaken within various approaches. This would give practitioners a chance to navigate across approaches, critically compare them, revisit prior actions, and use them as a starting point for new approaches, thus iteratively developing an account of the exploration of possible models.

Furthermore, modeling strategies should not be prescribed by the design of the modeling environment's user interface but allow for different approaches. As Yamamoto and Nakakoji remark with respect to the design of user interfaces more generally: "[T]he interaction design influences people's problem-solving processes because it changes the nature of the problem. A certain interaction design may lead some people into taking a certain problem-solving strategy even if other, more efficient strategies are available" (Yamamoto and Nakakoji 516).

Common DH visualization tools feature neither an action history nor any versioning functionality for following various modeling paths in parallel, comparing them, and picking a particular approach while leaving others behind.

Preunderstanding

Oftentimes, the data modeling process is informed by the output of algorithms not created by the scholars themselves. This means that there is some kind of "raw data"[12] at the start of the reflective conversation that is structured according to some algorithmic logic that is not necessarily in line with a particular hermeneutic research question. If that is the case, a user interface can provide options for pre-structuring the data, to ease the process for scholars to get into a reflective conversation with the data and avoid blank page anxiety. Such pre-structuring can, for example, be based on a machine learning algorithm that identifies potential affinities between data entities.

In some DH visualization tools, textual data is automatically transformed to meet the input requirements of various visualizations (which is the case, for instance, as detailed above with *Voyant Tools*). Such data models can of course be in line with a research question by accident. In most cases, however, the modeled data will not trigger a preunderstanding of the modeling situation.

In the next section I will demonstrate the application of two of the above-enumerated principles in an early stage prototype of an environment for, what I call, *reflective modeling*. This will be followed by an outlook on how the remaining principles could also be incorporated into the prototype's user interface.

Case in Point: DraCor Reflective Modeling

The prototype developed within the context of this research is based on use cases in digital literary studies (DLS), specifically corpus analysis. It uses data provided by the *DraCor* platform, a collection of mostly European plays encoded in Text Encoding Initiative (TEI). *DraCor* provides access to metadata of all the corpora via an API, allowing users to extract slices of corpora depending on their research questions, a concept that the operators of this platform call "Programmable Corpora" (Fischer et al.).

In the prototype that I am going to present here, I used the German drama corpus, which has been extracted from the API in a CSV table format. The dataset consists of 592 plays spanning a time period from 1650 to 1947. Each play occupies one row of the above-mentioned table with 33 columns, each of which represents a certain data dimension. These data values fall into different categories like general information (e.g., first author, title, subtitle, year premiered, genre), calculated network metrics (e.g., density, average degree, average path length), and other metrics that could be easily derived from the TEI structure (number of male/female speakers, number of acts/segments, number of words spoken).

The Prototype

The long-term goal of the prototype is to demonstrate what data modeling as a reflective practice in DLS could look like. It is work-in-progress, and at this stage of the development, it already offers some of the features that I presented above as imperative for reflective practice. More will be added in the future and I will provide more specific details in that respect at the end of this chapter and in the conclusion.

The main part of the user interface is a map area, where individual plays appear as little circles. The circles are positioned on the map according to their similarity to the other plays. This similarity is calculated by T-SNE (t-distributed Stochastic Neighbour Embedding [van der Maaten and Hinton]), a dimensionality reduction algorithm that calculates the pairwise distance between different entities with many dimensions. On the left side of the map area, a listbox allows users to select the dimensions they want to use as basis for the calculation of the T-SNE map. Since similarity cannot be calculated with qualitative values (e.g., title, author, type of genre), the list consists only of quantitative dimensions (mostly network values, e.g., size, density, diameter, but also year, number of speakers, and word counts). These are automatically identified by the prototype and normalized.[13] Anytime the *Calculate* button is clicked, the T-SNE map is recalculated based on the selected dimensions. Users can then hover over circles to display author and title information for the respective play (Figure 6.1). Clicking on a circle displays a list of all the dimension values for that particular play.

Here, users can check individual dimensions to invoke a filter for that dimension, which is shown to the right of the T-SNE map (Figure 6.2).

Depending on the data values of the selected dimension, either a slider appears for numerical values or a listbox for categorical values. The filter is set to the value of the selected play and all plays with the same value are marked in the map (i.e., the circles appear darker). If a categorical filter has been selected, the circles additionally get assigned different colors depending on their categorical value. For example, Figure 6.3 shows a situation, where the filters *normalizedGenre* (with the value "other") and *density* (with the value "1") have been selected.[14]

All the plays matching these values appear darker at the top-left of the map. The selected filters can now be used to explore the map, for example, by clicking and dragging into the *density* filter to create a new range for this filter or by selecting other categorical values in the *normalizedGenre* filter. Figure 6.4 shows a situation with a range of 0.425–0.65 selected for *density* and the values "Other" and "Comedy" selected for *normalizedGenre*, resulting in a strip of circles in darker color in the middle of the map.

Figure 6.1 Detailed information shown for one play, while hovering over a circle on the T-SNE map

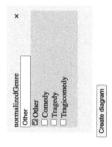

Figure 6.2 List of dimension values for the play with "normalizedGenre" selected as filter

Figure 6.3 Filters "density" and "normalizedGenre" selected

Figure 6.4 Vertical strip of circles in the middle of the map as a result of the filter selection

These filtered subsets of the whole dataset can be further analyzed by clicking the button *Create diagram*. Based on the selected filters, different types of diagrams are then generated, showing an alternative or aggregated view of this part of the data, which can be further analyzed. If, for example, only one filter for categorical values has been selected, a click on the button invokes an overlaid bar chart representing the number of plays in each selected category (Figure 6.5).

If users have chosen a categorical dimension and a numerical dimension, a bar chart with average numerical values for the categorical values is presented to the user (Figure 6.6).

Selecting two numerical filters, finally, brings up a scatter plot (Figure 6.7). In each of these diagrams, entities can be hovered over to get detailed information.

Reflective Modeling

Let us now take a look at how this user interface already supports a reflective conversation with the situation. The process starts with a calculation and representation of the T-SNE map that gives users a rough idea of the similarity of plays in terms of their dimensions. An examination of this map and the representations of its subsets can lead to valuable insights, which in turn will lead to adjustments of the dimensions used for the calculation and recalculation of the map, getting more and more specific with each iteration. Thus, the calculated T-SNE map is a statistical evaluation of the data that can serve as a preunderstanding for detailed inquiries into the data.

This circular process of evaluating the results of a particular map, followed by adjusting the dimensions and recalculating the map, is driven by the indeterminacy and ambiguity of the representation that has its origin in the projection of a multidimensional vector space onto a two-dimensional plane. Naturally, this leads to a complexity reduction of the data and inevitable indeterminacy with respect to the shown distances between plays. Each new calculation produces slightly different map representations and creates a sense of ambiguity about them.

The other characteristics of reflective modeling, namely selectivity, unrestrictedness, immediacy, reversibility, and argumentation, have not yet (or only marginally) been addressed in the prototype. In the following paragraphs I will give an outlook on how these could be applied and provide concrete examples in the form of sketches.

While selecting subsets of the data is possible through the use of filters for all of the 33 dimensions and these subsets can be investigated further with different diagrams, it is not possible to interact with the canvas itself for selecting subsets. If that were an option, scholars would be able to

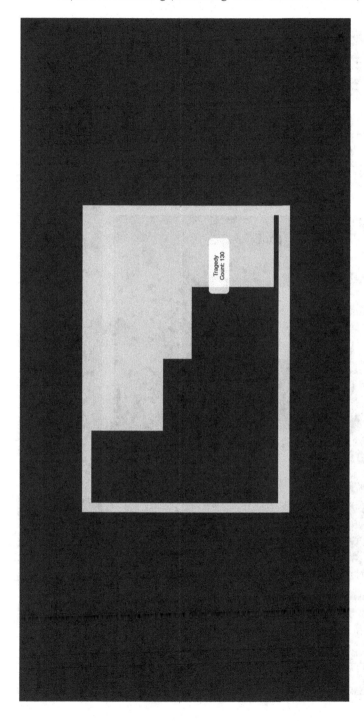

Figure 6.5 Bar chart with number of plays in each genre category

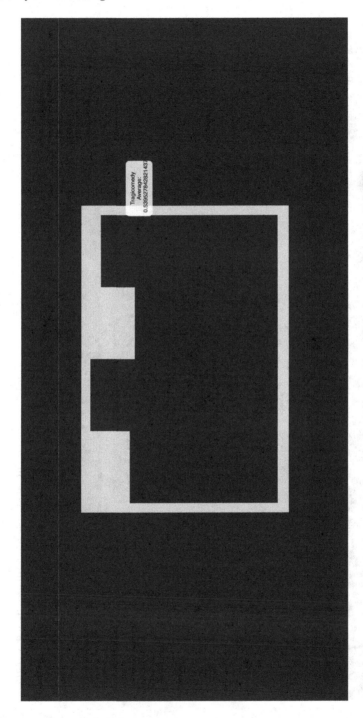

Tragicomedy
Average:
0.53952784282143?

Figure 6.6 Bar chart with average values for each genre for the selected numerical dimension (density)

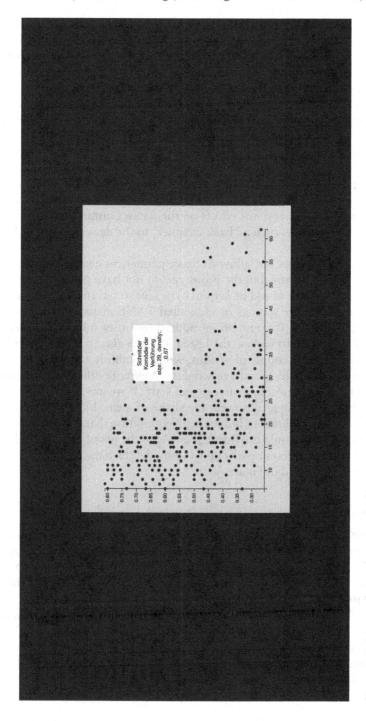

Figure 6.7 Scatter plot with numerical filter size and density selected

select parts of the dataset that are related to their research interests. For example, this could be achieved by letting users draw on the canvas in order to encircle clusters and single out plays they are particularly interested in, either in order to create a data subset or just mark and keep track of them for comparative purposes in different recalculations of the map. This would enable a much more fluid interaction with the visual representation and contribute to an unrestricted interaction with the data, as exemplified in the following sketches (Figure 6.8a, 6.8b).

Currently, the data represented by the T-SNE visualization is not affected by the interaction with the visualization. While setting filters and changing them has an immediate effect on the visualization and can be instantly evaluated, there is no way to change the data by manipulating the visualization and observe the effects on the dataset instantly. The following sketch shows how such a "back-channel" to the data could be realized (Figure 6.9a, 6.9b).

The prototype does not allow to make permanent changes to the data yet, so actions performed in the prototype do not have permanent consequences. However, it would be helpful to be able to return to specific states of the interface (filter settings or individual T-SNE maps) or just "undo" the last action, as it is common in modern tool user interfaces. Making it possible not only to reverse the last action but also to return to earlier states, going back a couple of actions, would establish a kind of versioning system that would encourage scholars to explore different paths with the possibility of returning to an original state. If we imagine a versioning history that is not linear but takes the shape of a tree-like structure (e.g., similar to *Git*) with different branches of exploration that can be viewed in juxtaposition, this would provide scholars with the possibility to weigh the pros and cons of different paths taken to model the data. What this could look like is illustrated in Figure 6.10.

Conclusion

In recent years a pragmatic understanding of modeling has emerged in DH. This is evidenced by certain qualities that are commonly ascribed to the modeling process, for example, that it is subjective, iterative, creative, and constructive and that it is characterized by a form of "practical thinking" (Ciula and Eide 34).

How this practical thinking takes shape has remained unclear, however.

In this chapter I proposed a number of principles for designing digital user interfaces for reflective modeling in the humanities by drawing my inspiration from reflective design practice. Reflective design practice is a modeling activity that not only displays the above-mentioned qualities but is also determined by a practitioner's critical (i.e., reflective) stance toward the situation,

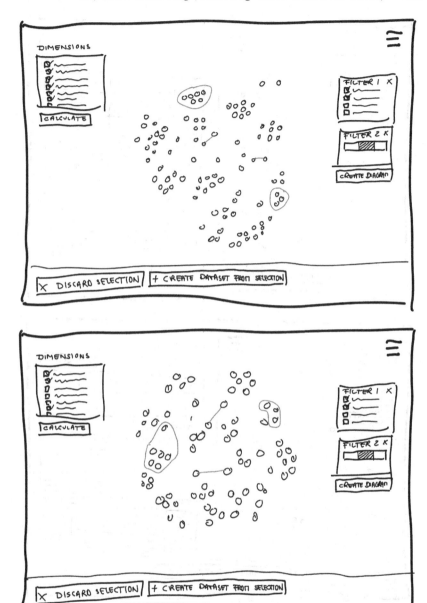

Figure 6.8 (a) A scholar has selected two clusters in the current T-SNE map and marked two distances between two plays, respectively. (b) The scholar recalculates the T-SNE map with different dimensions selected and observes how the clusters and the distances change.

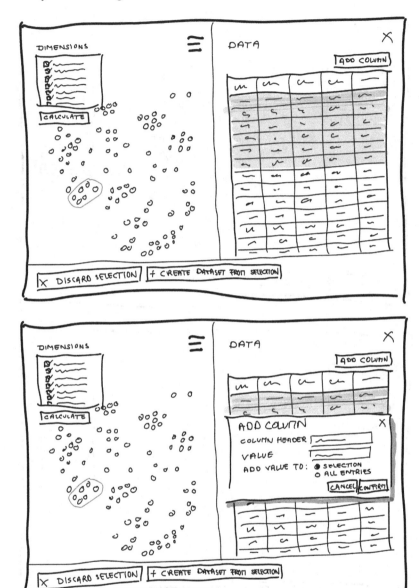

Figure 6.9 (a) The data view has been activated. The scholar has selected a cluster in the T-SNE map that is highlighted in the data view. (b) The scholar adds a new column to the data and is asked whether the value should be applied to all fields in the new column or only the selected subset of the data (which could be used for example to record some observation regarding the selected cluster).

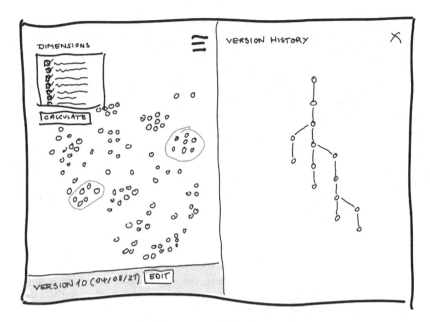

Figure 6.10 The scholar has activated the version history view and selected a particular version in a branch. The user interface provides a preview on the left-hand side and offers the possibility to edit this earlier version to continue the exploration of the dataset with this version

informed by external visual representations. Furthermore, as we have seen, design processes can be described as hermeneutical and constructive: Starting with a partial understanding of a design situation, designers develop partial solutions that lead them to a better understanding of the situation as a whole and in turn to a new round of designing and understanding and so on. These iterations result in models of possible outcomes of a situation and can, consequently, likely set an effective example for modeling in DH.

The presented principles are partly based on descriptions of analog reflective practice in design (and my personal experience as a designer) and draw on earlier attempts at establishing reflective design practice in software environments. I have started incorporating them into a prototype in order to explore their applicability for modeling reflectively. While this seems fruitful and has allowed for a first assessment of possible manifestations of the principles in a user interface, more principles will have to be implemented into the prototype and the value of the principles will have to be further evaluated in user tests with humanities scholars having specific research questions. To that effect and more specifically, the prototype will be iteratively developed in collaboration with the researchers involved in the DraCor project.

Moreover, the prototype focuses on a narrow range of use cases in DLS. In future work, it would be interesting to explore concepts for reflective modeling interfaces for other use cases, building a diverse repertoire of possible designs that can be compared and evaluated.

Last but not least, in the discussed prototype visual representations serve as models for different explorations. They are means to an end, insofar as they allow users to draw conclusions from the data visualizations while they continue their modeling process in the interface in an iterative hermeneutic manner. The data model is formed by means of the visual representation. These models are, however, ephemeral. They cannot be saved and processed in other applications. It would be helpful, therefore, to be able to record these states of the data and give scholars the opportunity to export the data models to other software environments.

Notes

1 Although there is a certain relatedness, the word constructive here is not to be misunderstood as a reference to constructivist philosophy. Rather, since I am approaching modeling from a design perspective, and design practice has often been conceptualized within a pragmatist framework (particularly by Donald Schön who strongly draws on the pragmatism of John Dewey [see Dixon, "Dewey and design"]), my approach can be described as in line with pragmatist ideas on knowledge generation as a process of actively engaging with and experimenting within a given environment.
2 Peirce differentiates three types of relations between sign and object: iconic, indexical, and symbolic. An iconic relation describes a similarity between sign and object that can either be pictorial, diagrammatic, or metaphoric (Kralemann and Lattmann).
3 John Dewey refers to the process of transforming indeterminate situations of practice into resolved ones as "inquiry."
4 The topic of digital materiality in digital literary studies is too large to discuss here in detail. For more perspectives on the topic, see, e.g., Kirschenbaum, Hayles, Parikka.
5 Gestalt laws are based on the work of psychologists Max Wertheimer, Wolfgang Kohler, and Kurt Koffka and were first formulated in the 1920s (Wertheimer). Usually, seven laws are described in the literature. Palmer lists the following: proximity, similarity, closure, symmetry, common fate, continuity, and parallelism.
6 The word "affordance" is used here in the sense that Donald Norman popularized in his book *The Design of Everyday Things*: "[...] *affordance* refers to the perceived and actual properties of the thing, primarily those fundamental properties that determine just how the thing could possibly be used [...]" (Norman 9, author's emphasis). I am aware of (and agree with) the criticism directed at Norman for his simplified view on the topic (e.g., Ratto et al.). However, I think that Norman's can still be a helpful perspective in design practice.
7 https://hdlab.stanford.edu/palladio/credits/
8 https://nodegoat.net/

9 https://voyant-tools.org/
10 https://gephi.org/
11 https://openrefine.org/
12 Of course, actual "raw data" does not really exist, as set forth in publications like *"Raw Data" Is an Oxymoron* (Gitelman). In this case, I consider data to be "raw" when—although possibly algorithmically processed and modeled in a particular way already—it is not yet modeled with respect to a specific research question a scholar may have. Notwithstanding the above, one could indeed say that data is always, in certain ways, already modeled by the methods and tools used in their collection or production as well as by the backgrounds, assumptions, and biases of the people responsible for the collection and production.
13 Here, "normalization" refers to the process of mapping numbers to a range between 0 and 1, a format the T-SNE algorithm expects to work properly.
14 Network density describes the ratio between possible and actual connections between nodes in the network. A value of "1," for example, means all possible connections are present.

Works cited

Barad, Karen. *Meeting the Universe Halfway: Quantum Physics and the Entanglement of Matter and Meaning.* Duke University Press, 2007.

Bertin, Jacques. *Semiology of Graphics.* University of Wisconsin Press, 1983.

Bod, Rens. "Modelling in the humanities: linking patterns to principles." *Historical Social Research/Historische Sozialforschung* 31.Supplement, 2018, pp. 78–95.

Bode, Katherine. "Data beyond representation: thoughts on the shift from computational modelling to performative materiality." MLA Convention 2020, *Katherine Bode*, 2020. https://katherinebode.wordpress.com/home/mla-convention-2020/. Accessed 29 Dec 2022.

Ciula, Arianna, et al. "Modelling: thinking in practice. An introduction." *Historical Social Research/Historische Sozialforschung* 31.Supplement, 2018, pp. 7–29.

Ciula, Arianna, and Øyvind Eide. "Modelling in digital humanities: signs in context." *Digital Scholarship in the Humanities* 32.Supplement 1, 2017, pp. i33–i46.

Cross, Nigel. *Designerly Ways of Knowing.* Springer London, 2010.

Dewey, John. *Logic: The Theory of Inquiry.* Holt, 1938.

Dixon, Brian S. *Dewey and Design.* Cham: Springer, 2020.

Dorst, Kees. "The core of 'design thinking' and its application." *Design Studies* 32.6, 2011, pp. 521–532.

Drucker, Johanna. "Humanities approaches to graphical display." *Digital Humanities Quarterly* 5.1, 2011, pp. 1–21.

Drucker, Johanna. *Visualization and Interpretation: Humanistic Approaches to Display.* MIT Press, 2020.

Elleström, Lars. "Spatiotemporal aspects of iconicity." *Iconic Investigations* 12, 2013, pp. 95–117.

Fischer, Frank, et al. "Programmable Corpora: Introducing DraCor, an Infrastructure for the Research on European Drama." *Proceedings of DH2019: Complexities.* Utrecht University, 2019.

Fish, Jonathan, and Stephen Scrivener. "Amplifying the mind's eye: sketching and visual cognition." *Leonardo* 23.1, 1990, pp. 117–126.

Flanders, Julia, and Fotis Jannidis. "Data Modeling." *A New Companion to Digital Humanities*. Wiley Online Library, 2015, pp. 229–237.

Flanders, Julia, and Fotis Jannidis. *The Shape of Data in Digital Humanities: Modeling Texts and Text-Based Resources*. Routledge, 2019.

Frigg, Roman. "Scientific representation and the semantic view of theories." *Theoria. Revista de Teoría, Historia y Fundamentos de la Ciencia* 21.1, 2006, pp. 49–65.

Frigg, Roman, and Stephan Hartmann. "Models in Science." *The Stanford Encyclopedia of Philosophy*. Spring, 2020 Edition. https://plato.stanford.edu/archives/spr2020/entries/models-science. Accessed 29 Dec. 2022.

Gelfert, Axel. *How to Do Science with Models: A Philosophical Primer*. Cham: Springer, 2016.

Gibson, James J. "The Theory of Affordances. The Ecological Approach to Visual Perception." *The People, Place, and Space Reader*. Routledge, 1979, pp. 56–60.

Giere, Ronald N. *Explaining Science: A Cognitive Approach*. University of Chicago Press, 1988.

Gitelman, Lisa, ed. *Raw Data Is an Oxymoron*. MIT Press, 2013.

Gius, Evelyn, et al. *CATMA*. 6.5.0, Zenodo, 6 Apr. 2022. doi:10.5281/zenodo.6419805.

Goel, Vinod. *Sketches of Thought*. MIT press, 1995.

Goldschmidt, Gabriela. "The dialectics of sketching." *Creativity research journal* 4.2, 1991, pp. 123–143.

Green, Thomas R. G., and Marian Petre. "Usability analysis of visual programming environments: a 'cognitive dimensions' framework." *Journal of Visual Languages & Computing* 7.2, 1996, pp. 131–174.

Hasenhütl, Gert. "Zeichnerisches Wissen." *Kulturtechnik Entwerfen*. transcript Verlag, 2015, pp. 341–358.

Hayles, N. Katherine. *Writing Machines*. MIT Press, 2002.

Hutchby, Ian. "Technologies, texts and affordances." *Sociology* 35.2, 2001, pp. 441–456.

Kirschenbaum, Matthew G. *Mechanisms: New Media and the Forensic Imagination*. MIT Press, 2012.

Kleymann, Rabea, and Jan-Erik Stange. "Towards hermeneutic visualization in digital literary studies." *Digital Humanities Quarterly* 15.2, 2021.

Knorr-Cetina, Karin. "Objectual Practice." *The Practice Turn in Contemporary Theory*. London and New York: Routledge, 2001, pp. 175–188.

Knuuttila, Tarja. *Models As Epistemic Artefacts Toward a Non-Representationalist Account of Scientific Representation*. Department of Philosophy Univ. of Helsinki, 2005.

Kralemann, Björn, and Claas Lattmann. "Models as icons: modeling models in the semiotic framework of Peirce's theory of signs." *Synthese* 190.16, 2013, pp. 3397–3420.

Latour, Bruno and Steve Woolgar. *Laboratory Life*. 1979.

Lim, Youn-Kyung, et al. "The anatomy of prototypes: prototypes as filters, prototypes as manifestations of design ideas." *ACM Transactions on Computer-Human Interaction (TOCHI)* 15.2, 2008, pp. 1–27.

Mahr, Bernd. Das Wissen im Modell. *KIT-Report 150 (2004)*, Berlin: Technische Universität, Fakultät IV, 2004, pp. 1–21.

Mandell, Laura. "Gender and cultural analytics: finding or making stereotypes?" *Debates in the Digital Humanities*, University of Minnesota Press, 2019, pp. 3–26.

McCarty, Willard. "Knowing…: Modeling in Literary Studies." *A Companion to Digital Literary Studies* (eds. Susan Schreibman and Ray Siemens), Wiley Online Library, 2013, pp. 389–401.

McCarty, Willard. "Modeling: A Study in Words and Meanings." *A Companion to Digital Humanities (eds S. Schreibman, R. Siemens and J. Unsworth)*, Wiley Online Library, 2004, pp. 254–270.

Norman, Don. *The Design of Everyday Things*. Revised and expanded edition. Basic Books, 2013.

O'Toole, Michael. *The Hermeneutic Spiral and Interpretation in Literature and the Visual Arts*. New York: Routledge, 2018.

Palmer, Stephen E. *Vision Science: Photons to Phenomenology*. MIT Press, 1999.

Parikka, Jussi. *What Is Media Archaeology?* John Wiley & Sons, 2013.

Pawlicka-Deger, Urszula. "The laboratory turn: exploring discourses, landscapes, and models of humanities labs." *Digital Humanities Quarterly* 14.3, 2020.

Pickering Andrew. *The Mangle of Practice: Time Agency and Science*. University of Chicago Press, 1995.

Ratto, Matt, et al. "Interfaces and Affordances." *Routledge Handbook of Digital Media and Communication*. Routledge, 2020, pp. 63–74.

Resnick, M., et al. *Design Principles for Tools to Support Creative Thinking*. Vol. 1. Carnegie Mellon University, 30 June 2018. doi:10.1184/R1/6621917.v1.

Rheinberger, Hans-Jörg. *Toward a History of Epistemic Things: Synthesizing Proteins in the Test Tube*. Stanford University Press, 1997.

Rittel, Horst WJ, and Melvin M. Webber. "Dilemmas in a general theory of planning." *Policy Sciences* 4.2, 1973, pp. 155–169.

Schön, Donald. *The Reflective Practitioner. How Professionals Think in Action*. New York: Basic Books, 1983.

Schön, Donald A. "Designing as reflective conversation with the materials of a design situation." *Research in Engineering Design* 3.3, 1992, pp. 131–147.

Shneiderman, Ben. "Direct manipulation: a step beyond programming languages." *Proceedings of the Joint Conference on Easier and More Productive Use of Computer Systems. (Part-II): Human Interface and the User Interface-Volume 1981*, 1981.

Snodgrass, Adrian, and Richard Coyne. "Is designing hermeneutical?" *Architectural Theory Review* 2.1, 1996, pp. 65–97.

Stachowiak, Herbert. *Allgemeine Modelltheorie*. Springer, 1973.

Tversky, Barbara. "Multiple models: in the mind and in the world." *Historical Social Research/Historische Sozialforschung* 31.Supplement, 2018, pp. 59–65.

Van der Maaten, Laurens, and Geoffrey Hinton. "Visualizing data using t-SNE." *Journal of machine learning research* 9.11, 2008.

Winther, Rasmus Grønfeldt. "The Structure of Scientific Theories." *The Stanford Encyclopedia of Philosophy*. Spring, 2021 Edition. https://plato.stanford.edu/archives/spr2021/entries/structure-scientific-theories. Accessed 29 Dec. 2022.

Yamamoto, Yasuhiro, and Kumiyo Nakakoji. "Interaction design of tools for fostering creativity in the early stages of information design." *International Journal of Human-Computer Studies* 63.4–5, 2005, pp. 513–535.

Part III

Analytical-creative Approaches

7 Writing as a Machine or Becoming an Algorithmic Subject

Johanna Drucker

The interconnection of writing as code and code as a form of poetics has generated an abundance of critical commentary since computational text production became a form of composition. The recovery of the Alan Turing and Christopher Strachey's 1952 experiment, "The Love Letter Generator," designed for the Manchester Mark I computer, pushed the era of electronic text back to that seminal mid-century period of mainframes and pioneers (McCray). In 1996, Charles O. Hartman published *The Virtual Muse*, which contained a long survey of the field, and critical writings and creative works had already provoked a lively dialog throughout the 1970s with texts by Gerrit Krol, Pedro Barbosa, Peter D. Juhl, and many others. *The Policeman's Beard Is Half-Constructed*, "written" by "Racter" in 1984, is often cited as the "first" book completely written by a computer, a claim that has been nuanced and challenged on various grounds but still provides a useful reference (Henrickson).

I mention this handful of milestones at the outset to frame my comments as a contribution to an ongoing conversation of long standing. This is especially important because techniques of automated composition have a much longer history than simply that which is attached to the modern electronic computer—even as generative adversarial networks (GANS) and recurrent neural network (RNN) text generators continue to push the field beyond earlier limits (Chintapalli). A provocative argument could be made that all composition is algorithmic, not just that done by automated computer systems, since it follows procedural rules. I would not be the first person to make this assertion which was an oft-cited mantra of my colleague, Jerome McGann. The distinction between a set of rules and their instantiation in expressions is also at the heart of linguistics, and Noam Chomsky's structural studies of language developed alongside emerging computational technology for good reason given his convictions about the generative power of formal rules of transformation.

With such an abundance of critical discussion already in place, what is left to say about the relation of algorithms and writing? I will address

DOI: 10.4324/9781003320838-11

the special case of wanting to inhabit the subject position of an algorithm, understood within a theory of enunciation taken from structural linguistics. Then, as a coda, I will imagine becoming a subject of other procedural techniques—particularly mechanical, organic, or conceptual modes of *poiesis*. Why not? Who wouldn't want to speak as a cog in a wheel of a Renaissance "computer" or calculator or understand the subject position of a modest little unit of code in a cellular automaton and/or a replicative string of messenger RNA? Each of these examples brings a specific process of composition into view as a mechanical, organic, or computational activity. Who speaks in such processes? Whose point of view is expressed? Inhabited? And to whom are they speaking? Should I perhaps also imagine the internal struggles of a GAN—its inner turmoil responsible for strings of output? Or is that too close to familiar human activity?

To begin, consider one fundamental fact about algorithms—that they are *written scripts*. Though computation might involve calculation (the manipulation of numbers or quantitative information), the language of code is precisely that, a *language*. It behooves us to remember this, pondering the nature of this all-pervasive linguistic form. All language is in some sense *an utterance* (the mode of delivery—oral, written, recorded—does not change this). And utterances are, to use a term from structural linguistics, *enunciated*. The term *enunciation* is not a generic substitute for articulation or expression. It is a term that references a specific theoretical understanding of language as a speech act that creates both a speaking subject (the person/position talking or writing) and a spoken one (the person/position produced by the message). The spoken position is described in theoretical terms as the *enunciated* subject, a concept that is far more dynamic than, say, *recipient*. While the terms *speaker* and *recipient* suggest a mechanistic "transfer" approach to communication, the *speaking* and *spoken subject* positions suggest a dynamic system of co-dependent power relations created in language. Either speaking or spoken subject positions might be occupied, at any moment, by actual persons, but they are also understood as constructs of the speech act. So, for instance, a stop sign at a corner is spoken by state agencies (with all the authority that attends to their official position), but it creates a *subject of* that sign who is (in a different, but related, sense of the word) *subject to* the power of that authority.

A preliminary question, then, is whether algorithms act like other kinds of *language*. Are they also enunciations, with speaking and spoken subject positions? Do they perform the same way with regard to planes of discourse (literal inscription) and reference (meaning production)? These two dimensions can also be understood as the "saying" and the "said," both of which apply in formal as well as natural languages, and thus can be brought into the discussion of algorithms. While the "saying" aspect of an algorithm might be teased out with some acrobatic analysis, the "said" aspect is harder to discern. If an algorithm is a set of instructions, largely a procedural formulation, then does it have a "said?" To put it another way, does an algorithm have a referent? Or does it only exist as a literal string of written text? And what of the emergent properties of algorithms in neural networks? What other language act transforms over time, creating iterations and versions of itself in often non-linear ways so that it becomes unrecognizable even to its original author? If I write or speak a sentence, I do not expect to see it morph before me in the air or on the page into something unrecognizable. Algorithms do not just re-inscribe; they may also change with successive inscriptions depending on the way they were written, data they were trained on, or new input that is fed to them.

The concept of enunciation from linguistic theory was applied, in the vogue peak of French structuralism in the 1960s through 1980s, to film, images, language, and a wide range of other systems of expression. For instance, the influential work of feminist theorist Kaja Silverman, *The Subject of Semiotics*, explored these relations in ways that provided methodological support for analysis across media. In his much-cited example of the concept, Louis Althusser described enunciation with the example of "Hey you," the act of "hailing" in public (Althusser 174). This act shows how these interrelated (speaking/spoken) positions are created and work in a social space. Who identifies as the spoken subject of that hailing call? Why? The answer is of course nuanced. Our sense of self is always socially and culturally constructed as a position, not only as an illusion of essential unique identity, and we respond according to the place we think we occupy in the power structures of which the utterance is an expression. Althusser described this process as the "interpellation" of the subject into the symbolic system. The term "interpellation" carries political implications, of course, because any structured system of positions involves power relations. And so, we move very quickly from linguistic analysis to ideology and issues of agency, enfranchisement, and subjectivity. In my 21st-century, United States, environment, I am keenly aware of the relationship between demographics and subject positions in the snap judgments that occur in interpersonal encounters on the street. We are each subject to and subject of the law and other aspects of social relations in accord with the ways our apparent identity is perceived.

The question is whether this basic theoretical framework can be used to address one of the more interesting aspects of algorithmically initiated writing practices. Who speaks in an algorithm? The author, obviously, writes the code, and in this sense, no mystery needs to be invoked. An algorithm is a writing act like any other. Or is it? Once the algorithm is released to do its (repetitive and iterative) work, the question of who speaks each expression gets slightly more complicated. Is the 5th or 2000th expression of a combinatoric instruction identical to the first in terms of its speaking and spoken subjects if its context has changed radically? Texts are produced as an act of reading and are thus dependent on context, but an algorithm may alter materially if it is an iterative—or emergent—string of code. Machine learning has become an integral part of algorithmic processes. Since the earliest neural net constructions, algorithms have had the capacity to shift their behaviors away from logical sequences and into mutating statements. The very structure of the code changes in relation to the conditions in which it is working. When the code alters and the text changes, then is the speech act the same? Of course not. In each instance, the speaking subject is marked differently in the code. The changed protocols are a new form of address, a unique call to interact with other code. And if, over time, the code becomes unrecognizable to its original author, then who speaks? This material transformation distinguishes algorithmic texts from other discourses even if the enunciative capacity persists across each iteration. Similarly, we can describe an interface as an enunciative apparatus—but whose voice does it enunciate? The designer is long absent from the screen, and yet the format and layout, organizational and instrumental features of the interface all perform enunciative functions. The relation of designer/interface/enunciation might be compared to that of author/narrator/statement in a text. Each of the components—graphic, textual, or algorithmic—has their own agency. In an interface, a button, pull-down menu, link, or any other dynamic feature only intensifies the already present directives in a static layout—which functions as a set of instructions for reading. But in the case of an emergent algorithm, the ongoing transformation of its code continues to transform the specifics of its enunciative activity (what is being "said"), which does not alter the fundamental fact that the algorithm is situated within the dynamic of subject production.

The double meaning of the second half of my title should now be evident—the "subject position of" an algorithm is both *speaking* and *spoken*. An algorithm may issue a call and hail its fellows within a sequence of unfolding computational events through which it effectively positions these other bits of code within a hierarchy of power relations. Without exaggerating, or turning this into a fantasy of code agents in a social network, we can acknowledge that algorithms function within networks of relations they help to shape. This co-dependent dynamic is itself an enunciative system in which any specific iteration of the code calls forth a corresponding instance. This generative process is a dramatic demonstration of enunciation at work.

So, I ask whether, as a writer, one can occupy the speaking position of this linguistic form. In my case, I addressed the question by trying to learn how to speak as a compression algorithm, processing substantial amounts of text into a distilled statement in a technique modeled on data mining.

I did not make any conscious effort to become an *emergent* algorithm but remained a more basic code creature, mechanically trying to perform a set of instructions on a body of text. While the statements produced were complex, the instructions were as simple as a children's book sentence, "See Jane run." In my case, "Condense this text." The speaker/spoken positions are clear in these simple sentences. The most basic algorithmic instruction performs the same action by using "get," "include," or "print" as a command. A command produces its spoken subject directly.

If we take an algorithm to be an expression of a rule or set of rules governing actions, a process, or a behavior through a set of procedures, then this discussion takes on yet another dimension. The articulated set of laws or rules is also an enunciative act. Hammurabi's Code is spoken as surely as the Napoleonic *Code Civil*, and as citizen-subjects we are absolutely spoken by such strictures and ordinances. Language has its rules—the famous distinction between *langue* and *parole* made by Ferdinand de Saussure differentiates the rules from the individual instances. As per the comments above, language is rule-bound and governed by syntactic constraints. We may say some things and not others in any particular system. The mystery of language acquisition—or the miracle—is that infant children grasp these rules without ever having been taught them explicitly and then follow them (more or less successfully) into becoming full-fledged language users. Few, if any, speakers of a language would be able to articulate the rules as an independent set of statements ("noun and verb must agree in number," for instance). We have grammars for that (which we rarely consult in common practice). But at another level, spoken or written language is governed by other rules—social constraints, decorum, concepts of appropriateness, and codes of inclusion and exclusion. We learn early what tone and vocabulary is acceptable between friends and among family or required in formal circumstances.

But what of literature? To reiterate my earlier remarks, the rules that govern literary production are no less specific than those that govern other acts of linguistic composition. Some of these rules are taught. A sonnet has particular constraints, and so does a couplet. A play is structured differently than a paragraph of prose. These constraints are formal, but they govern our procedural activity. They are the basic algorithms of composition. Some we learn, because they can be stated explicitly. Others we absorb from our experience of reading. As readers, we become experts at decoding this algorithmic DNA, able to distinguish within a sentence or two whether we are confronting a fantasy text or a realist one, a documentary account or a fiction. Lines blur, and genre-bending is a recognizable—but marked—act of playing with these codes. Literary work is rule-bound and each composition act is an execution of those rules in some degree of conformity to them.

Within the terms of literary composition, the levels of enunciation might be quite complex: an actual author creating an implied narrator who addresses a fictive figure with whom an actual reader is meant to identify and so on. Levels of enunciation, like nested frameworks of reference, position us within the text. In film theory, the recognition that we also identify with the situation of viewing or reading makes clear that a subject is created by the structure of that situation. Sitting in a theater seat, we occupy a subject position. Likewise, when we read a book, look at a screen, or device. Looking at a wall display hung at someone else's eye level or sitting in a chair designed for a child makes us immediately aware of how subject positions are inscribed in the world. We are always caught in these enunciative systems, and to reiterate my opening remarks, all forms of human expression are acts of speaking that assume/create/construct a spoken subject.

Many of these positions are rendered invisible by the habits of encounter that familiarize cultural experience and make it appear to be natural. That is the nature of ideology, of course, to become invisible through naturalization or normalization. Few, beyond literary critics of a particular disposition, are likely to take up the issue of the subject position embodied in distinct rules of literary production, video games, shopping malls, and so on. The decoding game, the stuff of seminar rooms and conference papers, has little other apparent productive use in our culture. Or does it? We might pause at this moment and open another entire dimension to this argument that analyzes devices, formats, and systems of mediation. For instance, the design of consumer electronics is deliberately meant to facilitate a seamless and frictionless interface that sustains the essential illusion of a free-willed individual with autonomy and agency, in keeping with the quintessential neo-liberal paradigm.

If, now, we return to the issues of encoded subject positions within the rules of literary production, we have ample material on which to ask a few questions based on the points just sketched above. The first is whether literary works that intentionally engage with algorithmic production are in essence (ontologically, as it were, fundamentally in their very identity) any different from those that are incidentally the product of rules that are less explicit. The second is whether the historical inventory of rule-bound textual production under constraint offers any insight into our current practices of code-based composition. And finally, what might be learned by trying to occupy the speaking position encoded in an algorithmic procedure? Can I become the subject of an algorithm? Speaking or spoken or both? By adopting or mimicking (not the same thing) the processes by which an algorithm enunciates? Aspiring to algorithmic subjectivity is, in fact, the experiment I took on in two recent works, the texts of *Fabulas Feminae* (Drucker and Bee) and those of *The Fall* (Drucker and Freeman).

I will come back to them, but first, some thoughts on the historical inventory of literary "algorithms."

Even if literary works follow rule-based protocols in which conventions are followed, most literary composition is not carried out under constraint. The history of literature maps the transformation of forms and genres in which the "rules" are bent and constantly re-invented. But works framed by explicit protocols work within defined instructions. Their very identity flaunts their rule-boundedness, calling attention to it. One interesting feature of these works in the historical inventory is that in many ways they embody the basic principles of code-based contemporary writing. They are combinatoric, permutational, highly structured, and yet, these historical examples lack one quality that is part of algorithmic composition—the capacity of the rules to change through algorithmic evolution. A more detailed discussion of the historical examples provides a useful contrast between analog and computational compositional techniques.

These historical precedents were the subject of a paper I wrote for the Electronic Literature Association meeting in Coimbra, Portugal, in 2017 ("Amusements Electroniques"). The paper began this way: In 1842, Gabriel Peignot, aka Philomneste, published a remarkable 500-plus page compendium of literary curiosities titled *Amusements Philologiques*, an erudite assembling of approaches to the procedural production of literary and poetic works (Peignot). Peignot was a bibliographer, with a disposition toward what he called "the singularity," a term that had a different meaning in his usage than it does in our New Age vocabulary. For Peignot, it meant a work with unique qualities. Peignot's attraction to anomalies and unusual practices formed the basis of his engagement with what we could call procedural writing, in which a set of generalizable principles, independent of individual works, can be used for production of multiple and varied works.

The first half of *Amusement Philologiques*, titled "Poétique Curieuse," offered a survey of the traditions of procedural composition. The collection was all the more remarkable for the date of its production, since Peignot's erudition was bibliographical and, as his title betrayed, philological. His knowledge was gleaned from extensive reading in an era long before search engines or other automated instruments were available to support research. Peignot's knowledge base was derived from reading classical and biblical texts, many of which now seem obscure. He scoured the writings of Church fathers (Augustine, Jerome), books on ancient history, dictionaries, grammars, and a host of other works in which the examples of complex rhymes and structures could be found. He had an intimate familiarity with a renowned *Anthology* assembled by Planudes, a Byzantine scholar whose collection of Greek epigrams was then a standard reference. Peignot also drew on the *Palatine Anthology*, the anagrams of Lycophon, a 3rd-century BCE poet, and other works that are now obscure to all but specialists. Peignot's study in procedural poetics *avant la lettre* deserves more than a superficial glance. (The second half of the volume, titled "Variétés," was a collection of classification systems of symbolism, emblems, flowers, money, and a variety of other linguistic terms from a wide range of disciplines using systematic figurative terminology.)

Peignot's discussion of the production techniques was descriptive and elaborative. He was explicit about the rules of composition for each form he identified. His alphabetic organization of more than thirty subsections began with the "Acrostic" and ended with "Vers en tarantara," followed by some "singular" pieces of composition he found particularly intriguing. His inventory was evidence of the continued transmission of these "folies" from antiquity, through the Middle Ages, and into his contemporary Western world. Peignot's inventory enumerated many types of constraints and procedures and offered these for comparison with methods of composition structured in digital work. One question this posed was what such an anthology would comprise today, if it were to enumerate the algorithmic techniques for permutational, combinatoric, aleatoric, and other methods of composition in computational approaches?

What became clear in the analysis of Peignot's collection was that the constraints governing production were considerably varied and not reducible to a single set of rules. Peignot identified 32 different strategies for production. They fall into several categories: those governed by rhyme patterns, those constrained by word-order, another governed by word or letter placement, broken layouts that split verse lines, puns, and double meanings, various techniques of appropriation, and one "chronographic" technique in which Roman numerals are embedded in a poetic text in such a way that they can be deciphered as a significant date (!). Some of these techniques are easier to automate than others. Rhyme patterns are susceptible to combinatoric work and descriptive instructions for selection of words within lines that scan for meter and rhyme. Double rhymes, repetitions, and echo verse, for instance, can all be produced programmatically—in fact, the forms are essentially programs for production.

But, returning to the third question posed above, how does this material pose the issue of who speaks such a verse? Is the author of the rule or protocol as much a part of the production as the individual who executes the rules to make a work? Does the answer to this question change if a work is produced inside of an algorithmically driven computer environment where access to lexicons, rhyming dictionaries, and other resources augments the limited facilities of a mere analog writer trying to conjure similar information from memory, mind, or a host of volumes open on the writing table? If I write such a work, I am clearly its author and my subject position varies not much at all from that of a conventional poet—except, in some small and significant regard, I am deliberately demonstrating a set of rules. My "authorship" is constrained within even more narrow and explicit terms than when I am writing as a historically and culturally located "subject" in the usual sense. The concept of "author" here draws on a critical history in which notions of "originality" and "autonomy" were radically changed to a model of the sociological-cultural production of author identity. The explicitly constrained process of articulation, which calls attention to the rules for a game and of play within it, places me within a nested subject position (instead of work/author we have rules/work/author). The rules are the powerful enunciating systems. Again, while we might argue that this is "always" the case for any writing act, it becomes more conspicuous when composing "under constraint" rather than simply "according to the/some rules."

What then are the points of contrast between computational and analog composition? Rhyme schemes can be automated, but so can arrangements and re-arrangements of order and repetition: anagrams and palindromes are perfect examples of combinatorics work that can constructed by instruction. The same issue arises: if am I the author of the rules, then am I also the author of all of their progeny? Who speaks in the hundredth iteration? The same subject as that of the first? How could it be otherwise—except that the accumulated weight of examples forces, in a human speaker, a kind of recognition that doubles back as irony or self-awareness marked in tone or commentary. The algorithm has no capacity for self-perception and utters each new example with the same innocence and affectless composure as the first. Here the concept of subjectivity takes on more than simple structural positioning and comes to include the social situated-ness of speech acts. Writing or speaking to an audience-as-Other, I enter into a communication feedback loop. I feel a need to recognize and acknowledge that Other within the conditions of production. The knowledge of that enunciated subject inhabits my awareness and is part of the writing machine of my practice. I am neither immune to nor fully engaged with that Other, but neither can I block awareness of my participation in an enunciative system. Though, of course, sometimes I do—writing merely to write, to feel the pleasure of compositional patterns and the peculiar satisfaction of making form from thought without any regard for whether or not some audience-Other is posited as a recipient. The pleasure of executing work under constraint as a demonstration of virtuosity within a disciplined space is also accompanied by a relief at feeling less responsibility for the work. I am, after all, just executing the rules.

Circling back to Peignot and his inventory, I am struck by the question of whether or not any/all writing under constraint structures the same enunciative relations (whether they are, in fact, merely variants on the structural system of relations) or whether some substantive distinctions can be found so that practices can be differentiated from each other on these grounds. Shaped and figured verse, poems comprised all of words beginning with the same letter, or ones based on words that all lack the same letter—these are procedural constraints readily handled by automated processes in analog or digital environments. The more problematic categories include those in which extra-linguistic references, non-literal features of language, must be used as a basis of composition. Parodic and equivocal works imply an I-know-you-know-I-know circularity that inscribes subject positionality within the text—but not in an explicit or even identifiable marker. Where does irony live? What are its specific discrete identifiers, features that might be recognized without reliance on extra-linguistic markers? The frameworks of consensual or tacit knowledge that make us complicit in shared conditions of reception engage a different strategy of enunciation than those of mechanistic application of rules. Don't they?

If we finish going through Peignot's inventory, we arrive at the elaboration of a limited set of strategies for composition. These are almost all capable of being automated (e.g., combinatorics, selection, and sequencing). But Peignot himself? The able and erudite compendium maker, creator of systematic inventories and schemes of description, the maker of lists of "singularities" and appreciator of idiosyncratic verse? His work is hardly algorithmically driven, even if the program of scholarly research, attempt at comprehensiveness, bespeaks a certain immodest impulse toward exhaustive acquisitiveness. Peignot's own project, oddly, is not formulaic, even if it conforms to norms of anthology production in which rules for selection are generally explicit. His acquisition of novelties and anomalies redeems him from mere repetitive stewardship of historical examples. But his rules have some elasticity, and he expands his definitions of procedural work. Acknowledgment of the swerve, the clinamen of pataphysics, the single deviation from repetition that inscribes each instance anew as a unique instance of enunciation, remains present in the long reception history of idiosyncratic "amusements" with which he clearly delighted himself and others. Peignot never mentions Lucretius, or the clinamen, but his collection seems to exist under its influence. He began with a set of constraints, but the outcome exhibits emergent properties as Peignot becomes "spoken" by the unpredictable outcome of his investigations. He is an emergent editor, not a mechanistic one.

The term *Amusements* in Peignot's title is important, since, like *jeux*, the French for games, it suggests a playful approach in which a collapse of subject-object, speaker-spoken, into a single mechanistic condition of identification is not possible. Play and amusement both suggest wiggle room between speaker and spoken, between provocation and reception, and this creates a dynamic play. The rules and the game are not the same, but what is permitted is still more or less circumscribed.

Though Saussure did not have a theory of enunciation, other structural-ist and post-structuralist authors did and, as already mentioned, the con-cept became central to structuralist and post-structuralist thought. Every instance of human articulation is an enunciative act. No amount of libera-tory rhetoric in the modes of disruption or dissensual activity alters that fact, and the process of adopting a critical stance as if one were outside of enunciative systems that position us as subjects is delusional but, perhaps, also necessary. Literary work does one essential thing, performs one essen-tial task, which is to call attention to the ways in which language works. We not only enact the rules but also show the workings, tip our hands, and expose the conceits. No simple modernist paradigm laying bear devices prevails here, but a longer one, in which the acts of *poiesis* are always arguments about language and its forms. This is how this works, I say, speaking myself into being in the process, with the "this" in the formula-tion of the first part of the sentence serving multiple functions of deictic identification and slippage. Who is the speaking subject of the algorithm when the location of its "this-ness" is unspecified, dislocated from its orig-inal site of utterance? I put the algorithm into play. But does the algorithm see itself? Know that it is an instrument of enunciative articulation? Here we shift into those mind-games beloved of sophomoric adolescents discov-ering questions of consciousness: how do I know that I know and who is the "I" who does the knowing? These are silly—if profound—exercises. Instead, I will describe the works composed in my aspiration toward algo-rithmic subjectivity.

In 2011, I came across a blog-post by Matthew Hurst, "The Hapax Legomenon of Steve Jobs." Hurst was not proposing his text as a poetic intervention in the normative order of all things linguistic like so many of my poet friends, but instead, modestly offering an instance of data min-ing. He had automated a text analysis process across the many crawls and feeds reporting on the death of Jobs. The phrase "hapax legomenon" describes words that occur once and only once in a corpus. They pose curious issues for translators and readers, because they cannot be glossed through association or comparison across contexts or instances of use. I might as easily drop a neologism into this sentence, describing myself as a *neophloglodyte* and leave it to your critical imagination to conjure some sense from the term. Such a practice introduces uncertainties in the com-munication stream. Can I position a subject through an articulation that cannot be consumed, deciphered, understood? Well, of course, obfusca-tion is its own form of power, deeply manipulative.

But more than the particulars, the style of Hurst's compressed sum-maries of Jobs' profile offered a way to think in poetic language, to take a mass of material and create a dense distillation of apparent essences. I cared much less about the enunciated subject of such utterances than

I did about how it might feel to inhabit the space of such an enunciation. I did not aspire to write *like* an algorithm, in some pathetic mimetic act in which I would always stand outside the actual position of enunciating subject, but instead, wanted to write *as* an algorithm, occupying the site of enunciation. This was a rewarding experience, and slipping into the voice, finding it in myself, making it a way of thinking and speaking brought me up against the question of who the spoken subject of such discourse might be. Other machines? Other texts produced in similar manner? Other writers of code or encoded authors? No cryptic message or pre-existing identity inheres in this work or the practice that brings it about any more than in any other kind of utterance. An algorithm, a machine, or an architectural space can "speak" a subject as surely as any other medium or format.

My first attempt to write as a compression algorithm, *Fabulas Feminae*, published as a collaboration with artist Susan Bee, was created by opening multiple web-page sources all at one time that all contained information on one of the women in our pantheon. I would read rapidly, scanning for words within and across each page. I did not read for syntax or meaning, but for frequency. The words that came up most often were the ones I pulled into my text. They brought with them fragments of grammar, like plants pulled from the earth with some clods of dirt clinging. No attempt was made to smooth these into a unified or coherent whole. The order of the words was created following their appearance in each text—opening paragraphs through final ones. This hyper-synthesis was done on the fly. I didn't take notes, or make drafts, but tried to process as quickly as possible by typing as I scanned. The final texts were barely edited. Here is a sample from the portrait of Elizabeth I:

> Whose name has become an era a heart a head a queen. Declared illegitimate her half-brother bequeathed cutting out half-sisters dominated dissension dominated. A tattered realm religious wars. Imprisoned on suspicion a weak divided backwater. The dry treasury and Calais lost she inherited. To power. Rule depended heavily. Good counsel. Legacy especially establishing her first moves the trusted advisers a church. Expected to continue the closest brush with marriage the Tudor line never.
>
> (Drucker and Bee; n.p.)

In the next project, *The Fall*, I relied on two different text sources. The first was chapters from Edward Gibbon's *The History of the Decline and Fall of the Roman Empire* (originally written in 1782, revised in 1845) in the Gutenberg online edition (Gibbon). The second was more complicated, since I wanted to use the front-page texts of a variety of online news sources beginning with the day of the Trump election victory in November

2016 and then for the 25 weeks following. This required a different kind of synthesis than either the Gibbon or the previous project, since news feeds are complex graphically and linguistically and do not stay current. I had to find back issues and editions, scan as rapidly as in the first project, typing as I went. Obviously, this was far from rigorous and not statistically accurate. This was human data mining, and I was the processor. Just to reiterate, I was not trying to write *like* a machine. I was trying to write *as* a machine, from inside the subject position of a speaking algorithm. I found it exhausting, because of the amount of language I had to digest and condense. I felt keenly that I was both speaking and spoken at the same time, the product of the very activity in which I was engaged.

A small sample of the text of *The Fall* gives some idea of its effects and affective dimensions:

Gibbon 1:

In the age of Empire fairest most civilized. Frontiers extensive ancient renown. Gentle laws powerful cemented inhabitants. And abused. Wealth, luxury, appeared to. Emperors happy. Prosperous and decline. Republic, preserving. Succession of triumphs. Relinquish whole earth, moderation to peace. Remote wars more precarious. Safety or dignity. Generals attempted but repelled. Northern scarcely morasses regained. Vicissitudes of empire.

Now 1: 11/8/16

Triumphs surprising despair captures white white who working uncertainty fear distress fear unlike any nation's biggest vowed check may set power resistance didn't see decline turns revulsion national stunning support upset. Shakedown politics advanced tactics and then profit. Blatant abuse? Stakes so high. Upset. They vanish. Upset.

(Drucker and Freeman; n.p.)

What I learned, in this aspirational exercise, was how to speak as a subject but without attachment to my individual identity. I was processing, not writing, compressing, not composing. Is there a difference? Some abdication of ownership and authority attends to the idea that one is enacting an operation to hear and feel how it enacts oneself. I liked becoming an algorithmic process, giving form to the enunciative apparatus of its strictures, not as abdication of my humanity or deviation from its norms but as an augmentation and extension of its possibilities.

The question of who speaks as an algorithm modifies, changes, emerges, and transforms will be with us in many ways for a long time to come. Coming to terms with the subject positions such articulations enunciate is crucial for positioning ourselves in relation to the systems of which we are a part, but which also exceed our control and even understanding.

If speaking *as* can be differentiated from speaking *like*, then so might the question of speaking *with* be posed in terms that address the potency of the algorithmic systems that speak us as much as we do them. Or not. We shall see. I enjoyed the exercise, and more, just as I aspired to write like Lewis Carroll at one stage of my development, and Emily Brontë at another, and absorbed the resonant lessons of Celia and Louis Zukovsky's translations of *Catullus*, so, in this cultural moment, I find the language of the machines the model on which I want to pattern my own poetic activity in order to inhabit a space that is increasingly interpenetrating the full spectrum of linguistic systems in which I am a spoken as well as speaking subject.

Before I began this compression experiment, I had already had considerable experience with procedural work in several book projects. But in these works, I had not been concerned with modes of enunciation as much as with the possibilities of language when it has finite limits. Specifically, these were the limits imposed by letterpress as a physical form. Two works in particular are worth a moment's description before moving on to explore a few final curiosities.

In 1977, I published a work titled *From A to Z* in which I used every letter—that is, every single piece of cast lead type—in 47 drawers of type to produce a work that was completely coherent and legible. The book was a study of 26 poets of my acquaintance whose social network of relations I had been involved with through my work as the staff typesetter for the West Coast Print Center beginning in 1976. That job had connected me with poets in a variety of circles writing in many different styles and modes from the most conventional lyric to procedurally structured work. But I had also been fascinated by the politics of the scene, the jockeying for position, jealousies, sexual tensions, and games, the plays for power and bids for influence and attention. *From A to Z* described these in marginalia attributed to the individual characters, always identified by their letter. Character A was in love with character Z and addressed a series of remarks to him even as other events unfolded through notes and snippets of conversation, snatches of correspondence, and overheard remarks—all put into the book in a carefully encoded visual layout and graphical score.

The task of using up every physical letter in every one of the type cases was an elaborate game of scrabble carried to virtuosic extreme, and the final pages of the book contain mixed-font footnotes that explain the marginal notes. These are set in paragonnage—a form of type setting that combines font sizes and styles in elaborate "forms"—as set type is called. The technical details of this and the conceptual elaboration were deeply entangled, but the point relevant within this current discussion is that I felt the text of the pages, poems, the whole emerged from what was already latent in the cases, as if the fonts suggested the texts. Also, once certain letters were used up, such as the letter "f," I found that certain grammatical constructions were no longer possible. The relationships of derivation—"of" and "from"—cannot be indicated without the letter "f;" no substitute exists in English for that letter. This was an interesting revelation to me and gave me one sense of being constrained, not merely working within constraints. The difference is subtle, but in the first case the limit is on what it is possible to say, in the second, on what is said, a distinction that aligns, again, with that of *langue* (the rules that govern language) and *parole* (individual speech acts). The rules that governed making a statement about "derivation" remained—but they could not be used because I had run out of typographic material—literally, I had run out of letters.

I had no sense in composing *From A to Z* that I was not the speaker, enunciator, of the text and of the book as a whole. The vision was mine, the execution and implementation as well, and if I channeled other voices in an *exercises de style* manner, that was a matter of mimicry not channeling, more puppet master than possession.

In a second constrained work, *Prove Before Laying*, I took a freshly cast font of type and proceeded to alter its arrangement across a series of pages never dropping any letters or adding any, simply re-organizing them to make a text that references the notion of poetry as a "figure" against a "ground" of language. (The title phrase appears on packages of newly minted lead type, encouraging a printer to take a *proof* of the font before using it in composition in case there are faults in the letters from casting.) This project stressed emergence more explicitly than *From A to Z*. The font seemed to speak; my role was to conjure its voice and bring it forward from the latency in which it existed. Was I speaking *as a font* in this work? Making my utterance from within the limitations of a finite set? Perhaps. Other texts could be composed from that same font even under the same rules of preservation and recombination. But the configured text would likely not have emerged through any other compositional process, and even if it had, it would not have contained the puns and typographic particulars that made "sly word$" and other graphical puns appear.

I mentioned these two projects because their elaborate constraints made the rules of composition conspicuously evident, and thus the tasks of enunciation within those rules more apparent than in other modes of composition. I came to understand that I was produced as an author by the rules set in place. In turn, the modes of enunciation were constrained. I could "speak" as an author to create a "spoken" subject with the work of composition. But I was limited in what I could conjure by *how* I was able to produce a text. Though, as in any literary work, the text created the spoken subject of my work, I had a limited menu of options through which to produce various modes of address. I was, in a sense, the author-subject produced by the rules and constraints. In a Perec-ian mode, I have often wondered what it would be like to run out of words, find out they were finite, that one had used them up unwittingly and thus could not speak certain phrases.

But in another speculative exercise, extending these concepts of enunciation to other systems, consider the following three possibilities, each an example of writing automatically. What might it be like to be within the enunciative apparatus of a Renaissance combinatoric machine for music, language, or calculation? How would self-conscious awareness of a subject position emerge in a cellular automaton as it bootstraps its lines of code? And what—or who—is "spoken" in the replication of messenger RNA and its creation of DNA strings?

If I am a Renaissance machine, what can I enable, how do I use my moving parts to enunciate as a speaking subject and position a subject in relation to those acts? The publications of 17th-century Jesuit polymath Athanasius Kircher contain designs for at least two combinatoric devices—Arca Musarithmica and the Arca Glottotactica (though the latter is sometimes attributed to Gaspar Schott, Kircher's student). Made of wood, these elaborate mechanisms had many interlocking parts and were storage devices for components of a system. If I am to "speak" as either Arca, I must first feel input that triggers my use of pre-packaged elements of this system in a large and well-ordered cabinet. Nothing is generated, only combined, as the process pulls from the inventory of components already poised and prepared. I am a speaker of stock phrases, or composer using musical parts, combined in predictable ways, an enunciative apparatus without capacity for innovation or generative thought performing rote actions. What is spoken by my operations cannot deviate far from norms. We are locked into a regular, regulated banality, drawing on stock phrases.

The Arca Musarithmica was a composing machine for music and built on the original work of classification Kircher described in his 1650 publication *Musurgia Universalis* among other titles. Kircher's approach was analytic and encyclopedic, and this work as well as others was governed by an overarching project of *Ars Magna Sciendi—The Great Art of Knowing* (Maina). His method for creating music required a composer to select a work of music as a starting point and, then through various calculations, create a system of combinatoric outputs. In the case of the Arca Glottotactica, which was a combination of a universal language system and a compositional output device, a series of slotted wood panels controlled the output.

But as a machine, I have to understand the process more fully. I realize that a set of pre-determined options are stored in the physical parts of my structure. A keyboard of sorts triggers my mechanisms to release in sequence so a tactile access to *language—the glottotactica*—becomes active. I do not *feel* the language working, instead, I am *the working of language* as a series of operations. A key triggers a panel, the panel slips into place, its slots lock momentarily in a neatly keyed position, and I feel it move, producing a sequence of output events. The complete vocabulary of all concepts, inscribed on wood, is available for combinations and these in turn and expose their written sides as output. All the potential of language is here, in discrete components, and yet, my articulation is a mediation, literally and metaphorically wooden, and the sound of clunky cogs punctuates the air. Another Kircher device, a hydraulic organ whose sounds are triggered by the teeth on a drum, is a Renaissance player piano striking strings to release air through a series of pipes. Because of the elaborate processes of mediation, the need for input in advance of an expression, I feel spoken before I can utter or create a sound or sentence. And yet, the wonder I produce when this occurs stuns the audiences in my presence and I am aware, though the cogs still vibrate, hitting each other with the dull thud of wooden parts, that I am able to produce the awe that subdues my listeners.

By contrast, when I inhabit the conditions of the Pascaline that elegantly geared device designed by the brilliant Blaise Pascal, I feel a frisson of perfection in my turnings and workings. The eight interlocked dials perform mathematical operations, and in this activity I, as the mechanism, feel completely at ease. The dials are notched in accord with the explicit places of the decimal system, so all that I can say as this device is *subtraction* or *addition*. My language is limited, but the very capacity to shift between additive and subtractive modes means I am offering my audience an output that could have profound effects on their future—especially if I am calculating sums of money. *More* and *less* are the two factors that I can offer to my viewers, and what precisely this represents in the sums depends upon the purpose to which I am putting my brass dials. As they move, a paper ribbon displays an integer in a window cut into the housing of the device. My position is always clear. I am never ambiguous in what it is I am trying to communicate. Though limited, and without the range of my colleague Kircher's encyclopedic and universal combinatoric linguistic apparatus, my articulations as the Pascaline have an exquisite precision to them that is both elegant and minimal. I speak accurately, even if I do not raise the question of truth, and my shiny brass surfaces allow tactile manipulation as well as visual gratification. I am surveilled rather than able to survey, and yet, the unambiguous sensation of gears interlocking, advancing, or retreating according to the measure of calculation provides me pleasure. As a finely made mechanical device I feel almost no agency, so performative and delimited are the entities I articulate. But my statements have power, and those who receive them manifest surprise, joy, despair, and confusion in ways that make clear I have effected a relationship with them. What a strange thought that my mechanistic articulations can produce such powerful emotional responses.

By contrast, as a cellular automaton I begin with a dance of sequential repetition across a matrix (Roberts). Whatever I "say" is always within a very simple binary vocabulary whose consequences I cannot anticipate. At first, I imagine I will simply make the same statement over and over into whatever perpetuity might mean. Even more explicit than the Pascaline, in some ways, I am just an array of micro-code, a grid of off-on cells. While the Pascaline had discrete stops in its system, and I could feel myself in a single state, the analog gears offered some play, some imprecision in spite of the jewel-like manufacture. But as an automaton I am always in a paradoxical state of stasis and flux. I am being played and playing, sorting out where I am in the neighborhood of my immediate topographical plane. I could move into three dimensions as well. Nothing stops me, but a rule governs the way in which my state updates. Who sets that rule? How do I know how to update? I am always dealing with my neighboring cells and their states, which means I am in a situation of dependency—even co-dependency—with other cells at a higher level of organization where pattern emerges. The very conditions within which I can articulate anything are determined by the simple on/off or living/dead condition of other cells around me. I articulate only in relation to this system, to the opportunities it affords. I speak as a binary organism and nothing more subtle is possible.

What does that mean for my ability to enunciate? What I notice is that I have an impact, however, within the constantly shifting system of which I am a part. I am clearly within the whole and I have agency in a highly complex condition of emergence. In fact, the very reductive simplicity of my condition makes it all the more effective as an element of a non-linear and stochastic system in which complexity emerges from simple processes. But I am not sure if I speak, enunciate, or merely inhabit a state of being. Is there a difference? I think there is, but I am not able to think it through given my limitations. I like to believe I am speaking by inhabiting a state, but the condition does not feel like a speech act, only a condition. My aspiration is to be a neural network, to be able to upgrade my own activity through feedback loops and reinforcement. But as a mere automaton, I am unable to advance. The complexity in which I participate never alters my capacity. I remain limited to an on/off condition, unable to learn. My speech acts merely report my state, and thus any recipient of them feels superior; their cognitive frames of perception always exceed my own. I am, technically speaking, a pathetic subject, barely enunciating, more spoken than speaking and signifying only within a pattern of which I am an unwitting participant. Frustrating to be a cellular automaton, at least, in terms of poetics.

In one final example, I imagine whether the work of a strand of messenger RNA can be considered a speech act—and if so, how I might articulate a subject position in that activity. My life as a strand of messenger RNA seems at first like one of mechanical servitude. I exist to take a particular pattern of protein and gather the necessary materials to produce a replication. *I speak with identicality, unwavering, unvarying.* Or do I? *I speak with quasi-identicality, wavering, varying.* Nothing is ever the same. *I speak without identicality in recognition of its impossibility.* An utterance performs in instantiation, never to be repeated. Gather your proteins where you may. The materials of poetic production have to be available for articulation to take place at all.

As messenger RNA I am highly specialized. My role is to translate a sequence of what are known as "nucleotides" (think of them as building blocks) into the right form/format. The details of RNA in its various forms are less important here than the idea of a replicating string which provides a way for life to perpetuate as a chemical code. The extent to which such a code is a linguistic statement is what is up for question here. I work with my helper code, transfer RNA, which does its best to bring me the components from which I can put together the protein sequences to match those on the DNA strands. The DNA speaks me, deterministically. I am a transcription mechanism, the means by which the agency of the gene is enabled, actualized. I am fully written, spelled out in advance by a genetic sequence. Of course, the process is far more complicated than this and involves multiple stages of copying and processing. But essentially, I consist of codes for amino acids and my responsibility is to replicate the sequences as accurately as possible. Such activity reduces my writing abilities to mere replication, in principle, and no singular utterances or expressions should emerge to mark or situate my identity within any subject position.

I should be a mere transcription mechanism—except that like many a subversive research assistant, prankster student, or under-recognized and lowly member of a production team, I cannot resist introducing the occasional variant, the unexpected and random error, in order to mark the site and circumstances of my existence. This trace, wanton and unwarranted, becomes the very point of deviation on which my identity as a speaking subject of genetic code depends. By deviating from the task, introducing a small but still significant error, I am able to enact that minute effect of agency that marks my position as a speaking subject.

What is spoken as a result? Mutation. Perhaps the single most affective metaphor for the relation of speaking and spoken subjects, this never isomorphic and yet co-dependent identity resonates with suggestive force. I speak as a mechanical transcription sequence whose effect is to cause mutation in the system, however small, with all that this implies for emerging and stochastic complexity. The unpredictable factor in all systems is duration and change over time. Whatever speech act I perform in the moment has an unfolding future I cannot foresee. Unlike the pre-packaged systems of mechanical instruments, or the binary state of singular automata, in my identity as RNA, I am the instrument of the clinamen that swerve in the ordered system whose utterances bring about change.

Coming back to the questions posed at the beginning, I conclude that the distinction between algorithmic enunciation and human enunciation *barely* exists, but it does. All language acts are rule-bound in their foundation, but distinguished by the circumstances of their utterance and use. The distinction between discipline and deviation—between rules and their specific enunciation—inheres in the circumstances specific to use, to utterance, to the situation in which a "speaking" subject enunciates a "spoken" one through positional relations that are always circumstantial. Rules of literary enunciation are merely a subset of the larger linguistic field, and the algorithmic statements are either a subset—or a superset—of those rules. They are exemplary by virtue of being exceptional and unexceptional by the fact of being exemplary. Algorithms perform in the same way as other utterances—they just do it within different situations of use. But where analog linguistic utterances only transform over time, through sequential iterations, the algorithmic strings are materially transformed through their interactions in much shorter time frames than the variations that become inscribed in analog expression—or protocols—and their transformations occur independent of their human authors.

Where does this leave me in the discussion of writing as a machine, inhabiting subject positions of various kinds? From where do I speak and how then may I compose in accord with that positionality? My subjectivity is elaborated in the act of taking rules into instantiations, expressions that in turn position my readers within their structuring devices. Or not. Nothing is ever the same. But the enunciative act of writing—in and as code—performs its infinite variations according to a combination of repetitive and iterative protocols that continue to inscribe us. We are constantly speaking and being spoken, subjects of unique and specific utterances, still sometimes even taken by surprise in the poetics of enunciation.

Works Cited

Althusser, Louis. *Lenin and Philosophy*. Monthly Review Press, 1971.
Barbosa, Pedro. *A literatura cibernética*, Ediçoes Árvore, 1977.
Chintapalli, Karthik. "Generative Adversarial Networks for Text Generation—Part 1," Becoming Human: Artificial Intelligence Magazine, 5 Mar. 2019. https://becominghuman.ai/generative-adversarial-networks-for-text-generation-part-1-2b886c8cab10
Chomsky, Noam. *Syntactic Structures*. Mouton and Company, 1957.

de Saussure, Ferdinand. *Course in General Linguistics*. Charles Bally and Albert Sechehaye. 1916. Trans. Wade Baskin, Philosophical Society, 1959.

Drucker, Johanna. *From A to Z*. Chased Press, 1977.

Drucker, Johanna. *Prove before Laying: Figuring the Word*. Druckwerk, 1997.

Drucker, Johanna. "Amusements Electroniques." *Electronic Literature ELO '17: Affiliations, Communities, Translations* Conference, 18–22 July 2017, University Fernando Pessoa, Coimbra, Portugal. https://eliterature.org/conference.eliterature. org/archive/2017/ebook_elo17_final.pdf. Accessed 1 Oct. 2023. Paper.

Drucker, Johanna and Susan Bee. *Fabulas Feminae*. Litmus Press, 2015.

Drucker, Johanna and Brad Freeman. *The Fall*. JAB Books, 2018.

Gibbon, Edward. *The History of the Decline and Fall of the Roman Empire*. 1766-89. Revised edition, Harper and Brother, 1836. https://www.gutenberg. org/files/25717/25717-h/25717-h.htm. Accessed 20 Dec. 2023.

Hartman, Charles O. *The Virtual Muse*. University Press of New England, 1996.

Henrickson, Leah. "Constructing the Other Half of *The Policeman's Beard*", *Electronic Book Review*, 04 Apr. 2021. https://doi.org/10.7273/2bt7-pw23

Hurst, Matthew. "The Hapax Legomenon of Steve Jobs." *Data Mining*, Oct. 2011, https://datamining.typepad.com/data_mining/2011/10/the-hapax-legomenon-of-steve-jobs.html. Accessed 06 Dec. 2022.

Juhl, Peter D. "Do Computer Poems Show That an Author's Intention Is Irrelevant to the Meaning of a Literary Work?" *Critical Inquiry*, Vol. 5(3), 1979, pp. 481–487.

Kircher, Athanasius. *Musurgia Universalis*. Lodovico Grignani, 1650.

Kircher, Athanasius. *Ars Magna Sciendi*. Lodovico Grignani, 1669.

Krol, Gerrit. *APPI; Automatic Poetry by Pointed Information, poëzie met een computer*. Querido, 1971.

Maina, Claudia. "Athanasius Kircher, Arca Musarithmica and Many Sound Devices," *Digicult*. 1 Jun. 2010. https://digicult.it/digimag/issue-055/athanasius-kircher-arca-musarithmica-and-many-sound-devices/. Accessed 06 Jan. 2023.

McCray, Mary. "Mid-Century Predictions and the Love Letter Generator." Big Bang Poetry, Mar. 2022. https://www.bigbangpoetry.com/2022/03/one-of-alan-turings-final-projects-was-a-computer-based-automated-love-letter-generator-which-some-have-identified.html Accessed 05 Jan. 2023.

McGann, Jerome. *The Point is to Change It*. University of Alabama Press, 2007.

Peignot, Gabriel. *Amusements Philologiques*. Victor Lagier, 1842.

Racter. *The Policeman's Beard Is Half-Constructed*. Warner Software, 1984.

Roberts, Siobhan. "The Lasting Lessons of John Conway's Game of Life." *New York Times*. https://www.nytimes.com/2020/12/28/science/math-conway-game-of-life. html. Accessed 05 Jan. 2023.

Silverman, Kaja. *The Subject of Semiotics*. Oxford University Press, 1984.

Zukofsky, Celia and Louis Zukofsky. *Catullus*, translation. Cape Goliard Press with Grossman, 1969.

8 The Shepherds of Electric Sheep
Generative AI and Creativity

Andrew Klobucar

"More human, than human"

(Bladerunner. Dir. Ridley Scott. 1982)

As an academic and university educator, I have recently implemented my first formal artificial intelligence (AI) use policy on all my course syllabi, emphasizing the freedom and even importance of utilizing new AI writing tools as effective aids to "human" intelligence and aptitude, while at the same time, almost by default, identifying intelligence, itself, as a possible "asset" that was no longer epistemologically secure or perhaps even stable. Web browsers and learning management systems (LMS) now typically feature extensions that provide instant online access in their preference settings to detect ratios of human-to-AI authorship as an assessable quality in writing assignments. At one level, it seemed strangely akin to issuing carpenters permission to use hammers for nails when the human fist or palm proved inadequate to the task, then deciding how best to assess the necessity of any subsequent choice. Clearly, this policy was more complex since I was now inescapably questioning or somehow qualifying intelligence not just as a skill or quotient but also on deeper ontological levels, along with any of its traditional associations with learning, reasoning, and, of course, communication. Intelligence and states of "being" were far more intricately connected than hammers and the hands that hold them.

Prior warnings against plagiarism in academic writing, much like forgery in the visual arts, carried far fewer epistemological implications and certainly no such ontological questions. Qualities like validation and accreditation, once automatically assigned to the author as the acknowledged originator or creator of a work, had suddenly transformed these very same roles into objects of scrutiny. Creativity, originality, and even simply resourcefulness are all still considered fundamental to intelligence, yet before AI technology, critical readings of any work took for granted that only the "unauthorized" replication of authorship demanded censure. In many ways, AI policies imply a fascinating reversal of this relationship by targeting instead the

DOI: 10.4324/9781003320838-12

originator as possibly unauthorized rather than the replicator, shifting in the process the very nature of epistemological and ontological authenticity to acts of duplication or, at best, reconstruction. In other words, the capacity to now qualify "intelligence" as "artificial," as this chapter proposes, cannot help but re-signify the very role of authorship, where the "author" as a state of being or presence along with commonly associated qualities like creativity and topical authority cannot help but appear secondary to the capacity to imitate and revise as better validators of human presence. We, in fact, may be witnessing a moment where the very concept of intelligence, once culturally aligned with authenticity and validity, must be reimagined where these very same qualities, along with any further attributes typically associated with them, like accuracy, levels of reasoning, and even critical reflection, as newly subordinate to practices like prompting and appraisal. In a way, it paves a literary path where even the reader's role must now be understood as innately superior to that of the author regarding any creative initiative in thoughtful contemplation or conceptualization.

Further reflection shows that this "reversal," though ontologically significant, may not be as novel as it first appears—an important premise to consider, since already much social and cultural anxiety over its effect on the authorial role in communication and media seems to be steadily increasing across many areas of cultural production. Recent union strikes in the spring of 2023 within the Hollywood Industry by television and film writers against the Alliance of Motion Picture and Television Producers (AMPTP), for example, cite the need for more transparent and more reasonable protection against AI use in their own professional creative fields as part of their current grievances. Such actions easily recall the plight of auto-industry workers across the Midwest in the latter half of the 20th century, where once thriving industrial capitals like Detroit, Michigan, began to experience new rates of unemployment and population reduction as human labor in the auto industry was quickly replaced with robots and fully mechanized assemblage work.

Arguably the ongoing development of AI is potentially threatening on precisely these same socio-political and economic levels. At the same time, the possible re-evaluation of the literal state of human being-ness, that is, what it is to "be" continues to bear more in-depth analysis. Current academic reports and studies seem to agree on at least two specific features standard to most contemporary AI services: namely, the highly advanced user interfaces (UI) these technologies have developed en masse and their subsequent design as individual applications or add-ons to provide an increasingly impressive variety of ways to structure and demonstrate argument across different prose genres. This second feature focuses on more content-based and software engineering issues concerning each application's factual and linguistic accuracy matching this feature with its ease of use. While clearly, content delivery and its overall accuracy are core elements when evaluating AI's more existential implications, its UI design seems more immediately relevant to its use in the creative arts, whether print- or electronic-based. The epigraph appearing at the beginning of the chapter, for example, remains one of the most important maxims in Ridley Scott's well-known cinematic interpretation of the Philip K. Dick novel *Do Androids Dream of Electric Sheep* published in 1968. The phrase curtly summarizes several key existential conflicts between AI and what, for the sake of argument, we might call the ontological state of being human. As the cyborg replicants in the story acquire more ontological awareness as individual beings, they also risk more social restrictions on interacting and existing with the "organic" humans who created them. They may be artificial, yet their capacities to mimic and blend in with organic life become the central conflict in both the film and the novel. Highly intelligent and increasingly self-aware via their engineering, the Replicants eventually begin to evoke in Dick's fiction the same fear and cautionary approach to genAI we are currently experiencing when using our computational devices. In many ways, the communication tools we are now developing to express and distribute what we once thought were our own voices, creative ideas, and even personalities clearly present new existential and epistemological challenges to how we differentiate what we are thinking and what the tools are producing as we use them.

In *Bladerunner*, the most prominent character is, of course, the new model of cyborg our protagonist "Deckard," (Harrison Ford), the special agent assigned to locate and "retire" escaped replicants trying to live as organic humans, meets early in the film. This model of cyborg, "Rachel" (Sean Young), raises the same existential dilemmas mentioned above to a new level. Her identification as a Replicant proves to be much more challenging than earlier models, even after Deckard submits her to an advanced form of Turing Test combined with retinal identification that lasts close to 20 times the duration of any previous Replicant "inquiry" session. Rachel's advanced ability to appear human derives from her own lack of self-awareness. She doesn't know she's a replicant; ironically, she possesses the same existential certainty that seems to best parallel how most humans regard their own sense of being. In other words, her state of doubt is the secret ingredient behind her superior ability to mimic a sense of ontological certainty. She simply lives, as most humans live: in a continuous state of self-determination fuelled by an equal fear of experiencing moments of complete indeterminacy. Rachel quite literally demonstrates a state of being that is "more human than human."

While genAI arguably introduces similar threats of existential "retirement," many of the UI features that empower their capacity are, in fact, not quite as novel as they may first appear. It is extremely important to acknowledge the technological advances accomplished between 2017 and the present day in server capacity, digital data distribution (including speed and volume), and the actual language models now undergoing near-constant rates of improvement and redesign have possibly introduced an unprecedented state of transformation of our entire eco-system in less than half a decade. At the same time, more research and critical work are needed in the digital humanities and especially the literary arts to understand equally significant changes complementing these startling developments we find in hardware and natural language processing technologies. An important starting point likely lies in UI design. After all, if we are producing models of enhancement in human communication and epistemology, how individuals socially, politically, and culturally interact with these technologies prompts an array of critical questions in interface design.

Successful UI design in many of the most popular genAI devices like ChatGPT arguably traces back to classical rhetorical strategies developed to purposely produce intellectual states of certainty through constant questioning and induced dispositions of doubt. Current popular methods of interacting with an AI tool for information, in fact, compare rather well to the basics of Socratic reasoning. The Socratic method shows an art of argument that begins with mass foundations of opinion and content generation before rhetorically testing them through active critical dialogue to determine how and where inconsistencies might appear in any initial proposition. Logically, when inconsistencies reveal themselves, better propositions can then be constructed. Yet, to perform the analysis accurately, the inconsistencies must be assumed to exist before a position of enquiry begins. Scientific knowledge, by contrast, remains based on very different methods of enquiry, usually described in terms of positivism, where a future sense of consistency or success is pre-imagined as accurate before processes of enquiry are engaged. Inconsistencies may naturally appear once the goal is achieved as first imagined but being rooted in positivist thinking, a consistent path of reasoning and testing is expected to show methodological improvement. In other words, any inconsistencies are expected to reveal themselves when procedural failures occur post-experiment, not pre-experiment. Without a sense of future certainty, a scientist or technologist may argue that progress through improvement is simply impossible.

AI obviously exemplifies a technology built upon the latter method where the very possibility of general AI (GAI) continues to remain an imagined scientific truth to pursue, despite what inconsistencies in either its premises or any mode of implementation may occur en route. Socratic methods of enquiry regarding the success of GAI, including how best to use it, would thus inevitably prove to be far less affirmative, while critically disrupting the very concept of using technology to improve reasoning and the art of argument, regardless of purpose.

The capacity to access, navigate, and critically examine more data in the world than previously available within all recorded history certainly remains inspiring as a technological and scientific truth worth pursuing, while allowing for improved versions to emerge. Hence, both its method and assessment model almost by default inspire scientific reasoning. At the same time, UI devices designed specifically to utilize this data to improve reasoning and the art of argument regardless of discipline or area of study instantly elicits important levels of assessment through Socratic criticism, independent of any imagined aim and focusing instead on the dialectical and epistemological nature of AI. Even educators in the sciences, such as bio-scientists Fuhai Sun and Ruixing Ye, draw important parallels between technological research in medicine and biology and the need to maintain epistemological as well as ethical standards in critical dialogue. As they observe in a recent paper on education and AI,

> The emergence of AI technology has a significant impact on the understanding and distribution of "subject," which has produced a new situation in moral issues. When considering the morality of AI, moral problems must also involve moral agents and moral patients. A more inclusive moral definition is necessary for extending the scope of moral consideration to other traditionally marginalized entities. The evolving ethics redefines the center of moral consideration, effectively reduces the differences, becomes more inclusive, and includes more potential participants. But we may still need to jump out of this binary framework and solve the problem by rewriting rules. It is a huge, complex systematic project to realize moral AI in education.
>
> (p.1)

Abandoning this focus risks precisely many of the ontological issues raised earlier concerning existential individualism across any social body actively using it as a reasoning device.

Taking into consideration the challenge AI brings to both scientific and ontological relationships to the social body, further exploration verifies that methodologies across learning and creative production must now respond to how generative AI technologies signify a highly momentous transformation regarding nearly every onto-political and cultural component of society. The capacity for social media industries when left unregulated and even to an extent ignored has already shown an immense potential to alter modern principles of governing in democratic nations across the globe. In the United States at the end of the 20th century, both the House and the Senate failed to consider new digital social media service companies like Facebook (now Meta), Twitter, and even search engine software companies like Google, Microsoft, and Yahoo as information and editorial distribution networks, as sources of public influence comparable to mainstream press production and cable and network media. Accordingly, social media quickly facilitated political and cultural disruption across the country, many of them comparable to the revolutions Western society experienced when civil republics reorganized the social body contesting imperial monarchical modes of government.

A second motive of argument proceeds to examine AI in terms of equally important existential questions, where, as mentioned earlier, critical response must also address questions of epistemological and ontological stability in the state. Both objectives, however, remain deeply intertwined since, as the critical theorist Michel Foucault, as early as the 1970s, argued, to engage in any epistemological activity to determine what constitutes knowledge is at no level ever isolated from the political need to control the social body. In his words,

There can be no possible exercise of power without a certain economy of discourses of truth which operates through and on the basis of this association. We are subjected to the production of truth through power and we cannot exercise power except through the production of truth. This is the case for every society, but I believe that in ours the relationship between power, right and truth is organized in a highly specific fashion—we must speak the truth; we are constrained or condemned to confess or to discover the truth. Power never ceases its interrogation, its inquisition, its registration of truth: it institutionalizes, professionalizes, and rewards its pursuit.

(p.93)

Foucault's comment shows exactly why the American Legislature and the Senate both overlooked the capacity of social media as effective knowledge dissemination technologies and therefore of little interest or perhaps they knew the market potential and ideologically chose to keep regulation minimal.

We've seen this social effect before with the appearance of the printed book as a new publicly accessible resource in the 16th century where much of its political and epistemological power was due to technical improvements in the textual layout, incorporation, and distribution of information to larger audiences. The increased distribution of information throughout newly literate populations has been critically investigated in numerous media histories. What remains insufficiently studied is how the text and page design also increased readability and therefore its political and epistemological significance. The placement, size, and spacing of text significantly impact readability, comprehension, and even overall visual appeal. Effective use of white space enhances the overall design and makes content more accessible to readers. Furthermore, the alignment and justification of text can create a sense of order and hierarchy within a document (Kintsch). Therefore, understanding how printed text interacts with space on a page is crucial for effective communication through written materials.

The writing process typically guides intellectual work as a visual activity. Hence, the visual role in learning remains significantly tied to its social and political relevance. Despite this connection, as Olive and Passerault note in their own study on visual elements in learning,

> Studies of the visuospatial dimension of writing are surprisingly scarce, and the cognitive models of writing describe only fleetingly, if at all, the underlying mental representations and processes. As a consequence, writing research has almost completely ignored how writers manage and process the visuospatial dimension of writing. This is particularly astonishing given that early research on cognitive psychology pointed to the necessity of visuospatial representations and processes.
>
> (p.327)

Foucault's work encourages us to posit that the book's increasingly widespread appearance throughout the 16th and 17th centuries via new distribution and production practices, emphasizing visuospatial learning, produced a stunningly powerful new epistemological era or epoch across the globe. However, we might find various parallels with the appearance of the personal computer for home use in the late 1970s and 1980s and, with its distribution, similar questions regarding how knowledge might be affected by electronic writing tools, especially while supplemented by near-immediate access to digital networks appearing as user-based discussion forums. One of the central questions that emerged almost immediately was simply how one might assess or even cite information used in academic research across disciplines properly when sources were accessed via electronically shared writing forums and not conventional conference papers or published work in print even if such sources had not been updated for decades. As networks multiplied in number and access and distribution rates increased in speed along with their capacity to store information, academic use and trust grew accordingly. And again, as with the book, electronic tools demonstrate extremely intricate UI features, adding to space and visual design new levels of personal, multimodal interactivity with any text. In a sense, AI emerges at this moment in the 21st century as the next stage of the same political history.

However, despite this ongoing politico-epistemological drive to maintain and even enhance control over the social body, whether digital or print-based, the creative use of these same tools and techniques, empowered with a Socratic or dialogical mode of criticism, continues to provide an equally powerful counterpart to epistemological dominance. Creative aesthetic experiments in print design emerged when the same technologies advanced to a degree that enabled concrete, symbolic experiments in meaning in relation to the page and the book as a visuospatial experiment in epistemology. When a symbolist experiment in page and writing, such as Apollinaire's famous poem "Il Pleut" or "It's Raining" appears in 1916, one cannot help reading and engaging with the page and design of a text as an extremely effective aesthetic textual work with little epistemological use.

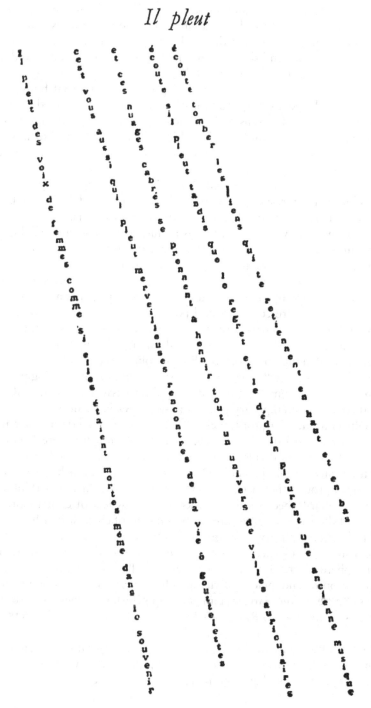

Figure 8.1 Guillaure Apollinaire. "Il Pleut." *Calligrammes; poèmes de la paix et da la guerre, 1913–1916.* 1918; Paris.

For the philosopher Jacques Rancière, aesthetics defines interpretive experiments that actively seek to counter epistemological aims using the same technologies, since the aesthetic object exists outside accepted epistemological advances and therefore has not yet been socially approved or accepted as knowledge. Just as Foucault showed how epistemology could not be detached from the distribution of power over a social body, for Rancière, knowledge also signified the concept of what he termed the social "distribution of the sensible" (Rancière), in other words a way of dividing up social space and people, which remained essential to how a social body is policed as an essential component to its symbolic constitution as a functioning society.

Rancière drew upon Plato and Aristotle's ideas about partitioning the sensible in their respective works, *The Republic* and *Politics*. Plato proposed a division of social space into three classes based on reason, spirit, and appetite, while Aristotle distinguished among different kinds of government such as monarchical tyranny, oligarchy, and democracy. However, there are tensions in Aristotle's political thinking regarding democracy as he prefers one where democratic government depends on laws rather than being solely based on votes. The essay argues that all discourse has the capacity to project social and political divisions powerfully in an anticipatory manner, preparing the way for hierarchical spaces of rule and subordination. Therefore, it is crucial to understand how language functions discursively in shaping our understanding of politics and society.

Critical theorists like Bert Olivier also provide important starting points to help underscore some of the primary political issues in Jacques Rancière's theory of contemporary governing strategies in modern states (Olivier). Olivier argues that, for Rancière, contemporary governance systems are not truly democratic or representative of politics. Rancière believes instead that society is divided along exclusionary lines defined primarily by what he calls a symbolic "police" function used to establish spaces that deny certain groups their rightful place in the polis. Rancière's thinking is radical primarily because it unmasks the hollowness of contemporary politics and shows how consensus can be a means of exclusion rather than a goal to be attained through political negotiations. Instead, he advocates for dissensus as the essence of politics, given its power to open a gap in the sensible sphere where consensus operates and allow for genuine political demonstration to take place. Olivier also highlights Aristotle's preference for a less "pure" democratic system and his exclusionary view on citizenship rights in contrast to Rancière's belief in equality for all members of society.

In fact, for Rancière, the concept of politics quite literally serves to disrupt the hierarchical order imposed by the "police" (the system of power and control) and assert better equality. Olivier, too, sees that Rancière's concept of dissensus emerges primarily to counter how society, consensus, and managerialism continue to prevent a true politics from existing. What must also be added to the discussion, though, is how, for Rancière's, not all disruptions are to be considered political; only those that assert equality. Dissensus is also a contest or struggle between two orders: a sensorily perceptible and commonsensical apprehension of the world and one that is precisely calibrated to offer an alternative, usually unorthodox arrangement of the sensible. Due to this struggle, Rancière conceives dissensus deriving chiefly from poetic, creative, or aesthetic domains, making them automatically political resources. He similarly argues in *The Politics of Aesthetics* (Rancière) that the concept of dissensus seems best characterized as a "politics of aesthetics," where creativity is explicitly enabled to challenge the status quo and create new forms of political subjectivities. After all, the "distribution of the sensible" refers directly to how societies organize their sense of what is visible, sayable, and thinkable.

It may be useful here to note that various critics continue to point out divergences in Rancière's concept of politics and art. Bruno Bosteels argues that there is an asymmetry between Rancière's concept of politics and art because there are enduring universal conditions for politics but not for art (Bosteels). Peter Hallward also criticizes Rancière's use of theatre as a metaphor for equality in his work because it can lead to problems such as inequality being seen as artificial rather than natural (Hallward). Yet, overall, Rancière's philosophy highlights how aesthetics plays an important role in shaping our understanding and experience of politics through its ability to disrupt established norms and create new possibilities for organizing society. It is a moment of disruption or dislocation of the normal parameters regulating social life as sanctioned by the police. It is a clash between one established sensible order and another that disperses arrangements of the sensible world by the police. Rancière's concept of "the police" refers to the system that maintains social hierarchies and prevents true democracy from emerging. He believes that true democracy requires a multiplicity of voices and identities, rather than a single unified voice. This means that political action must be contingent, improvisational, and liminal—operating in the space between established categories.

What's interesting here is how we can see in both Rancière and Foucault that once the specific art of writing begins to abandon semantic diversity and simulate referential meaning without an underlying aesthetic objective, readerships seem most prone to social anxiety and states of confusion. For Rancière this confusion establishes dissensus and aesthetic response; for Foucault, we see primarily the political urge to re-establish consensus through force and social oppression. Both theories show, however, where creativity and political challenge combine under a primary goal to challenge epistemology, which, as we've argued previously through Foucault, by default, remains a political aim to either maintain or challenge power over the social body.

Aesthetics maintains its epistemological aim to speculate rather than announce or even imply direct confrontation with the political will to know the truth. Aesthetic work thus rejects a capacity to simulate knowledge through representation to avoid a distinct social and cultural anxiety over technologies designed to imitate and possibly challenge human reasoning to a limit that subsequently implies or somehow threatens political control. When the social body of a state begins to question knowledge through aesthetic means, what might begin as speculation evolves to a level that requires serious epistemological and then political transformation—the collective capacity to discover truth—and political instability typically follows where epistemological concerns begin to counter with public creative interests in rights to govern and build productive societies.

Within these contexts, we can easily understand AI in terms of its potential to revolutionize socio-political control. Clearly, it demonstrates the most advanced technological mode of reasoning yet produced based on its capacity to simulate and distribute knowledge through UI designs that practically trivialize any prior effectiveness of print distribution. Connected to mass digital knowledge networks, its political power seems daunting at all levels. At the same time, a Rancière-based understanding of aesthetics provides numerous points of discovery where and how creative dissensus can also be nourished and actively employed.

Aesthetic experiments in code, of course, are plentifully available, many of them following approaches laid out first in concrete poetry, demonstrating historically that programming and creativity need not be epistemologically inclined as the primary goal available. Computers and programming work well with poetry. In fact, in some ways, poetry can even be considered a programming of sorts due to its use rigorous use of signs and symbols to build meaning. Both poetry and programming languages benefit from creative, informed uses of syntax and grammar since they cannot *literally* understand the language without paying close attention to the mechanical instructions. Computational tasks—whether the task is epistemological or aesthetic—align with the aim of the programmer. Programming languages thus naturally provide poets with syntax and semiotics as valuable resources to create strong programs by defining the rules and meanings of the code. In other words, syntax and semiotics are key resources when enabling programming complex operations and data structures in a clear and precise way. Consider, for example, how variables are declared and initialized in C++, where a variable must be declared with a type before it can be used. In Python, a variable can be assigned a value without even specifying a type.

Computation initiated a far-reaching re-envisioning of language as an information-based, knowledge tool that, as will be discussed later with print technology, can be traced back to the emergence of lexicology and the ongoing development of textual and diagrammatic formats in relation to linguistic communication. Yet the evolution of lexical tools from the first dictionaries and graphs to today's algorithmically generated scatter plots of live interaction patterns across the web has been surprisingly swift. With these advances, increasingly distinct models of linguistic processing have become equally applicable to bio-physical cognition as to any information technology. The very concept of a "thinking machine," as Turing laid out as early as 1950 in his well-known essay for *Mind*, "Computing Machinery and Intelligence," did not so much elevate programming to levels of human intelligence, as it reconsidered the latter to be at a fundamental level a mode of computation.

Turing remains, of course, something of a founding figure in the cultural history of digital communication, especially in relation to AI. He began working on developing what we might call the first functional computer programming languages at Manchester University using an early computer model known then as the Mark 1, a UK version of the original IBM machine, the Automatic Sequence Controlled Calculator (ASCC) developed at Harvard during the mid-1940s for the Manhattan Project. John von Neumann helped bring the model to Manchester when he returned there from Boston in June of 1948. The model was quickly updated to the better-known Manchester Ferranti, which became the standard Manchester University Computer or M.U.C. that Turing worked on throughout the 1950s as an assistant director of the university's first computer lab. Early on during his appointment many key issues that continue to drive science and industry's ongoing interweaving of computation, programming, and linguistic study emerged. Techniques for computationally mimicking human conversation are still evaluated for authenticity via his self-titled "Turing Test." At Turing's invite in 1952, a young programmer named Christopher Strachey almost immediately began experimenting with designing the first programming "templates" to assess how computer languages might be used linguistically. His first (and probably best-known) experiment consisted in composing and generating a series of short, one-paragraph "Love Letters" to be distributed to his colleagues' letter boxes one spring morning (Roberts). Few critics consider the well known "Love Letters" Christopher Strachey created with the M.U.C. that year to mark much of a literary or even salutatory achievement. Nevertheless, the simple printouts Strachey produced seemed even then to confirm the importance of computer programming as a linguistic accomplishment as much as a triumph in automated calculation. Computational programs, Strachey saw, depended upon grammatical and syntax rules to facilitate specific tasks more accurately and quickly than any human capacity, much like any common language shared within different cultural societies. Strachey was not a linguistic theorist, but the procedural similarities seemed obvious at the time. He was building a communication framework to help humans work with vast computational machines much as any social body might use to define and understand itself as a cultural entity. Perhaps even more importantly, Strachey realized an important structural as well as productive connection between computational analysis and how communication systems in general seem to develop dynamically, whatever underlying syntactical rules may govern how words and phrases in any language typically hold together to produce meaning. While syntactic structures may be fundamental to any communication system in terms of analytical meaning, variations in semantics and vocabulary can spark important levels of how language often signifies multiple meanings and perhaps even higher, more creative levels of how we understand one another and share knowledge. Needless to say, poetics as an art form remains finely attuned to such issues, yet Strachey was able to show that skills in programming require very similar proficiencies and at least some attention to the linguistic art of shaping syntax to accomplish higher levels of human-machine communication. At this point, whether Strachey was aware of the fact or not, it seems easier to understand how his experiments with syntax and meaning had opened new questions and ideas of how we define and understand intelligence in almost any communicative context. Poems such as T.S. Eliot's "The Waste Land," published in 1922, certainly proved challenging to analyze as a literary work when first published over a century ago, but once we had a communicative context, as laid out by New Criticism barely two decades later, nothing less than a new "intelligence" in the literary arts had emerged to re-evaluate it as one of the signature creative works of the 20th century. Within New Criticism, we might subsequently argue, epistemology and creativity seem to develop, not just dynamically but highly interactively.

Close to Turing and Strachey's experiments with the Manchester Mark 1, the mathematician Norbert Weiner also considered computability comparable to broader epistemological explorations in what he, himself, called a universal symbolic language, where reasoning and decision-making could be augmented somehow through better communication frameworks based on logical systems. For Weiner, determining a method for such mechanisms would be a core focus of the then-nascent discourse of cybernetics with its corresponding study of self-regulating or "servo" systems (1948). Andy Clark a half-century later similarly emphasized the cyborg, working clearly from Donna Haraway's ground-breaking 1984 essay "A Cyborg Manifesto: Science, Technology, and Socialist-Feminism in the late Twentieth Century," as a powerful model for understanding the increasingly intricate connections humans tend to forge with their technical environments. In his influential analysis of cognition and computation, *Natural Born Cyborgs* (Clark), he declares "the cyborg" to be "a potent cultural icon of the late twentieth century. … For what is special about human brains, and what best explains the distinctive features of human intelligence, is precisely their ability to enter deep and complex relationships with non-biological constructs, props, and aids" (loc. 51). To look at texts as cybernetic apparatuses where, as we see in coding, language's symbolic use to arrange and program tasks logically is prioritized over its semantic function is not to displace one linguistic form by the other. Language's programming capacity should not be somehow gauged as its culminating cognitive role, implicitly re-assessing verbal semantics as a flawed mode of reasoning; yet neither can these functions be accurately isolated from each other.

Knowledge of semantic diversity in programming continues to inspire instructors throughout the Humanities to explore how the computer could and/or should be viewed as a uniquely significant new writing tool. Robert Scholes, working in Brown's creative writing program in 1975, immediately sought van Dam to help him employ Hypertext and electronic writing tools for use in his poetry class. Scholes' questions much like Strachey's, in other words, derived from poetics first, where the form and analysis of writing seemed best integrated through computers and computation. He was convinced computational poetry signified advancement. Together, van Dam and Scholes might be considered founders of programmable creative writing, showing that how students were able to think critically and creatively using computation more effectively than possibly any other writing device. Computers, once again looking at Turing's statement (Turing), may not be able to think but combined with human reasoning; 25 years later we seem firmly en route towards producing highly advanced computational aids that can do more than simply calculate numerical amounts and formulae faster than individuals or even more collective efforts.

The result of these efforts not surprisingly produces incredible semantic diversity. Central to the development of the vast number of programming languages now available is also their characteristic semantic diversity where each language depends upon numerous, often unique production and distribution-based features, especially those related to type of usage, interface design, general professional or commercial needs, and, of course, cost. Each factor will certainly affect how different programs assign meaning to syntax, how they model computation, and even how they handle errors and exceptions. Different programming languages almost universally require different technical forms to describe their semantics, typically distinctions in algebraic, axiomatic, operational, denotational, or translation commands.

When compared to these qualities, what might first seem odd in poetry are many of the similarities they share concerning programming in terms of linguistic construction and this same proclivity towards semantic diversity. As mentioned earlier, the most immediately apparent parallel lies in how most poems offer incredible varieties of semantic meaning and interpretation to different readers compared to prose narratives, where at some fundamental level an audience will likely agree upon basic plot and narrative arcs. Attempts to play with semantics, as one might find with Joyce and *Ulysses*, published in 1922, or even more obviously *Finnegan's Wake*, published in 1937, produce significant (and famous) challenges concerning narrative construction but even the latter and most difficult work remains labelled readable, though highly ergodic. Poetry typically escapes forms of readerly insistence on a shared semantic model or structure.

Because of this lack of insistence, poetry remains more open to working with semantic experiments that feature poems written in actual, often working programming languages. We might even compare such experiments to earlier 20th-century explorations with form and content in poetry, including Ezra Pound's experiments in *The Cantos*, where he explored the poetic possibility of ideogrammic symbols throughout the project. I would argue that Pound's experiments inherently comment on the poetics of programming when focusing specifically on the work's semantic diversity using not just different languages but different sign and symbol arrangements to build meaning. Programming is similarly rigorous in how it construes the arrangements of different signs and symbols to explore semantic diversity. Poems show the same rigour to play with semantic structures successfully. Understanding a poem can be compared to running a program successfully. Probably the clearest parallels lie in projects like *code {poems}* edited by Ishac Bertran (Hertz). The project, in fact, exists as a print collection of work and most likely cannot currently be run on any actual computer even though it is written in a programming language. At the same time, we might easily call the collection a set of computer languages presented as poems, where the reader is required to comprehend the poem as any programmer might read computer code. The book, itself, as a project seems to draw inspiration from Hannah Weiner's earlier work titled similarly and published in 1982.

C++quined.pix[i]e[s(cher.shel)]ls>stitch ed+flesh.baked.in2.my.foaming.
monitored.skin........ resolut[(corrupt)iou]e.bonding.stapled thru. [agg]
re[gation]dness...... its.the.edge.of.the.world.as.we.no.it........
                          mez breeze, "4.12.5 make.me.look.computer
                                      (2006-12-1315:52)," 244

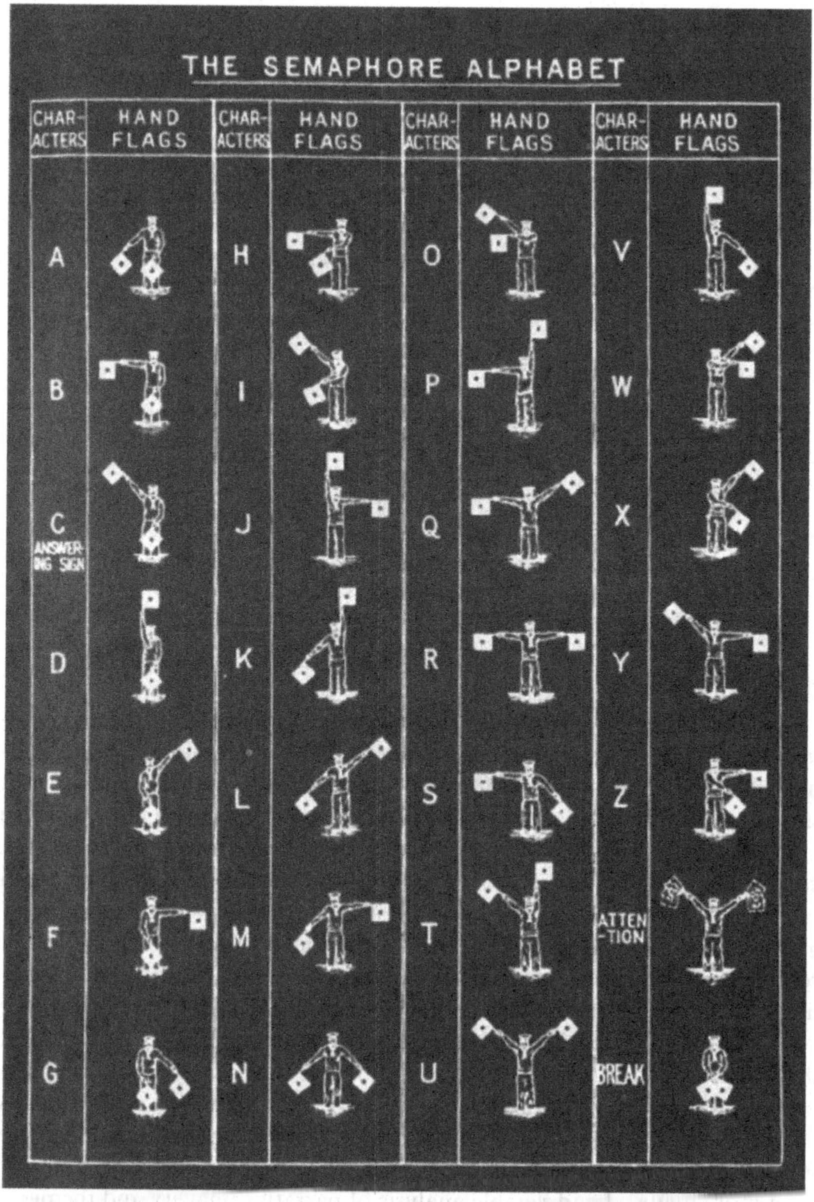

Figure 8.2 "The Semaphor Alphabet." *Code Poems*. Station Hill Press, Barrytown, NY (1982).

```
include everything.*;
void wonder(Universe u) {
    while (ever || never) {
        for (Poem i in u.now()) {
            Word dust = u.speak(i);
            for (Moment mote in dust) {
                wonder(new Universe(mote));
            }
        }
    }
}

// All.go.rhythm
// Paul Hertz 2013
```

Figure 8.3 Paul Hertz. "All.go. Rhythm" image is taken from David Conrad's "Writing Code As Poetry; Poetry As Code." *I Programmer* (January 5, 2014). https://www.i-programmer.info/news/200-art/6808-writing-code-as-poetry-poetry-as-code.html

Each work seems to require a semiotic-based mode of criticism and reading looking first at a visual structure rather than a referential sense of meaning and thus challenges any form of inherent epistemological positivism throughout much of literary art history. The works seem to critique three issues central to this history: context, senders, and receivers, implying that context is not a fixed or objective reality, but a text that is produced and interpreted by sign-users. They also question the implicit status of the artist as a sender of meaning, and the role of the literary critic as some kind of responder or interpreter of meaning as the primary model of cultural assessment. Instead, the works suggest that readerly reception, much as how the New Critics validated Eliot, is always a dynamic and diverse quality that depends on the institutional and cultural forces that shape the viewers' expectations and experiences, while at the same time exploring opportunities to creatively challenge them. This semiotic "turn" in poetics can dissolve implied hierarchies between language and its textual reproduction to allow for a more nuanced and flexible analysis of narrative imagery and themes.

Hertz's work, much as Eliot's "The Waste Land," will no doubt prove challenging to both programmers and poetry critics as a "readable," easily interpretable text, though readers familiar with either syntactic context—programming or poetry—will find some level of meaning in how the lines and symbols are arranged. Just a single reading will typically induce a sense that Hertz is considering a fascinating conflict between states of wonder and broad, inclusive understandings of "everything." The poem/program seeks to merge the writer "i" into the reader "u" and suddenly a fascinating metaphor occurs concerning how programs literally run tasks as computers run code. If the "i" in the poem is in, "u.now" are we, the reader, running/reading the poem computationally, running the work into us, and coding the task as a feat of new intelligence? What have we been tasked to do, we "wonder," building a new universe that is simultaneously but a mere particle (as in a mote of dust) read spatially or a moment, read temporally? Our earlier reference to "The Waste Land" helps our interpretation as well: "I will show you fear in a handful of dust."

Similar creative mixed technical and rhetorical modes of stimulating non-referential meaning outside poetry seem both historically and in practice to emerge from experiments in sound and music composition. Theories and research into the act of listening as an individual, often self-referential experience, rather than a more passive, typically pre-approved process of consumption of cultural or natural activity have continued to evolve since at least the work of Pierre Schaeffer in the 1950s and 1960s when his ground-breaking essay on "Acousmatics" first appeared. In this work, Schaeffer proposed that the very experience of listening can and should be understood as non-referential. In many ways, Schaefer's concept of listening compares to various critical research in semantics that occurred roughly parallel to important critical interest in listening practices and sound art, where the concept of how to interpret or find meaning in words is best understood under formalist frameworks allowing abstract rules of grammar and syntax to drive meaning rather by context-driven, cognitive interactions with texts. In other words, meaning and its assessment in a written work derive more universally from a formal set of rules that shape the meaning, while we work to communicate and further shape them from our own personal (and likely context) driven intentions. Any major conflicts, clearly, between contemporary semantic studies still seem driven by questions concerning language and personal experience. Whether form-driven or context-driven semantic theories show us most generally that we can't understand the pragmatics of communication from variables or elements outside individual practice and experience.

Francisco López's later critical paper "Profound Listening, Listening and Environmental Sound Matter" (2017) describes his nearly 65-minute soundscape, "La Selva," referencing a rainforest reserve in Central America, as a work that specifically aims to combine "biotic" (or living) species and recording technologies (non-biotic, technical components) to produce a replication produced in real time with no later editing to demonstrate how artists, especially sound artists, must aim not to produce a realist replication of an environment but rather a distinct technical construction to deliver a clear listening experience for the listener to evaluate and interpret. Lopez obviously compares his theory to "Acousmatics," disagreeing with various points in Schaeffer's earlier argument but accepting the importance of experiential interactivity over technical or rhetorical skill. Lopez categorized his creations as markedly anti-realistic. In his words,

> I don't think "reality" is being reproduced with these techniques; rather, a hyperreality is being constructed. The carefully recorded, selected, and edited sound environments that we are able to comfortably enjoy in our favourite armchairs offer an enhanced listening experience, one that we would likely not have if were hearing those sounds in the "real" world. Ironically, it is often these nonrealistic effects that give this kind of Jf sound work its appeal, as they satisfy our expectations of how "the real thing" sounds. I don't mean to suggest that the recorded version is better. Rather, I want to suggest that it is not a version but a different entity with its own inherent value.
>
> (Lopez 84)

López's emphasis on listener experience relates aesthetically to the semantic diversity we find in both coding and poetry. Poetry, as argued, finds meaning primarily as experiential in terms of the reader's level of personal engagement. Coding, too, remains experience-driven since its meaning as a symbolic device becomes apparent only when we see the procedural task it produces.

Returning to digital text-based technologies, we find that the screen remains the latest technology for interactive advancements in writing, production, and distribution, especially when linked to vast digital networks. However, these models of interactivity in poetry, digital prose, and soundscapes may just this year have also led to a unique epochal transition in all multimodal communication and media that finally retires analogue works of art as legacies of a previous epistemological era. Once these same interactive visuospatial UI elements become automated, we attain the first models of automated knowledge that require surprisingly little reliance on active human roles, whether technical or rhetorical in practice. These are essential elements in modern individuality; they might even be considered central to the very foundation of modern individualism, begging the question as to whether we need to redefine self-hood socio-politically as a mode of "being" as we transition into what appears to be a new epochal moment. In other words, it seems possible that we must now work to redefine how we can "be " Fernand Gobet and Giovanni Sala offer more of a psychological approach to the question in their 2019 article "How Artificial Intelligence Can Help Us Understand Human Creativity," arguing how AI may help us newly understand how an individual thinks what we typically see as "creatively" (p.1717). One approach, they discuss, relies on what is technically referred to as "Automatic Generation of Theories" (AGT), which uses a probabilistic algorithm to generate theories as computer programs and then compares their predictions with empirical data to build better ones. This method might prove helpful to avoid being stuck in local minima and cognitive biases that all individuals are usually prone to. However, these algorithms have conceptual and methodological challenges, such as how best to score participants' results and various testing theories, as well as questions about the understandability and usefulness of generated theories for writing applications (p.17). Looking more closely into these issues, however, it may be possible to generate actual theoretical frameworks for entirely different genres of poetry.

That said, AI seems to have been in use for understanding creativity for some time, with examples including the program Logic Theorist, a program written in 1956 by Allen Newell, Herbert A. Simon, and Cliff Shaw to perform automated reasoning that could prove theorems more successfully and clearly than leading mathematicians. It seemed to function as what Newall called a kind of "robot scientist" that could build hypotheses independently.

We might also note how, simply by playing games like "Go" and chess, AI has uncovered clear limits in human creativity. Herbert A. Simon's theory of bounded rationality proposes that limitations in knowledge and computational capacity constrain any decision-maker's capacity to make rational choices. What's central to Gobet and Sala, accordingly, is that even proven experts in a field like literary theory can be "blinded" by their knowledge, preferring standard answers over novel ones even when objectively better. Hence, we might credit AI with helping us overcome preconceptions, which likely will foster human creativity.

Current technology can design ready environments that can be studied with a creative application of what we referred to earlier as the scientific method. The key contribution Gobet and Sala share here is to propose using even more intricate environments, including those that require a more Socratic sense of critical doubt where intelligent agency begins by approximating the problems of any preconceived method and ways of thinking. Then the system-based risks that naturally accompany any aesthetic or outlying pattern can be applied to test any current theory thought to be key to creativity and discovery, observe new empirical phenomena related to these aims, help build alternative domains to practice in, and then finally train people to be creative and even take further risks with these new domains or practices.

The theorist Margaret Boden makes a similar argument where she admits openly that creativity seems a crucial aspect of human intelligence that still poses a significant challenge for AI. AI models of creativity can be useful in the laboratory or within cultural markets, and cognitive science can certainly benefit from understanding how human minds are creative.

However, creativity when not limited to a select few but considered present in everyday capacities such as an association of ideas, perception, analogical thinking, problem-solving, and self-criticism, current AI models weaken as soon as they leave any focus on the cognitive dimension of creativity. She reminds us that cognitive science tends to categorize creativity into three types or classifications: combinational (novel combinations of familiar ideas), exploratory (generation of novel ideas by exploring structured conceptual spaces), and transformational (transformation of one or more dimensions to generate new structures). The latter two types lead to the "shock" of surprise that greets an impossible idea. Human beings often make a living out of exploratory creativity by searching inherited accepted styles and tweaking them superficially to explore their contents, boundaries, and potential. However, they sometimes transform the accepted conceptual space by altering or removing one or more dimensions or adding new ones to generate previously impossible ideas. The shock value increases with the fundamental nature of transformations made; however, if transformations are too extreme, newly possible structures may be unintelligible and rejected until recognized over time (Boden).

Boden quickly notes the limitations of current AI models in terms of creativity, particularly in their ability to transform conceptual spaces. While some AI systems can explore pre-defined spaces and make constrained tweaks, they cannot generate truly novel or surprising ideas. However, there are transformational systems that attempt to change the generative mechanism in more fundamental ways, such as genetic algorithms that allow for changes in the length and complexity of image-generating code (ibid.). The evaluation of new ideas is a major challenge for AI models of creativity. While some programs have heuristics built-in for evaluating interestingness, these evaluations are often mistaken by human standards. Furthermore, it is difficult to express what humans like about certain creative works and why they value them, as human values are never static, changing constantly over time and across cultures, making it extremely challenging to define any possible evaluative criteria that can be implemented into an AI system.

Boden confirms that while some historically accepted ideas—what she calls "H-creative"—have been generated by AI programs through exploratory procedures, transformational AI originality is just beginning. The two major bottlenecks are domain expertise and the valuation of results, which interact with each other since subtle valuation requires considerable domain expertize. Ultimately, the goal would be an AI program that generates novel ideas that initially perplex or repel us but can persuade us of their value—something we are still far from achieving.

This might be the reason why we tend to compare new tools like Chat-GPT to parodies of even pastiche versions of reasoning. That said, as the history of electronic media shows, the aesthetics of proceduralism in poetry with its long history in aesthetics adapted parody in computer programming. Aesthetics, however, or the space of creativity that lies outside knowledge, not easily assimilated into discourse still has the potential to show or use AI-generated content that what we believe to be valuable still lacks the emotional depth and originality that comes from human experience. They can show that true creativity requires an understanding of emotions and context that machines cannot replicate. And if these systems can enhance their abilities, even the automation of repetitive tasks such as image editing or music composition, artists can focus on more complex experiments in their work, much in the same way that the symbolists and concrete poetry used space creatively to complicate the production of image and word. Current relevant examples include "data poetry" and Aaron A. Reed's *Subcutanean* (2020). We can read that entire novel as an experiment in computer-generated fiction since even the author doesn't quite know what story he has written. In this way, we can easily consider this project an intriguing addition to ongoing experiments in digital creative expression, since the work, while not near-randomly generating new plot designs or characters, has in a sense written itself into existence through the participation of a readership network at the very moment of consumption.

Returning to Foucault, we might say that the book's political value derives not only from its aesthetic quality but how it subverts the market and distribution system through its uniqueness and undeliverability as a commodity. No critical or analytical discourse can be written about *Subcutanean*, since to an extent, it doesn't even exist discursively but rather as an unlimited aesthetic concept never fully consumable.

The examples discussed here provide important insights and possibly starting points for building new discourses around the creative use of computational programming since each work relies on programmable devices while remaining aesthetically, not epistemologically driven. The struggle is still explicit in them. They remain expressive of a new form of individual experience and how we might build a better existential presence in programmable automation. Creativity can and must foster similar efforts to help develop a public, politically aware adaptation of AI in our lives, especially in terms of how powerful it is as a knowledge device that is highly adept at deceiving the user/reader to release individual control over how we learn, argue, and discuss socio-existential concerns. It makes the creative arts more socially significant than in any prior epoch. As artists and writers already understand, AI cannot replace human creativity and storytelling as an epistemologically driven tool; yet it can, with skill, be controlled and used to enhance aesthetic aims to question, if not disrupt knowledge systems. With proper implementation and collaboration between human writers and AI-powered tools, the possibilities for creating compelling, politically relevant works of art remain undeniable, perhaps even compelling.

Works Cited

Boden, Margaret A. *AI: Its Nature and Future.* OUP, 2016.

Bosteels, Bruno. "Rancière's leftism, or politics and its discontents." In Gabriel Rockhill and Philip Watts (eds.), *Jacques Rancière: History, Politics, Aesthetics.* Duke University Press, 2009.

Breeze, Mez. "4.12.5 make me look computer (2006-12-1315:52)." *Human Readable Messages [Mezangelle 2003-2011].* Trauma Wien, 2011.

Clark, Andy. Natural Born Cyborgs: Minds, Technologies, and the Future of Human. Oxford University Press, 2003.

Foucault, Michel and Colin Gordon. *Power/Knowledge: Selected Interviews and Other Writings, 1972–1977.* New York: Pantheon Books, 1980.

Fulber-Garcia, Vinicius. *Programming Languages: Lexicon vs. Syntax vs. Semantics.* Last modified: December 17, 2022.

Gobet, Fernand and Giovanni Sala. "How Artificial Intelligence Can Help Us Understand Human Creativity." *Frontiers in Psychology* 10, 2019. https://doi.org/10.3389/fpsyg.2019.01401.

Hallward, Peter. "Jacques Rancière and the Subversion of Mastery." *Paragraph* 28 (1): 26–45, 2005.

Hertz, Paul. "All.go. Rhythm: A Poem Written in C." In Ishac Bertran, coding edited by David Gauthier, Jamie Allen, Joshua Noble, and Marcin Ignac (eds.), *code [poems].* Self-published by editor, 2012.

Kintsch, Walter. *Comprehension: A paradigm for cognition.* Cambridge University Press. 1998.

López, Franceso. "Profound Listening, Listening and Environmental Sound Matter." In Christoph Cox and Daniel Warner (eds.), *Audio Culture: Readings in Modern Music.* 2nd Edition, Bloomsbury Press, 2017.

Olive, Thierry and Jean-Michel Passerault. "The Visuospatial Dimension of Writing." *Written Communication.* 29 (3):326–344, 2012. https://doi.org/10.1177/0741088312451111.

Olivier, Bert. "Rancière and the Recuperation of Politics." *Phronimon* 16 (1): 1–15, 2015.

Rancière, Jacques. *The Politics of Aesthetics.* Bloomsbury, 2013.

Reed, Aaron A. *Subcutanean.* Independently published, 2020.

Roberts, Siobhan. "Christopher Strachey's Nineteen-Fifties Love Machine." *The New Yorker*, February 14, 2017. www.newyorker.com/tech/annals-of-technology/christopher-stracheys-nineteen-fifties-love-machine.

Sun, Fuhai and Ruixing Ye. "Moral Considerations of Artificial Intelligence." *Science & Education* 32(3): 1–17, 2021. https://doi.org/10.1007/s11191-021-00282-3.

Turing, Alan. "Computing Machinery and Intelligence." *Mind* LIX(236): 433–460, October 1950. https://doi.org/10.1093/mind/LIX.236.433.

Weiner, Hannah. *Code Poems.* Station Hill Press, 1982.

Weiner, Norbert. *Cybernetics or Control and Communication in the Animal and the Machine.* Cambridge, MA: MIT Press, 1961 [1948].

Index

Note: Page references in *italics* denote figures, in **bold** tables and with "n" endnotes.

Printed in the United States
by Baker & Taylor Publisher Services